THE HUMAN RIGHT
TO INDIVIDUAL FREEDOM

THE HUMAN RIGHT
TO INDIVIDUAL FREEDOM

THE
HUMAN RIGHT
TO
INDIVIDUAL FREEDOM

A Symposium on World Habeas Corpus

Edited by LUIS KUTNER

Foreword by ARTHUR J. GOLDBERG

Introduction by ROSCOE POUND

UNIVERSITY of MIAMI PRESS
Coral Gables, Florida

Designed by Bernard Lipsky

Manufactured in the United States of America

Permissions to reprint were generously granted by:
Center for the Study of Democratic Institutions, for
"The Rule of Law in World Affairs" by William O. Douglas;
Denver Law Journal, for "World Habeas Corpus—Its Past,
Present, and Possible Worldwide Future" by Leonard v. B.
Sutton; *Notre Dame Lawyer,* for "The Legal Ultimate for the
Unity of Mankind" by Luis Kutner; Fred B. Rothman & Co.,
publishers of *Virginia Law Review,* for "International Due
Process and the Law" by William J. Brennan, Jr.; and
Rutgers-Camden Law Journal, for "Islam: Concept, Law,
and World Habeas Corpus" by M. Cherif Bassiouni.

Contents

Foreword

World Habeas Corpus

By ARTHUR J. GOLDBERG*

THE IDEA of worldwide habeas corpus, internationally recognized and enforceable in an appropriate international court, can only be applauded by those who are dedicated to the rule of law and the attainment of lasting world peace. For the very term "rule of law" or "due process of the law" implies a procedure such as habeas corpus; a means whereby official detention can be challenged and, if not justified on the basis of valid laws, terminated. Without this simple procedural mechanism, many of the substantive rights that have been recognized as so important to the cause of peace must remain little more than mere aspirations. With the advent of international habeas corpus, and the universal respect for human rights that it would encourage, a long stride toward a peaceful world would be taken.

It is peculiarly fitting that we in the United States should heartily support the movement for international habeas corpus. We have had long domestic experience with the "great writ," an experience in which we take a good deal of pride. Habeas corpus finds its place in the "bright constellation" of American rights to which—in the words of Jefferson's first inaugural address—"the wisdom of our sages and the blood of our heroes have been devoted." Indeed, it is

---

* D. Jur.; American lawyer and politician; Bar of Illinois, 1929; United States Supreme Court Bar, 1937; associate justice, United States Supreme Court, 1962-1965; U.S. ambassador to the United Nations, 1965-1968.

not too much to say that we have come to regard habeas corpus as an indispensable means of supervising the administration of justice, and a cornerstone of just government.

But it is not only our traditions that should lead Americans to regard the concept of international habeas corpus with favor. Our devout national commitment to world peace points in the very same direction. We have not forgotten the thought that President Kennedy put so eloquently in the form of a question: "Is not peace, in the last analysis basically a matter of human rights?" It is painfully obvious that, if we are to have lasting peace, we must use all appropriate and effective means to strike at the human rights abuses that divide man from man and nation from nation. For this reason, even if we were not as familiar as we are with the habeas corpus procedure, we would be naturally drawn to an international institution of the type proposed.

It is not, of course, a question of utopian dreams. We must recognize that there is not yet universal agreement on the content and extent of international rights, much less on the form of the necessary guarantees. Nor should we expect to eradicate abruptly the abuses that have prevailed for centuries. But a beginning is being made, in the efforts of international organizations to define and categorize human rights, and in the work of private bodies such as the Commission for International Due Process of Law. I believe it is important that such efforts go forward, and that the nations of the world take notice of these efforts. For unless men and nations are prepared to lend at least their attention to such endeavors, meaningful international human rights standards will remain forever beyond man's grasp.

Preface

IN REPLY to letters to the president of the United States and to the secretary of state concerning World Habeas Corpus, the editor received acknowledgment from Mr. Carl F. Salans, deputy legal adviser from the Department of State. The text of Mr. Salans' letter [Department of State, Washington, 9 May 1967] is as follows:

"Dear Mr. Kutner ... Your efforts in the cause of individual rights and dignity are greatly appreciated. Were the writ of habeas corpus available throughout the world, it would indeed be a giant stride forward in the effort to realize for the peoples of the world their human rights and fundamental freedoms, a goal to which all the Members of the United Nations have committed themselves in Article 1 (3) of the charter.

"Though the international community has increasingly recognized the rights and dignity of individuals through international agreement, significant elements of that community, not limited to the Communist states, remain unwilling to subject themselves to meaningful international scrutiny. The United States should be in the forefront of the effort to overcome this unwillingness. However, there are, as you know, some groups in this country which continue to resist strenuously the notion that protection of certain basic human rights is a proper subject for the exercise of our treaty power. The failure of the United States to ratify certain of the existing human rights conventions inhibits our efforts to achieve further progress internationally. It would appear that a great deal of educational spade work must be accomplished before the goals which World Habeas Corpus seeks can be achieved."

Introduction
A Forward Step toward a Legal Order

By Roscoe Pound*

IT IS a common notion that law is a system of polic-
ing. The legal order is too often assumed to be a system of policing
the population of a politically organized society. But do we require
a world state to have a world law?

Justice, said Daniel Webster, in his address to the bar on the
death of Joseph Story, "is the great interest of man on earth." If so
there must be a great interest, too, in law, the chief instrumentality
by which justice is maintained and promoted in action. Justice,
however, as well as law, is a word of more than one meaning. Here
we are speaking, on the one hand, of the ideal relation among men
and among organized groups and bodies of men, particularly of
groups and bodies of men when organized for economic or social or

* Roscoe Pound holds a preeminent place among the world's legal scholars,
educators, and philosophers. He has served his country and the legal profession
in many distinguished posts. In 1937, after twenty years as dean of the Harvard
School of Law, a period that has been termed the school's Golden Age, Pound
succeeded to a university professorship that enabled him to teach in any faculty
of Harvard University. He retired from this position in 1947 to serve as advisor
to the Ministry of Justice of the Republic of China. His monumental five-volume
work, *Jurisprudence*, has been acclaimed as the "law book of the twentieth century." Roscoe Pound has been repeatedly honored as America's foremost "Archi-
tect of the Law."

political purposes. On the other hand, we are speaking of principles of maintaining and promoting that ideal relation, whether recognized as universal, or formulated and authoritatively declared by some agency of politically organized society. It is an ideal relation maintained by social control, the agencies of which are religion, morals, and law. Since the sixteenth century, law, backed by a politically organized society, has become the paramount agency. But conflicts between politically organized societies, which have come to be worldwide, are raising a problem of external peace in an economically unified world, where there had been only a long struggle with problems of internal peace in particular societies.

There is thus today a quest for a universal regime of justice. If we think of justice according to law, are we to think of it as a regime prescribed and maintained by organized force? May we conceive of law as transcending and putting limits to organized force? Does our quest of a universal justice involve a quest of a universal state? Can we find how to secure universal ideals of right and justice without, as a first step, setting up an omnicompetent, universal, political organization of mankind? Are there individual claims to life, and liberty, so general as to be substantially and universally recognized, and so possible as to be secured by an international process of law? Does not the history of civilization teach us that there are?

Even in savage society peace is maintained in the family by household discipline. In the progress of social development peace is established in the neighborhood, in the village, and, in classical antiquity, in the city and city-state. There comes to be a regime of peace in the tribe, in the people of a kin group, in the people of a nation of many kindreds. The ultimate step in the development of civilization would be peace among all mankind—a peace of the world.

How to achieve this peace of the world is something which has given concern to saints and prophets and philosophers and statesmen from antiquity. Universal religious organizations, universal military organizations, and universal political organizations have been sought to be imposed on mankind. Can there be a general regime of peace that is not imposed or enforced but is recognized?

It was thought at one time that a model organization was afforded by the Greek Amphistyonic Council, a religious organization of independent states. In origin religious, but also maintained for the common defense and internal peace, it became political in the fourth century B.C. It kept up a formal existence under the Roman rule and became extinct in the second century A.D. Grote says that it was "at first religious, then religious and political, and then lastly more the latter than the former." When it became political, it lost all significance.

Of the plans advanced from the sixteenth to the nineteenth century, the Grand Design of Henry IV (1603) proposed a political organization of Europe in six hereditary monarchies, five elective monarchies, and four sovereign republics. They were to be governed in their external relations by a general council as elaborated by the Abbe St. Pierre (d. 1745). It was to be a consensual superstate. William Penn (in 1693-1694) planned a permanent Sovereign International Parliament, or Congress, which was to be a judicial body and at the same time have law-making functions.

In the eighteenth century, Bentham, between 1786 and 1789, planned a universal and perpetual peace through a superstate. Kant in 1795 published a plan for a federation of free states with provision for a tribunal. It will be seen that the plans, down to the nineteenth century, had been religious or political but not legal.

In the nineteenth century there came to be many plans for arbitration treaties or tribunals, presupposing a doubtfully existent international law or, in case of treaties, formulating certain rules for the case in hand. In the twentieth century we have seen what may be called embryo superstates, political and partially judicial. Behind these different plans for a general peace we may see two conflicting ideas: the Germanic cult of the local self-governing community, what Beseler called *Kleinstaatismus* (or, as I translate it, Mainstreetism), and what came to be the Roman belief in a universal empire.

Have we not since the seventeenth century, which was obsessed by the Roman autocratic state, expected a universal political organization to bring about a universal justice according to law, whereas perhaps the law must come before the regime of adjudication?

What is called for is a world legal order—a regime of adjustment of relations and ordering of conduct in an orderly process of administering justice according to law. A general conviction must arise that due process of law in application of law rather than legislative formulation is the crucial point. The common law as the legal order of the English-speaking world has no one politically organized society behind it. The civil or modern Roman law, which long was and still is to no small extent the legal system of a great part of the world, has had no unified political organization behind it.

We must distinguish between law and a law—between law and a body of rules of law. "Law" is a word of much more than one meaning. Two of these meanings are important for our present purpose: (1) What Continental jurists call the legal order (*Rechtsordnung, ordre juridique*)—the regime of social control through legal institutions of justice in a civilized society—and (2) the body of authoritative legal precepts which obtain for the time being in a particular politically organized society. It is easy to assume that because each is called by the one name of law the one is bound up in the other, so that inquiry as to the adequacy of the working or the justice or the expediency of the authoritatively established precepts of the time and place, for worldwide as distinguished from local purposes, involves an attack upon the legal order itself. But the vital, the enduring part of the law is in principles—starting points for reasoning—not in rules, i.e., precepts attaching definite detailed consequences to definite detailed states of fact. Principles remain relatively constant or develop along constant lines. Rules have relatively short lives. They do not develop; they are repealed and superseded by other rules. In truth, there is no necessary connection between the legal order and any particular body of legal precepts established in any particular time and place.

How little necessary connection there is between law and general legislative law-making power is well brought out in the United States by the uniformity of law on commercial subjects brought about by the activity of the American Law Institute and the Conference of Commissioners of Uniform State Laws.

It has been assumed that to have a world law we must have a world state; that universal political organization must come before universal law. May it not be rather that universal law must precede the universal state that will undertake to put any required force behind it? There is abundant evidence that there may be a generally recognized and accepted body of principles to which men are expected to adhere in their relations with others and in their conduct without any general law-making or declaring political organization.

If a complete regime of universal peace may be an ultimate objective, any step toward it in achieving a regime of securing paramount individual natural rights through a legal remedial process would be of the highest significance.

The general proposition of World Habeas Corpus that the concept of the international personality of man is growing in acceptance and must make obsolete much of the reasoning based upon the idea of sovereignty seems to me well taken. To my mind, the main difficulty in the way of world legal order is in the notion of law as an aggregate of laws proceeding from a legislative authority, whereas I conceive law to be experience developed by reason and reason-tested by experience such as we see in the common law in the English-speaking world and the modern Roman law in Western Europe, Latin America, Quebec, and Louisiana. It is significant that Louisiana follows the civil law while the rest of the United States adheres to the common-law system, and yet they have a common political obedience to the United States. The same thing occurs in Canada, where Quebec is governed by the civil law although the other provinces are governed by the common law, and yet they have a common political superior in the Dominion of Canada. In other words, no omnicompetent superstate is involved in European adherence to the civil law, in the Anglo-American adherence to the common-law system, or in the similarity between Canadian provinces and states of the United States just pointed out.

Why cannot a world law develop exactly as the law of the common law has developed without any supergovernment? The proponents of World Habeas Corpus seem to me, therefore, to be moving in the right path in insisting upon a general principle of law rather than a sovereign political authority as the basis of a world legal order. Certainly, not the least feature of the world legal order should be the securing of individual personality.

Editor's Comment

World Habeas Corpus
and the Rule of Law

THE INTERNATIONAL Commission of Jurists have long maintained that the mere declaration of a fundamental right is not sufficient to ensure that it is respected. To ensure the effective protection of all the rights enunciated in the Universal Declaration of Human Rights and in the Charter of the United Nations requires specialized remedies and institutions to deal with abuses of these rights. The judicial protection, to be effective, must be exercised, above all, by an independent and objective judiciary not subject to political pressures nor the object of political patronage. As an essential feature, it must, however, have the legal competence to investigate and act on individual complaints unimpeded by official and political considerations and provide an effective summary remedy where human rights have been infringed or denied.

As co-chairman of the working session on Law and Human Rights of the World Peace Through Law Center at Geneva, Switzerland, on 16 September 1968, the Honorable Chaudri Nazir Ahmad Khan of Pakistan emphasized that all imbalances of the present day world are, in one form or another, traceable to the violation of human rights. Without a strict observance of these rights, there can be no rule of law and, therefore, no hope for world peace. This makes it necessary to create something more legally binding than a mere declaration. Partial adoption of international treaties, conventions, or covenants on human rights are not adopted or embodied in the fundamental or civil law of these nations and, therefore, have no validity. To ensure every human being a free and dignified life and to put an end to every type of totalitarian regime, adequate machinery for implementation of human rights must be perfected soon.

Unless there are effective, respected, and legally competent implementations of these rights at the regional and at the universal levels, all professions and declarations about human rights will be no better than mere abstractions—vague generalities.

Arbitrary detention of human beings must be prevented by available summary remedy. Individual security must be guaranteed. Since the days of Hammurabi, all great law-givers have sought by legal means to protect the individual against the strong. There is no higher moral or ethical obligation of mankind.

The concern for advancement of individual dignity and security within legal dimension was concurred in by the Honorable René Cassin, Nobel Laureate, president of the European Court of Human Rights, former president Conseil d'Etat, France; the Honorable Earl Warren, chief justice of the United States Supreme Court, chairman, World Association of Judges; the Honorable Terje Wold, chief justice of Norway, former minister of justice of Norway; the Honorable Giuseppe Flore, presidente di Sezione della Corte Suprema di Cassazione, representing the Honorable Silvio Tavalaro, Prima Presidenza, Corte Suprema di Cassione of Italy; the Honorable Anthony McNulty, secretary, European Commission of Human Rights, Council of Europe; the Honorable Thomas H. Doyle, chairman, General Council of the Bar of Ireland; and Professor Jean Adrien Lachenal, University of Geneva.

The agreement among peoples on the perspectives of human dignity and on creating concord on their application to concrete cases is the dedication of Law Laureate Charles S. Rhyne, founder and president of the World Peace Through Law Center and a great supporter of World Habeas Corpus.

Hence, the following:

World Habeas Corpus is a proposed legal remedy suggesting that the security of the individual against arbitrary detention or imprisonment is a paramount concern in a world public order embodying the optimum and maximum for human dignity. It is a competent remedy that prevents or corrects wrongful individual detention.

The concept of World Habeas Corpus accommodates diverse and competitive political systems, implementing the human rights, articles of the U.N. Charter, the Universal Declaration of Human Rights, the Convention on the Prevention and Punishment of the Crime of Genocide. Asserting that the individual is the *subject* and not *object* of international law, it affords the right of individual petition to regional international courts of World Habeas Corpus. Repudiating Thomas Hobbes' *Leviathan dicta* that "coercion is the only prerequisite to make law effective," that "covenants without swords, are but words, and of no strength to secure a man at all" (ch. 17), that "the bonds of words are too weak to bridle men's ambition, avarice, anger and other passions with fear of some coercive power" (ch. 14), World Habeas Corpus is premised on Aristotle that "will, not force, is the basis of law," and "if a constitution is to survive, all of the elements of state (the people) must join in willing its existence and its continuance" (Barker, *The Politics of Aristotle* [Clarendon Press, 1957], p. 94).

Effective international law is a prerequisite of the institution of government. It is a means of prescribing international behavior that should be obeyed because it is the valid expression of the will of the people. Effective systems of sanctions (swords, coercion, economic boycott, military blockade, war per se) are immaterial to the consensus that obedience is essential because of the moral institution that the law ought to be obeyed and there can be sanctions for illegal behavior without resorting to war. A nation's self-interest in a world community is the most compelling element for consent to an international legal system.

Since World Habeas Corpus consists of a set of norms prescribing patterns of international behavior for individual security, it also fulfills the functions of domestic law to respect the integrity of the individual from arbitrary detention or imprisonment. The proposed treaty-statute of World Habeas Corpus spells out the convention as the source of the material international legal rules for *jus gentium*, or the law of peoples. With this codification will come increasing clarity for "reason," "equity," and "social conditions," a needed emotional basis for judicial decisions respecting the integrity of the individual.

Judicial decisions, when communicated to all the members of the world society, develop a climate of opinion. World Habeas Corpus will thus develop an international system—a consensus on the nature of the system of World Habeas Corpus—the mutual interdependence of national and international institutions about the human rights of mankind.

The treaty-statute of World Habeas Corpus, when adopted by convention and duly ratified by world signatories, can be "self-executing." Though the term "self-executing" may be ambiguous, the clarity of the phrase is illustrated by Chief Justice John Marshall in the case of *Foster* v. *Neilson* (1829) :

> Our constitution declares a treaty to be the law of the land. It is consequently, to be regarded in courts of justice as equivalent to an act of the legislature, whenever it operates of itself without the aid of any legislative provision. But when the terms of the stipulation impart a contract, when either of the parties engage to perform a particular act, the treaty addresses itself to the political, not to the judicial department, and the legislature must execute the contract before it can become a rule for the Court. (A. H. Robertson, *Human Rights in National and International Law* [Manchester University Press Oceana, 1968], p. 23.)

"Self-executing" is the core of the European Convention on Human Rights. If certain clauses are so worded that the convention addresses itself to the contracting states as subjects of international law and requires them to introduce laws and regulations to give it effect on municpal law, then it *cannot* be said to be "self-executing." Many clauses are "self-executing" which contain "obligations to refrain." If the prohibited action is one affecting individuals, this restriction of the freedom of action of the public authorities may manifest itself in international and in municipal law simultaneously. Some examples, among many, are the clauses providing that "no one shall be subjected to torture or to inhuman or degrading treatment or punishment" (art. 3) , that "no one shall be required to perform forced or compulsory labor" (art. 4 [2]), and that "no one shall be deprived of his liberty save in the following cases . . ." (art. 5 [1]). (Robertson, ibid., p. 24.) Another cogent illustration of the European Convention on Human Rights is article 25, wherein states are bound to allow the exercise of the right of individual petition to the Commission of Human Rights.

It is a curious commentary that the concept of World Habeas Corpus was first proposed in 1931, in Chicago, Illinois, by the editor of this symposium, a Chicago lawyer then 22, and that the achievement of its principal objectives was first established by the European Communities in 1950 when the European Convention on Human Rights was signed in Rome on 4 November 1950. When the right of individual petition first became effective in 1955, this remedy became available to more than 150 million persons. The United States and Canada, in the White House Conference on International Cooperation, 29 November–1 December 1965, as part of the United States observance of the International Cooperation Year, the committee on human rights expressed its belief that:

> As the United States and Canada share with the European Countries a common heritage in the field of human rights, it should be possible for them to join the European countries in their enterprising and successful effort to give international protection to human rights.

Since the foregoing is a still desirable goal, it is believed that World Habeas Corpus is a concrete proposal to accelerate international reluctance toward a common understanding of human rights that will unite nations on both sides of the Atlantic and the Pacific and the remainder of the seven seas.

As mentioned above, the concept of World Habeas Corpus was first proposed in 1931. The catalyst was Hitler's *Mein Kampf* and the exposure of the author to the oral and written speeches of Joseph Goebbels, Hermann Göring, Ernst Röhm, and Adolph Hitler. The author was frustrated in attempting to sound the alarm to the Nazi blueprint for human decimation and in attempting to create a rule of law, a personal legal beachhead for mankind. The inevitability of the rising tidal wave of national socialism was clear to few men in its expiation of German guilt in World War I, repudiation of the Treaty of Versailles, and determination to create a bloodbath in order to cleanse the guilt. The monstrosity of the Nazi mentality was not comprehended. The Jews were to be removed from Germany. *Mein Kampf* spelled out the blueprint for all the world to see. Arbitrary detention and murder was to be the order of the day. The love of law was to be flouted. But the conscience of the world remained sound asleep.

As a result, the apathy of the world in general and of the Bar in particular was incredible. However, several profound scholars encouraged the concept, namely, Dean Roscoe Pound, Professor John Dewey, Judge Francis Biddle, Dean Shailer Matthews of the Divinity School of the University of Chicago, then General (Vice President) Charles G. Dawes, George Cardinal Mundelein, Professor Hersch Lauterpacht, and several others. The author of World Habeas Corpus toured the United States trying to sound the alarm of the blueprint of *Mein Kampf.* There was little response and particularly no response from the Jewish community. Human decimation was unthinkable.

In 1937, Senator Arthur Vandenberg (Michigan) became a sound supporter, and from that year on the concept took on academic and political stature. Senator Vandenberg opened many doors and obtained the support of Mrs. Eleanor Roosevelt and Senator Warren Austin. At Dunbarton Oaks and during the drafting of the Atlantic Charter, Senator Vandenberg attempted to have the concept of World Habeas Corpus at least referred to.

In San Francisco, during the drafting of the United Nations Charter, the phrase "habeas corpus" was on the threshold of being inserted in the text of the Human Rights Articles. The building of the institution of World Habeas Corpus continued.

In 1949 the Vatican consulted with the author of the proposal, who worked with Samuel Cardinal Stritch and John Cardinal Spellman. A brief in behalf of Joseph Cardinal Mindszenty was drafted and circularized throughout the world. The premise of jurisdiction in the International Court of Justice was that the Paris Peace Pact of 1946 between Hungary, Romania, and Bulgaria declared these countries to be republics. At the time of the trial of Cardinal Mindszenty, however, Hungary was a police state. It was alleged, therefore, that it lacked jurisdiction to try him.

In 1950 Robert Vogeler was imprisoned by Hungary. The author of the World Habeas Corpus concept was consulted, but Vogeler had a semblance of due process and, therefore, the facts available did not warrant the drafting and filing of a petition of World Habeas Corpus before the Commission on Human Rights, particularly because of the resolution prohibiting individual petitions.

It was in 1950, at a conference in London, that Sir Winston Churchill eloquently summed up: "World Habeas Corpus is the difference between civilization and tyranny."

In 1952 the Associated Press correspondent William N. Oatis was tried and convicted in Prague, Czechoslovakia. The Associated Press, through Frank Starzell, then general manager, consulted the author of World Habeas Corpus, and a definitive petition for a U.N. writ of habeas corpus was drafted. In this endeavor invaluable assistance was given to the author by the late Congressman Joseph Martin, then Speaker of the House, Congresswoman Edith Nourse Rogers of Massachusetts, and Mrs. Eleanor Roosevelt. The author was permitted to use Congressman Joseph Martin's office for press conferences, and Mrs. Rogers presented the entire petition and brief on behalf of William N. Oatis before the House of Representatives on 8 May 1952. On 9 May 1952 Mrs. Roosevelt took over, and, with her invaluable support, the petition for Oatis was filed. Madam Vyaclev Pandit was then the incoming president of the General Assembly. In due course, twenty copies of the petition were served upon the respondent Czechoslovakia. Dean Acheson was then U.S. secretary of state. A press release in Washington did not disavow the unprecedented maneuver on behalf of William N. Oatis but merely stated that, at this time, the proposal of World Habeas Corpus was "unworkable." Several weeks passed, and the author obtained the practical assistance of the then ambassador of the Dominican Republic to the United Nations, Raphael Trujillo.

Ambassador Trujillo agreed to present the resolution before the United Nations, calling for the adoption of World Habeas Corpus as the definitive remedy to implement the human rights provisions of the U.N. Charter. In the interim, the mission from Czechoslovakia did not know what to do about the pending unanswered petition for the U.N. writ on behalf of Oatis. With the persistence of Ambassador Trujillo and goaded by the author, Oatis was released. On the floor of Congress, it was said that the legal fagot that helped free Oatis was the petition for the U.N. writ of habeas corpus as was filed on his behalf.

The institution of World Habeas Corpus spurred forward. From all over the world came support from international law scholars. Of course, in the interim, the loyalty and support of Dean Roscoe Pound and Professors Harold D. Lasswell, Myres S. McDougal, and George Dession, of Yale University were just way and beyond the call of duty. Famed jurist and scholar Hans Kelsen met with the author for a full week, and his support was immediate.

Then Father Harold Rigney was imprisoned in Red China. It was proposed that a petition be filed before the U.N. Commission on Human Rights requesting an ad hoc tribunal and naming Soviet Russia as respondent because of its alliance with Red China, which was not a signatory to the U.N. Charter. Numerous consultations were held at the Commission on Human Rights, and, during the drafting of the petition on his behalf, Father Rigney was released.

The moral weight of the institution of World Habeas Corpus was being felt. In 1959 the American Bar Association put World Habeas Corpus on its program at their annual meeting, and the proposed treaty-statute for World Habeas Corpus and the creation of regional international courts of habeas corpus were presented and given wide dissemination. This took place twenty-eight years after the concept was first proposed.

In the interim, numerous law journal articles were being published and worldwide recognition—at least academically—took place. Committees were being set up throughout the world. Former Chief Justice and now Justice of the International Court of Justice Kotaro Tanaka was involved in setting up the Japanese Federation of Bar Associations' endorsement. In India, S. G. Vase, senior advocate of the Bar, launched a World Habeas Corpus center, and centers followed in Rome, Hong Kong, Tokyo, Guayaquil (Ecuador), Laos, and Cambodia. Out of 126* signatories to the United Nations, some 90 presidents or chief judges of the courts of the signatory states have endorsed and are sponsoring the structuring of World Habeas Corpus as a permanent institution. The great and indefatigable Charles S. Rhyne launched the World Peace Through Law Center and promptly included World Habeas Corpus within the overall agenda.

In 1964 the author represented the American Bar Association at the International Bar Association Conference in Mexico City. One of the principal topics was World Habeas Corpus and international extradition. This followed the unqualified endorsement of U.S. Associate Supreme Court Justice William J. Brennan, Jr., at the American Bar Association meeting in San Francisco in August 1962, and the presentation of tributes to the proposal by the late Senator Estes Kefauver on the floor of the United States Senate.

---

*As of 31 January 1970.

In January 1969 an International Penal Law Conference was held at Siracusa, Italy. One of the topics was extradition. Professor M. Cherif Bassiouni represented the American Section of the Association Internationale de Droit Penal. The topic on extradition centered around the Bassiouni Special Resolution introduced at Freiburg, Germany, in April 1968, which was largely inspired by the concepts of World Habeas Corpus.

The Siracusa International Penal Law Pre-Conference (a preliminary stage preceding the Xth International Penal Law Congress scheduled for Rome, September 1969) resolved unanimously to adopt a resolution which restated the principle and terms of the Freiburg resolution, emphasizing the importance of human rights and their actual implementation through international organs such as the regional international courts of World Habeas Corpus.

H. E. Colli, justice of the Supreme Court (Presidente Corte di Cassazione), who presided over the Siracusa proceedings, concluded with an eloquent address wherein he outlined the future of a world where the law would know no frontiers and man no fears that he can be subjected to treatment outside the law. On the premise of World Habeas Corpus, he concluded that jurists must adhere to and work hard within organizations such as the Association Internationale de Droit Penal and the World Peace Through Law Center. Justice Colli hoped that international structures be developed so that ultimately and for the benefit of all mankind world public order be preserved by subjecting man and political structure to the competent rule of law.

A world conference on World Habeas Corpus with accredited representatives of the United Nations signatory and nonsignatory states is imminent. The institution of regional international courts of world habeas corpus is on the threshold of realization.

The rule of law has many images, and it has many spokesmen. In world history, from time to time, it has been ignored or violated by iron-willed, narcissistic, or psychotic rulers; but it is the only ligament that permeates the ever enlarging domain of the purpose and society of man.

The rule of law is not technology, it is not gadgetry of some mysterious cult. Nor is it any forbidding social monster. The evolution of law—rules of conduct that are permissive and prohibitive— is a constant adventure of the human spirit. It seeks to buttress faith in an order of reason out of a chaotic universe of which man is a part in his quest for individual security, opportunity, and meaningful peace.

In other words, the rule of law is a wellspring of human discontent that stirs man to seek more of life than merely a place of abode and of eating and sleeping. And that human discontent flames higher with each generation. It fails, however, to keep step with advancing scientific, chemical, military, and agricultural technology, albeit the discontent is nurtured by the desire to contemplate realistically the achievement of the highest of social ideals for the condition and existence of man.

The emergence of the human being as *subject* and not *object* of law—domestic or international—is of significance in the current space-age explorations of the entire universe and probably the entire galaxy. The accelerating age of science and technology comes to grips with the very nature and purpose of man as to what basically constitutes a good life in a turbulent world society.

It is a matter of contradiction, in the excitement of the space age, that there is a growing philosophy that seems to make man more serene in his transition through his lifetime without being hampered by religious or by totemic or idolatry shackles. The elite of the clergy no longer has a persuasive role in the purpose of mature, sophisticated men. The ever growing class of educated people repudiate the dogmatism, mysticism, and irrelevancy of religions in a world of physical and chemical sciences.

While collective science concerns all of mankind, all nations—be they emerged or emerging or expanding or contracting—recognize the truth that the progress of law, to permit people to live peaceably, productively, and without fear, is the only durable conquest of the story of humanity in the earthbound and space worlds.

History records the jailing, torture, degradation, and executions of men of science, men of law, and men engaged in "revolutionary activities" who dared to suggest social designs for shaping social and cultural patterns. It is a tragic cliché of a contemporary age to reject the dreams of the progressive thinkers. As genuine revolutionaries, developing cultural patterns and fostering vigorous sciences, explorations, and inventions, men (and women) have been condemned by a society devoid of discernment to recognize ability or to govern itself rationally and with justice.

The enigma of history has been the relentless pace of progress in the face of obstinate and obsolescent opposition. Since man, with his limited knowledge is the cause of violence, it is a wonder and excitement that the world has reached the incredible plateau of being able to convene a General Assembly of United Nations to exchange and debate viewpoints in the quest for peace and the implementation of the security of human rights. The divinity of rulers and the perfection of politicians are no longer dogma or accepted on an absolute basis. It is the constant compliment to man to discover his own inadequacies and to develop the implementations that point to ultimate truths.

Law, being self-revising, recognizes that there is no absolute right or absolute justice, but it does recognize that interpersonal relations between men and nations are connected and responsible to each other. To live comfortably and peaceably with law it is necessary to live with dynamically changing systems of cultural, national, and political concepts.

Responding to the interpretations of the needs and complexities of mankind, conservative attitudes are necessary to thwart and resist the easy abandonment of national and international concepts of law and religion. Not only are the rules of law and religion constantly subject to change but its prophets of law and religion for a better world are under challenge themselves.

Organizations such as the World Peace Through Law Center, International Bar Association, and International Law Committees of National and Local Bar Associations now enjoy the stimulation of intellectual exchanges dedicated to the end that the collective rule of law be made understandable to the world public. This mutual goal is one of constant education and intellectual discipline. This includes a constant reassessment of the government's obligations to live up to its contracts with its citizens so that there will be no violation of the human person nor impairment of the national sovereignty.

Those engaged in bringing into being the world cultural pattern of the rule of law are a sensitive elite different from those of the rest of society. This elite is not capricious or whimsical but endowed with historical optimism. They have the courage to tackle forcefully the awesome problems of creating an affirmative, behavioral world court. This is the true approaching tide of progress; it recognizes that man will always be a small island isolated in a vast hostile sea.

This, then, is the continuous creation of the men of law, the age of the rule of law. With it comes the promise of what the life of man can be with peace, education, food, adequate housing, and human freedom for all. It leads to a more even balance between individualism and collectivism.

The men of the rule of law for World Habeas Corpus commit themselves to build a world where mankind will not live at the razor's edge of danger. The men of the rule of law have a vital, flexible, and ever evolving concern about the nature and purpose of man and what constitutes a good life and a good society. It is to them that the human dimension of World Habeas Corpus is entrusted.

THE HUMAN RIGHT
TO INDIVIDUAL FREEDOM

THE HUMAN RIGHT
TO INDIVIDUAL FREEDOM

being subject to restraint in their personal liberty, is punished; —the maximum limits of detention prior to trial are established by the law." Furthermore, § 111 of the Constitution recites that "measures affecting the personal liberty of individuals and issued by ordinary or special courts shall be always subject to challenge, by means of an appeal to the Court of Cassation."

The constitutions and statutes of all civilized countries contain rules and norms very similar to those quoted above. We must prevent, however, the possibility that those principles remain practically ineffective in some countries, although such countries define themselves as civilized and in theory declare the validity of said principles. In other words, we must cause the habeas corpus to have an actual effect all over the world. To this end, besides the International Court of Justice and the European Court of Human Rights, it is necessary to create a world court of habeas corpus, as proposed by the Commission for International Due Process of Law. With this proposal, supported by many outstanding jurists from all over the world, I expressed at the Washington Conference, and confirm now, my full and enthusiastic solidarity. In my opinion, the possibility of appealing to said court should be available not only to individuals of whatever nationality who have been arrested or are imprisoned without cause but also to the states of which said persons are citizens and, in general, to all states which in a given case have even a moral interest to safeguard the dignity of man, by causing the arbitrary arrest or imprisonment to cease.

In order for the international court of habeas corpus to be actually operative, it will be necessary also to establish branches in all the states that will accede to the charter of World Habeas Corpus. Nor could anyone claim that the sovereignty of states might be impaired by the establishment of said court. To express such thinking would be to display the same skepticism as already arose on the occasion of the Universal Declaration of Human Rights, at San Francisco, in 1948. Against such skepticism we must react, if we do not want to deprive mankind of any yearning for improvement and any trust in human freedom and dignity. Those who will draw up the draft charter should therefore adopt very clear and explicit formulas in order to remove any idea of superimposition and predominance, so that, under full equality of rights among all the acceding states with respect to the charter, the

World Habeas Corpus, finding its accomplishment by virtue of their sovereign will, should actually constitute an expression of sovereignty of each state as well as of the community of all states.

I sincerely wish that our efforts give life to clear ideas and firm purposes, such as may enlighten the action of all rulers of the world and convince them of the absolute necessity of entrusting an international court with the task of settling every dispute concerning human freedom and dignity.

Some Thoughts on World Habeas Corpus

By the Honorable Sir Udo Udoma*

THE WORLD, it must be admitted, has made tremendous advances in technological knowledge, perhaps more than at any other period in its long history. It is also correct to say that the moral conscience of the world has been stirred by acts of brutality committed in many parts of the world against individuals. The idea that it is morally wrong for one nation to keep another under subjection or bondage and that such a subject nation ought to be given its right of self-determination, which may be said to have originated from the acts of a few men in Boston, won for the United States of America its independence. So too the concept of freedom for all and that slavery is fundamentally evil, which was propagated and championed by moralists of the nineteenth century, some of the greatest of whom may be said to have been Abraham Lincoln and William Wilberforce. What started as a small local ember has now developed into a great conflagration, or, in the words of Mr. Harold Macmillan, a great gust of the wind of change, sweeping across the world. These concepts are today virtually taken for granted and have brought about the emancipation of many countries formerly under colonial rule.

In spite, however, of the great advances both in technology and moral consciousness the world is still today in great turmoil. Human liberty is everywhere in peril. There are the fears of war. In

* M.A., LL.B., Ph.D.; chief justice of Ugandi.

some parts of the world individual freedom is practically nonexistent. It is trodden under foot by the great machine known as the state, which is daily growing in strength both in the political and, in some parts of the world, in the economic fields. The reason for the great powers assumed by the state is claimed to be that they are necessary for the preservation of its sovereignty. The new emphasis on state sovereignty has created a fear complex and distrust among nations as well as individuals, to the extent that any offer however genuine and laudable by one state to another for the preservation of peace is treated with nonchalance as a Greek gift. There is tension almost everywhere.

It cannot be denied, on the other hand, that mankind everywhere desires peace and the orderly development of society in order to ensure prosperity for all. But even so, the more desirable peace is the more elusive it appears to be, partly because of the feeling of distrust among nations and partly because of man's ambition for political and economic power, which still lurks in the hearts of those who, with almost religious regularity, pay lip service to, and even worship in the shrines of, world peace.

Man's desire for power is insatiable. Politicians sometimes disguise it under the smoke screen of the welfare of the people and the sovereignty and security of the state. A closer examination may reveal that the so-called advocates and champions of domestic as well as world peace and orderly development of society have but feet of clay. They are budding, if not practicing, dictators who, in their determination to have themselves entrenched as political rulers, would strengthen their hands by legislation in which the fundamental human rights—in terms of the U.N. declaration originally embodied in their constitutions for the protection of individual and minority rights—are suspended or abrogated altogether, and human rights and liberty become subject to the whims and caprices of politicians of the day.

Another technique that has been employed in denying the individual citizens or nationals their fundamental rights is the exclusion of the jurisdiction of the courts from all questions arising from or incidental to the exercise of executive power by state officials. So that matters touching and concerning the exercise of executive power become immune to justice. The courts are thus rendered powerless even in the face of grave injustice crying aloud to the high heavens for relief. Thus insulated from liability, state officials acquire and exercise almost absolute power with impunity.

By such techniques possible or potential political rivals are eliminated very often by incarceration or detention without due process of law—that is to say, without any form of criminal charge or trial. In detention, detainees are more often than not subject to solitary confinement and sometimes torture as a means of extracting information from them. They may never be informed of the actual reason for their detention or the precise nature of the offense committed by them other than the vague generalization that they were engaged in activities subversive and detrimental to the security of the state. Such a generalization may cover a multitude of sins on the part of the state officials.

During detention, detainees are denied access to any form of relief and to their wives, families, or other close relations. The psychological effect of such detention is general depression, sometimes resulting in temporary insanity or even death. Thus detained, the detainee becomes completely helpless and hopeless.

The thought that a citizen or national can be detained without charge or trial must of necessity affect the morale of the local population. Courage and boldness among the population become rare commodities. Detentions of this kind destroy individual originality and engender the belief among the people that any criticism of the activities of state officials is a crime, even though proper criticism ought to be accepted as a *sine qua non* for the proper functioning of a democracy. Fear and a feeling of insecurity are generated; and individual freedom, the very foundation of a democratic society based on the rule of law, which should germinate and flourish in every society, is thwarted and destroyed. Man thus becomes a mere cog in the wheel of the state so that to all intents and purposes he is given the impression that he was created for the state instead of the state for him.

In such circumstances, if the free world is to have a meaningful survival, it becomes the duty of all men of good will throughout the world—the idealist, the humanist, the Christian, and the true and sincere democrat, of whom there are many, who believe in a free society and a world in which the rule of law must reign supreme—to unite together to find a way of releasing mankind from this new chain of bondage and oppression and thereby bring an end to the prevalent venomous practice of arbitrary arrest and detention.

I think I am right in saying that it is only a peaceful, free, democratic society which can release a man's latent energy and creative instincts and direct them into right channels for the production of the higher things of life. It is only in a free atmosphere that the arts, literature, and intellectual pursuits can flower and flourish for the benefit of mankind.

In my view, the one effective remedy provided by law for preventing and possibly exterminating the present practice of arbitrary arrest and detention without trial, which would preserve human dignity and guarantee human freedom within the law, is that ancient constitutional bulwark of individual liberty that originated about the thirteenth century, even before the Magna Carta, and is known to the law as *habeas corpus ad subjiciendum*. This remedy is well known and revered in all common-law systems throughout the world.

Habeas corpus ad subjiciendum is a writ of such sovereign and transcendent authority that no privilege of person or place can stand against it. It is a remedy available to even the weakest citizen or individual against the most powerful. It remains still today of the highest constitutional importance, for by it the liberty of the individual in the state is vindicated, and his release from any manner of illegal and unjustifiable detention is assured. It is a "writ of right and it is granted *ex debito justitiae*" (see re Corke [1954] 2 All.E.R.440). It is a prerogative legal process for securing the liberty of an individual person, be he a citizen, an alien, or a foreigner, by affording him an immediate release from an unlawful detention whether such detention be in a prison or private custody.

Habeas corpus ad subjiciendum operates in this way: If a person is arrested and detained arbitrarily or illegally or unlawfully or unjustifiably and thereby deprived of his liberty, the person so detained is entitled to apply to the High Court for the writ for his release. Where the writ is granted, it commands the warden or the person to whom it is issued and directed to produce the body of the person detained with the day and cause of his detention—*ad faciendum, subjiciendum et recipiendum*, that is to say, to do, submit to, and receive whatsoever the court or judge awarding such writ shall consider in that behalf. The warden or the person to whom the writ is directed must, under the pain of attachment for contempt and the penalty of treble damages forfeitable to the detainee, produce in open court at the return of the writ the body of the detainee, and must then certify the true cause of detention or imprisonment. Within three days after such production the court must proceed to examine and determine whether the cause of such detention or imprisonment as appears upon the return is just and legal or not; and if not, must forthwith release the detainee.

The writ is very often used today for the purpose of testing the validity of any arrest or detention in countries in which its application has not been suspended or abolished altogether. It would lie in the case of a military arrest and detention, where the detainee is not brought to trial, or where someone is detained under the order of a naval, military, or ecclesiastical court. It may also be used in an application by a parent or guardian as to the custody or care of an infant, where the question may not even be as to the illegal or wrongful detention or the restraint of the liberty of the infant but as to the manner of the infant's education and upbringing. In England the writ is available to anyone detained under the Fugitive Offenders Act and the Extradition Act.

It may be noted in passing, however, that the writ of habeas corpus ad subjiciendum is not available to a criminal already convicted by a court of competent jurisdiction by due process of law. The only avenue open to such a convict is to institute an appeal to a court of appeal for the examination of the basis on which he was convicted. In the event of such an appeal proving unsuccessful, the law expects such a convict to serve his term in order to atone for his crime.

Another observation worth making is that under the common-law system, there is no right of appeal against an order absolute of a court for the issue of the writ (see *Secretary of State for Home Affairs* v. *O'Brien* [1923], A.C., p. 603).

Now comes the big and by no means an easy question: How can the writ of habeas corpus ad subjiciendum be made applicable to all countries of the world, and in what manner can it be enforced, having regard to the current theory of state sovereignty?

The doctrine of the sovereignty of states is of course in modern terms undergoing a sea of change. It is beginning to wear thin. Our present postwar world is contracting, and I think I am right in stating that the trend since the founding of the United Nations Organization is toward the humanization of international law as a result of the universal reaction against fascism and nazism, which had brought indescribable sufferings to innocent people in many cases because of their races.

At this juncture, it is worth noting that under nazism those who suffered were completely helpless and powerless even though there were courts still functioning in Germany.

While it is still true that states are directly the proper subject of international law as established by treaties and conventions duly ratified, and that the United Nations can in practical terms only deal directly with states as organisms embracing its whole population, yet it is hardly deniable that as far as fundamental human rights are concerned the proper subject in international concept should be the individual in the state. It is the individual in the state who suffers; and more often than not, the offender or oppressor is the state. A way must be found, therefore, for the protection of the individual citizen even against his own state.

If the Universal Declaration of Human Rights initiated and sponsored by the United Nations, which covers the right to life, liberty, safety, equality before the law, respect for privacy and family life, freedom of thought, expression, conscience, and religion, to name only a few, is to have any meaning at all, it should be made effective and enforceable throughout the world. As these rights strictly concern individuals within the state, I venture to suggest that there ought to be courts or institutions set up by the United Nations in specific, strategic areas charged with the duty of the enforcement of these rights. Ideally such courts ought to be of mixed nationals. The status of individuals ought to be recognized in this regard as a proper subject of international law, and an individual citizen or national should have a right of access to such regional courts either personally or by representatives.

The right to life and liberty of the individual in the state is of such fundamental importance that its enforcement should not be allowed to be controlled entirely by individual states.

Every member of the United Nations should be compelled not only to accept and ratify the conventions of human rights but also to have them implemented by incorporating them in and making them form part of its municipal law. Such member state should also regard it as its duty to submit to the compulsory jurisdiction of regional courts set up by the United Nations. It is of vital importance that these rights be declared to have binding effect on the high contracting parties and their nationals, because in some countries an international treaty or convention has no binding effect on citizens in the state unless their legislatures have given the force of law to such treaty or convention according to the procedure laid down in their respective constitutions. Unless these rights are accepted as of universal application and effect, and enforced in courts as part of the municipal law, a situation might develop whereby the state concerned may refuse to be bound by the decisions of regional courts on the ground that such decisions are inconsistent with their domestic laws.

A case in point in support of the above proposition is the famous Irish case of O'Laighleis. *Re O'Laighleis* (1960), Ir.R. 93, was an application for a writ of habeas corpus by O'Laighleis, who was suspected of being a member of the Irish Republican Army (IRA), then an outlawed organization. O'Laighleis was arrested and detained under the Offences Against the State (Amendment) Act, 1940, of Eire.

The detention was challenged as illegal having regard to articles 5 and 6 of the European Convention on Human Rights, of which Eire was a high contracting party and had also ratified it. Counsel for O'Laighleis submitted that the government of Eire, having ratified the convention, was bound to perform the obligations imposed thereunder, and that it was therefore estopped from exercising powers inconsistent with and in violation of the said convention.

That submission was rejected both by the High Court and the Supreme Court of Eire on the ground, *inter alia*, that by the Constitution of Eire "no international agreement shall be part of the domestic law of the State save as may be determined by the Oireachtas"; and that since the Oireachtas as the sole law making body in the state had not enacted a law implementing the convention, the convention had not become part of the municipal law of Eire and therefore could not be enforced by the courts. In upholding the decision of the High Court, the Supreme Court, on appeal, by way of emphasis maintained that the court could not give effect to the convention "if it be contrary to the domestic law of Eire or purports to grant rights or impose obligations additional to those of domestic law; and that domestic laws must prevail against inconsistent provisions of international law."

Thereafter O'Laighleis petitioned to the European Commission of Human Rights. The petition was held admissible and the Hu-

man Rights Court, while finding that the detention of O'Laighleis
had violated articles 5 (1c) and 5 (3) of the convention, was
nevertheless of the view that the act "of the Government of Eire
was not unlawful as the Government had acted within Article 15 of
the Convention". It was further held that the government had
acted primarily within the exigencies of the situation then prevailing in Eire even though in derogation of its obligation under
the convention.

I think it is only right and proper that in this paper tribute
should be paid to some of the newly independent countries that
have adopted these fundamental rights and have had them entrenched in their constitutions, so that such rights can only be suspended in times of real emergency, as envisaged in article 15 of the
convention. The conduct of affairs by some of these newly independent countries, in spite of their difficulties and pressures both
externally and internally, has been exemplary and is praiseworthy.

It is also reassuring that in Europe institutions like the European Commission of Human Rights, as well as the Court of Human
Rights, have been established at Strasbourg; and that these institutions and courts entertain individual petitions. Reports about their
performances have always attracted the highest praise. Among the
member states of the commission mention may be made of Austria,
Denmark, the German Federal Republic, Sweden, Norway, and
Great Britain. It is both noteworthy and praiseworthy that, in spite
of the system of law that guarantees human liberty and freedom of
expression as well as of religion, Great Britain should have decided
to become a member of the European Commission of Human
Rights. It is to be hoped that others will emulate this good example in leadership.

Another matter of interest is that there are proposals in the air
for the setting up of similar commissions and courts in the inter-
American and Central American regions. The idea of regional
commissions and courts seems to have gained ground in recent
years and rightly so for many reasons, the most important of which,
I think, is the reduction in expense and distance. The commission
and the courts thus become easily accessible to the people of the
area concerned. Regional commissions and courts would naturally
result in cohesion and continuity.

There is, however, one word of warning that, while regionalism
appears now popular, maybe on the grounds of expedition facili-

ties and above all accessibility, such commissions, when established, ought to be accorded the status of an important organ of the United Nations, to which alone it must owe allegiance. Otherwise, there is inherent in regionalism a tendency of separatism and fragmentation. Perhaps in the light of the progress being made in the operation of the European Commission of Human Rights and the Courts of Human Rights, and the proposals for the setting up of similar institutions in the inter-American and Central American regions, it would not be out of place to venture the suggestion that similar regional commissions and courts ought to be set up for Asia and Africa, where at present it seems that nothing is being planned in this direction.

In *re Mwenya* (1959), 3 All.E.R. 525, Lord Evershed, M.R., had said at p. 537:

> In conclusion then I do not attempt anything in the way of definition beyond saying that the jurisdiction in *habeas corpus* (of the Courts in England) ought not to be limited to territories, outside England, which are strictly labelled colonies, or foreign dominions, but will be extended to territories, which, having regard to the extent of the dominion in fact exercised, can be said to be "under the jurisdiction of the Crown," and in which the issue of the writ would be regarded in Lord Mansfield's words as "proper and efficient."

I would, therefore, like to end this paper by paraphrasing, if that were not too presumptuous of me, the above speech of Lord Evershed, M.R., with the statement of what the United Nations—of which all free and independent states but one are members and to which they may be said loosely to owe allegiance—do in order to exert its proper influence for the good government and peace of the world at large. It should conceive it its duty to see that the exercise of jurisdiction in the enforcement of the writ of habeas corpus for the protection of individual liberty and freedom be not limited to national or state courts but be extended to regional courts to be set up as organs of the United Nations for the proper and impartial administration of this great constitutional remedy— the bulwark of individual freedom.

Possibilities of the World Habeas Corpus Movement

By GEBHARD MÜLLER*

THERE IS no doubt that the worldwide acceptance of the habeas corpus principle would add a great deal toward securing peace and justice in the world. The great importance of the principle of habeas corpus for fair legal proceedings and for the safeguard of the fundamental human rights in general is obvious. An international system of habeas corpus forms a substantial part of "World Peace Through World Law."

The international movement for habeas corpus, like every movement for peace and justice, depends on whether the political realities will permit the realization of the idealistic goals. Unfortunately, at this time the political realities are not favorable for many idealistic movements, among which is the world movement for habeas corpus, even though the constitutions of many countries of the free world contain the right of habeas corpus. In some countries this right has a long judicial tradition. It might be possible to adopt this principle in many young countries that find themselves in a transitional state in which they are struggling to achieve interior stability and order. Despite all encouraging examples, however, there are still many countries whose constitutions put the

---

* Chief justice, Constitutional Court, Federal Republic of Germany.

raison d' état over the right of the individual and, therefore, do not allow for the principle of habeas corpus. We Germans experience over and over again legal proceedings and sentences—passed in that part of Germany occupied by the Russians—that repudiate all principles of justice and human dignity as well as the principle of habeas corpus.

In view of the political realities I also believe that a world court of habeas corpus could not, at present, operate too successfully. It is well to point out here that the International Court of Justice in The Hague has so far decided only one case in which Western and Eastern countries were opponents. In that instance the judgment in the Corfu Channel case decided in 1949 could not be carried out. The same would probably happen if a world court for habeas corpus were established. Such a court could be an additional guaranty only for the safeguard of justice in those countries that recognize the principle of habeas corpus. It would appear that the authority of a world court for habeas corpus would suffer if it would encompass only part of the nations that are divided ideologically, as then it probably would be charged with being merely a tool of the cold war.

The fact that a general world court of habeas corpus does not appear feasible at present affords nevertheless a good opportunity for the establishment of regional courts for habeas corpus. All things considered, however, such regional courts probably should not be created until further study is made to see whether their jurisdiction should also include some additional important legal rights of persons as are now guaranteed by the participating countries. The Anglo-American judicial tradition, which has always emphasized the formal protection of the individual by fair legal proceedings, could also be considered here, as well as the endeavor of other countries, e.g., the Federal Republic of Germany, to create a constitutional order of values with the central focus on human dignity. The European Court of Human Rights could serve as an example for such regional courts. The creation of courts similar to the present European one in the Western Hemisphere, or in Africa, Asia, or Oceania, or attempts toward this goal, would be one step in the right direction. The moral respect enjoyed by the international movement for habeas corpus and its leading members should certainly add to this development.

In the meantime it seems to be of the utmost importance that the countries of the world recognize the principles of habeas corpus. The inclusion of habeas corpus in more constitutions should be encouraged, especially in those countries where constitutional development is still in progress. The actual safeguard of habeas corpus by independent courts, however, is almost more important than written guarantees. That is a task for all courts, especially those which are entrusted with the interpretation of constitutional law. Particularly useful in this type of situation are constitutional courts like that of the Federal Republic of Germany. Here, too, the world movement for habeas corpus could contribute to accelerate and promote the development of such courts and their independence.

In all countries, various legal traditions and social structures constitute different problems. Further investigation should therefore be made to determine which countries should be considered as the best prospects for an endeavor to promote the principle of habeas corpus.

In these countries the world movement of habeas corpus should focus its work. Countries such as the United States, as well as the Federal Republic of Germany, in which the principle of habeas corpus has already been adopted as a part of their constitutions, should serve as examples for others. This example should not merely be the abstract principle embedded in the written or unwritten law, but must also be something concrete that actually can be seen by others to be in daily practice and operation.

Cambodia's Viewpoint
of World Habeas Corpus

By Norodom Sihanouk*

THE World Habeas Corpus proposal for the setting up of a judicial structure within the framework of the United Nations Organization is designed to ensure proper observance of article IX of the Universal Declaration of Human Rights, which lays down that "no one shall be subject to arbitrary arrest, detention or exile."

Small countries, such as Cambodia, are well placed to appreciate the immense benefit that would be derived from the setting up of such machinery to protect citizens from arbitrary abuses of power by their respective governments, exposed as such countries often are to threats to their national existence by predatory neighbors. Indeed, I would suggest that international agreement to this proposal should be preceded by the strengthening of the existing means for ensuring the protection of small states from arbitrary abuses of power on an international scale, based on universal acceptance of the principle that the age of territorial conquest is past.

Cambodia can justly claim, furthermore, to have set the example and to have shown the way by which the rule of law can come about by declaring its readiness to accept certain restrictions on national sovereignty in exchange for an international guarantee of its territorial integrity. Thus, Cambodia recently offered to allow

---

* Phnom Penh, Samdech Preah, Chef de l'Etat du Cambodge.

members of the International Control Commission charged with ensuring strict observance of that neutral status—which would be the necessary corollary to a guarantee of this nature—complete freedom of movement throughout its national territory, together with the right to search Cambodian villages and homes without prior reference to the local authorities.

May the endeavors of World Habeas Corpus to achieve its noble aim prove successful in aiding the efforts of my government to ensure the peoples and governments of like small countries the right to pursue their national destiny secure against such arbitrary abuses of power as air attacks on their villages and raids from neighboring territories, which have been so devastating during recent years.

The Chinese Constitution and the Habeas Corpus Principle

By Ku Cheng-kang*

THE World Habeas Corpus aims at world peace through law, which, I believe, is congenial to the Chinese traditional utopia of One World, the Great Unity ('Ta-tung' in Chinese), envisaged by Confucius two thousand years ago.

It also recognizes the absolute value of the individual, which is similar to the Chinese traditional principle that the people are the foundation of the state, that is, the doctrine of supremacy of the people ('Ming-pen' in Chinese) initiated and developed by Confucians.

The above two traditional Chinese principles have been further developed and transformed elaborately into Dr. Sun Yat-sen's Three Principles of the People ('San Min Chu-i' in Chinese), which were adopted as the basic principles of the Constitution of the Republic of China.

With regard to the present constitutional government of the Republic of China, it apparently illustrates in some ways the Chinese principles identical with the purposes of the World Habeas Corpus.

First, in article 8 of the Chinese Constitution, it is clearly provided that personal freedom shall be guaranteed to the people.

* President, Asian Peoples' Anti-Communist League, Republic of China.

Some basic principles of the guarantee of personal freedom followed in the regulation of the article.

Article 9 of the Constitution goes on prescribing that except those in active military service, no person shall be subject to trial by a military tribunal.

In addition, there is Law of Habeas Corpus, promulgated on 22 June 1935 before the promulgation of the Constitution, and amended on 26 April 1948 after the enforcement of the Constitution. It is similar to the British habeas corpus acts.

Secondly, article 141 of the Constitution provides: "The foreign policy of the Republic of China shall ... respect treaties and the Charter of the United Nations ... promote international cooperation, advance international justice, and ensure world peace." Evidently, it is by all means in harmony with the purpose of the World Habeas Corpus.

Thirdly, the constitutional government of the Republic of China is primarily devoted to the rule of law. Article 62 of the Constitution prescribes; "The legislative Yuan is constituted of members elected by the people. It shall exercise legislative power on behalf of the people." Again, it is provided in article 172 of the Constitution that ordinances that are in conflict with the Constitution or with law shall be null and void.

All in all, both in Chinese cultural principle and in Chinese political system, the World Habeas Corpus is fully respected.

The Idea of Habeas Corpus in Colombia

By SAMUEL BARRIENTOS RESTREPO*

WE IN Colombia have long maintained the democratic philosophy of making a world secure under the rule of law. We believe that no legal order, international or other, is true to its essential function unless it protects effectively the ultimate unit of all law: the individual human being. Since the Second World War there has been widespread conviction that the effective international protection of human rights, including some form of an international bill of rights, was the major purpose of the war, inasmuch as it is an essential condition of international peace and progress. We have long believed that the time is ripe for the advancement of the rights of man through anchorage that is natural and fitting, to wit, a universal law of organized mankind in the law of nations.

Colombia adheres to the principle that man's fundamental right, the right to be let alone, bespeaks that freedom from unjustifiable interference from the government is the fundamental right of every man. Colombia is a unified republic centralized in the political field and decentralized administratively. Its government is a representative democracy. The "sovereignty resides essentially and exclusively in the nation and from it emanate the public powers that will be exercised in the terms that the Constitution establishes."

It has been said that the state is the power that possesses the

*Magistrado de la Sala de Casación Penal de la Corte Suprema de Justicia, República de Colombia.

right or, as it were, is an organization that seeks the empire of justice, so that each man has those benefits that will be subordinate for his perfection, spiritually and materially. From this it is deduced that the authorities in Colombia have as their function to guarantee the life, respect, and benefits of its citizens and to insure the carrying out of the social duties of the state and the citizen. Among the rights of men that the Colombian Constitution recognizes are his individual liberty, dignity, and privacy. The Constitution guarantees these rights through these rules:

> Article 23: No one shall be molested in his person or family, nor placed in prison or arrested or detained, nor his domicile invaded, but by virtue of a written ruling by a competent authority with the legal formalities and by motives previously defined by law.
>
> .   .   .   .
>
> Article 26: No one shall be judged except in conformity to preexisting laws concerning the accused act, before a competent tribunal, and in observance of the fullness of the appropriate processes of each trial.
>
> .   .   .   .
>
> Article 28: Even in time of war, no one shall be sentenced *ex post facto*, except in accordance with the law, order, or decree which has previously prohibited the act and determined the corresponding penalty . . .

In Colombia, as is seen, it is only possible to deprive a man of his liberty by previously defined laws, by competent authorities, and observing the fullness of the correct processes of each trial.

Colombia procedural law is consecrated to agile procedures to ensure individual liberty; defense is not only a right but a duty of the citizen, as the state defends him when he does not defend himself; these procedures are written and are carried out without permitting the least coercion or influence; unions cannot be subjected to punishment or pressures of any kind; innocence is presumed where there has been no condemning judgment or sentence; the trial is public and the public has access to the defendant.

In this manner we have the acceptance of the principle contained in article IX of the Universal Declaration of Human Rights of the Charter of the United Nations, which says: "No one shall be arrested, detained or exiled arbitrarily"; and we have the stated measures for its effectiveness.

It is possible that this is not the case in some countries. We therefore recognize the importance of the proposed international courts of habeas corpus, whose principal author and advocate has been Professor Luis Kutner, who is worthy of recognition because of this.

It is accepted that, in the Universal Declaration of Human Rights, habeas corpus can actually be no more than rhetorical inspiration or pious longings while measures are not promulgated to guarantee it. To this point, an international court of habeas corpus, or regional courts, might very well be considered. Or perhaps the adoption, through a multilateral treaty, of a summary and effective procedure that will guarantee habeas corpus—that is, protect individual liberty as well as all the other rights inherent to the human being.

In this way, the principles of the Universal Declaration of Human Rights would cease being mere literature in many cases and be converted into realities in the modern world. The day this is achieved, the importance of the task initiated by Professor Luis Kutner will be fully recognized.

The question of access of individuals to international tribunals, including the International Court of Justice, should no longer be a matter to be determined by reference to an abstract, dogmatic, obsolescent, and inaccurate rule that individuals are not subjects of the law of nations and that it would be contrary to the very structure of international law to confer upon them a procedural capacity in that sphere.

World Habeas Corpus translates the provisions of the U.N. Charter and the Declaration of Human Rights into an effective rule of international law. It dramatically illustrates that international law is not a rigid notion but can admit, in the interest of international peace and justice, the concept that human beings are subjects of the community of international law.

It is hoped that these thoughts about habeas corpus in Colombia, as well as the thoughts about the necessity of the free world to make effective article IX of the Universal Declaration of Human Rights through the creation of a world court of habeas corpus, or of regional courts of habeas corpus, or of the signing of a treaty-statute that contains a plan (or procedure) to guarantee all the rights of the human being and principally the right to be free, will be helpful in hastening the day of reality.

We in Colombia praise the work that is being done toward the creation of the international courts of habeas corpus and wish to participate in the success it deserves.

World Habeas Corpus and the United Nations

By Raoul Benattar*

IT IS an honor for me to become a member and sponsor of your association for World Habeas Corpus and the regional courts of habeas corpus. I do agree with your ideas and with incorporating a habeas corpus treaty-statute into the United Nations structure.

All the member states of the United Nations have adhered to the Universal Declaration of Rights and acknowledge the guarantee of the fundamental liberties of the individual. Such a principle, so solemnly affirmed and unanimously recognized, asserts itself as a veritable judicial rule constituting one of the fundamental principles of international public right.

Now, as a consequence, all judicial rule necessarily has power. Also, the states which adhere to the declaration and which, by the same token, are bound by such a rule are obliged not only to apply it in their own countries but, moreover, are all engaged, jointly and separately, in ensuring respect for this rule of law everywhere in the world.

It follows then that, just as in the internal order of states there are judges and sanctions to ensure respect for laws, one must equally acknowledge international law, judges, and sanctions to prevent and check violation of the rules of the U.N. Charter. Without this, these rules are deprived of all efficacy and the com-

---

* Faculté a Droit de Tunis.

pulsory authority appropriate to judicial rules and become no more than "empty rhetoric," as has been so well expressed by Mr. Justice Brennan.

One cannot but approve the international judicial principle similar to the European Court of Rights of Man, only making it flexible and improving its procedures, at least those which would be susceptible of being put into effect against governments that act arbitrarily in depriving individuals of their liberty and dignity.

It is doubtful, however, that in the actual state of affairs in the world the states would agree to acknowledge—althought one can hope that justice will become, by its own power and virtue, veritably international—that a redress against the decisions of their national tribunals should be brought before an international court through the legal tool of World Habeas Corpus.

A first step on this path could nevertheless be accomplished by imposing on states, as a consequence of the Universal Declaration, a compulsory control to be exercised by jurists and experts designed and delegated by a special section of the United Nations to ensure that the fundamental freedoms and, in particular, the rule of law, are neither threatened nor affected in a given country each time a danger of this type is indicated.

It is not only in the case of a state refusing this control or if, following the imposition of the control, the experts themselves set aside a report verifying the alleged violations that the world habeas corpus international courts would then be invoked. The principle of World Habeas Corpus would be a determining factor that would constitute and influence the judgments of these international courts, making the national tribunals revise their processes and without delay grant just reparation and indemnities to the injured parties. One could further conceive that, as long as the defaulting state would not comply, it could be suspended from exercising its rights at the United Nations.

The above mentioned observations constitute another spring to the coil; they go along ideologically with my preferences.

At the present time, I am afraid, neither governments nor people are yet ready to accept such judicial internationalization. But efforts should be renewed with increased vigor on behalf of World Habeas Corpus. In-depth education suggests internal solutions that would then be a solid basis on which the judicial international organization of World Habeas Corpus could be put on its feet. The objectives and principles of World Habeas Corpus are imperative if ever a peaceful world is to be achieved.

Section II

The Rule of Law
in World Affairs

By William O. Douglas*

Tennyson wrote of the time when "the battle-flags were furl'd in the Parliament of man, the Federation of the World." There have been several times since those lines were penned when some had the notion that we were on the edge of having a full-fledged world parliament. The illusion always was dispelled; and cynics rested more secure than ever in the smugness of their brand of nationalism. Yet the world has made greater progress than we are prone to think in developing important parts of the framework of a world system of law.

We have had in this country among legal circles a narrow, limited view of law. Thomas Hobbes in 1651 published the *Leviathan* in which he took what became a rather classic but restricted idea of law—that a "sovereign" is the source of all law. This meant, in Hobbes' view, that "equity, justice," or other "qualities that dispose men to peace and obedience" are "not properly laws." John Austin gave the Hobbes philosophy great impetus. Several generations of lawyers have been influenced by Austin and his book, *Province of Jurisprudence Determined*, first published in 1832, where law in the strict sense was defined as the body of rules enforced by a sovereign state. World law, in that view, requires a

---

*Associate justice of the Supreme Court of the United States.

full-fledged superstate in which all nations are merged—a supranational organization that has political and military control over all
of its units. Under this view world government would require
perhaps a more centralized organization than that proposed by
Grenville Clark and Louis B. Sohn in their important book, *World
Peace Through World Law.* Yet, as Roscoe Pound observed in a
chapter in Northrop's *Ideological Differences and World Order,*
"all states need not be merged in a great world state, in which their
personality is lost, in order that their conduct may be inquired into
and ordered by authority of a world legal order." Moreover, the
true gauge of law is not command but conduct. Those who move
to the measured beat of custom, mores, or community or world
mandates are obeying law in a real and vivid sense of the term.
Law is a force that shapes and moulds the affairs of men. The fact
that there may be no court to enforce a rule of conduct does not
prove that no international law exists. As Professor A. L. Goodhart said, "Law has frequently existed before the particular courts
of the State have been created."[1]

No institution springs full-blown from the pens of draftsmen.
Every institution is the expression of need and of experience; it
may evolve slowly; its periods of growth may be separated by
decades. The cohesive force may be linguistic, economic, religious,
military. Reason alone may also be the instrument. For the latter
we need not look far. The United Nations is today the expression
of world opinion that the cult or regime of force must be replaced
by a measure of world law. The United Nations has a far greater
prestige and stature, I think, than it could have been expected to
acquire in such a short period since its formation.

Mr. Justice Holmes said in 1895, "Now, at least, and perhaps as
long as man dwells upon the globe, his destiny is battle, and he has
to take his chances with war."[2] That viewpoint has dominated
men's thinking for centuries. Yet it deserves no enduring place in
any decalogue. For man is capable of great cooperative efforts in
peace as well as in war. Love and the instinct for preservation of
life—these are even deeper in man's character than violence.
William James in *The Moral Equivalent of War* wrote in 1910,
"[W]hen whole nations are the armies, and the science of destruction vies in intellectual refinement with the sciences of production, I see that war becomes absurd and impossible from its
own monstrosity." Nuclear war surpasses that prophecy. The physi-

cists have told us how obsolete the cult of force, armed with nuclear weapons, has become. Harrison Brown and James Real, in their paper, "Community of Fear,"[3] show how and why this country could *today* probably be utterly destroyed by less than a 20,000 megaton attack.[4]

We hear of proposals to put us all underground. We are told that we could sustain a loss of 20 million people and rebuild our economy in ten years.[5] But we know that as bombs get bigger and bigger we would have to go deeper and deeper into our holes. Factories, stores, apartments, houses, etc., would be all underground. Man's journey from the caves to the light would be ended; man would revert to his Mousterian condition of tens of thousands of years ago. Today there are only a few nations that have these nuclear weapons. In ten to twenty years how many nations will not have the secret? We are told that there will be at least fifteen nations producing nuclear weapons in the 1960s, including Red China.

What are the chances that there will be a nuclear war? A military analyst says that during the next ten years the chances of a nuclear conflict, based either on diplomatic miscalculations or on a limited war's becoming an all-out war, are 50-50. Diplomatic miscalculations and the spread of a limited war are only two of several factors. What about accidents in defense systems such as false radar readings, faulty intelligence, misinterpretations of military orders, and the like? What about human errors, such as aberrant bombers or missiles, irresponsible commanders, or sabotage from within our own ranks? When atomic bombs, as a result of new discoveries, get into ."the ten dollar" class, what international gangster will be without one? What Hitler will appear with mad dreams? What adventurer will think he may be able to pull it off so that he in truth runs the world? What leader with cold calculation may be willing to sacrifice twenty, forty, sixty, eighty, a hundred million, or even more of his own people to gain leverage on the whole world through a sudden nuclear attack?

Rational people the world over are disturbed by these thoughts. Reason, as well as fear, is propelling them to place their hopes in joint action to protect the very earth from being so poisoned by radioactive fallout that human life is jeopardized or even ended.

We are told of new dangers by such experts as Dr. Abel Wolman of Johns Hopkins, who in his 1959 testimony before Congress showed that even peaceful use of nuclear energy poses staggering problems. As of 1959 we in this country had 65 million gallons of high activity radioactive water in storage. By 1980 he estimates that these by-products of the peaceful use of nuclear energy will amount to from one to three hundred million gallons. By 1980 these storage waters will have about 10 billion curies; i.e., they will emit the same number of alpha rays per unit of time as 10 billion grams of radium. These wastes cannot be detected by human taste or odor. Their life is long—perhaps a thousand years, perhaps longer. Failure to control what we store today may lead to vast human disasters next year, a hundred years hence, or in the far distant centuries. Will concrete containers buried in the ocean last that long? What is the life of stainless steel that holds these wastes? Can they be disposed of in the ionosphere? These are problems that concern the experts. As Dr. Wolman testified, the problem "will require a deep governmental supervision, a very long, continued, and uninterrupted supervison over the fate and location of these materials." As of 1960 no nation in the world has found a solution to disposal of these high level radioactive wastes.

What is the amount other nations have stored? What will the world total be in 1980? We do not know. But we do know this is a problem the international community shares.

Fission by-products may be temporarily disgorged in the stratosphere or sunk deep in the oceans. But they eventually return to plague the skies, the shores, and the waters of every country. Plainly, international regulatory action will soon be necessary. Only supranational action can save all of us—white, black, brown, yellow—from the new perils generated by these new engineering achievements.

Another force, though of lesser proportions, is at work bringing the nations together. We witness in this half of the century a great emergence of new nations. Fifteen new African nations plus Cyprus were admitted to the United Nations at its recent meeting. Centuries of colonialism have ended; nations or races long subjugated by outside regimes are gaining their independence. They are weak, inexperienced, fragile. They came into their inheritances at a time when world forces are aligned into powerful blocs that might make these new countries pawns in the old game of power politics. Many at least remember the old African proverb, "When the bull elephant fights, the grass is trampled down." Moreover, none wants to become either a puppet of an imperialistic regime or a Communist satellite. Neither alternative is attractive to those young nations. If independence is to be kept, as well as achieved, they must have a refuge, a sanctuary where they can feel secure. The United Nations satisfies that craving for security. And its early success in the Congo, in protecting the new nation from the internal machinations of foreign powers, dramatized its usefulness as nothing else at this juncture of history could do.

The United Nations today has eleven consultative groups in the Congo for civil operations. Agriculture, communications, health, finance, foreign trade, labor, judiciary, national resources, and public administration mark the area where the United Nations is trying to give the Congo a viable system of government. Doctors and nurses from at least two dozen countries are working there. The community of nations has united on a mission of education and mercy as well as power. The Congo episode shows some of the potential for law, order, and justice that exists in the United Nations.

One handicap of the United Nations today is that it excludes groups that should be included. With the admission of Nigeria the number of members has reached ninety-nine. Red China is still excluded. Yet Red China, in which nearly a fourth of the people of the world live, is apparently more than a transitory government. She is established more firmly than a mere *de facto* regime. Prof. Tuzo Wilson of Toronto University in *One Chinese Moon* (1959) makes startling disclosures as to her progress in science. We can assume she will have her own atomic warheads before long. Meanwhile she is an obstreperous, aggressive nation. Her tactics against India have added up to calculated aggression. While she was talking peace and friendship, she actually was annexing Indian territory in northern Ladakh. Her tactics against Tibet have exceeded in ruthlessness and cruelty the actions of Russia in Hungary. Tibet—never rightfully a province of China in spite of several centuries of Chinese propaganda—has been cruelly incorporated into it. The Buddhist church has been all but exterminated. The priests have been executed or put into labor battalions. A fierce regimentation has been placed on the people. A proud and independent nation of two million Tibetans has been transformed into a servile province by the invasion of six million Chinese.[6]

These Tibetan and Indian ventures on the part of Red China

make her an outlaw in any accurate use of the word. Being an outlaw may seem in logic to be a reason for barring her from the United Nations. But in reality how can an outlaw be kept outside the United Nations and yet disciplined by it? There is today no tribunal to which Red China can be made to account. There is no assembly or council before which she can be summoned.

Traditionally, "recognition" of a government did not necessarily imply approval of its regime. President Grant said in 1875 concerning the recognition of Cuba that in such a case "other nations simply deal with an actually existing condition of things, and recognize as one of the powers of the earth that body politic which, possessing the necessary elements, has, in fact, become a new power. In a word, the creation of a new state is a fact."[7] That reflected the traditional view. The historic tests have been (1) whether a government exists independent of another state, and (2) whether it has internal stability and is a functioning government.[8] By Jefferson's standards a government was to be recognized if it represented "the will of the nation, substantially declared."[9]

But conditions change, and the concept of "recognition" has been used to serve other ends; it has at times "become a political weapon used to force a new government to make concessions to the demands of the recognizing state."[10] So far as precedents go, one can find what he is looking for. But as recently stated,

> In the absence of effective international guarantees for securing just government and proper administration of the law within the various States, it is impossible to insist on the perpetuation of any existing regime by a refusal to recognize its revolutionary successor. Neither is it in the long run practicable to adopt the indirect method of refusal of recognition as a means of compelling the fulfillment of international obligations. The more rational method is to grant recognition and then to insist, by such means as International Law offers, on the proper fulfillment of its obligations on the part of the recognized Government."[11]

Cold practicalities make admission of Red China necessary, accompanied, of course, by a settlement of the many tangled but pressing problems between this country and Red China. What about the Americans held as prisoners by Peiping? What about the Korean and Vietnam situations, and Formosa? Today these problems fester and worsen. It is time that we undertook political settlements of them. The peace of the world may soon turn on them. In any event, a United Nations that is such in fact must be able to bring its influence to bear on all world problems that affect the peace or that impair the integrity of nations. Today we can say no more than that the United Nations is a form emerging from the mists. What shape it will have in the bright hours of man's maturity we do not yet know. It is, however, real, vivid, and effective in providing some instruments of international law.

The United Nations has weathered stormy seas. On 27 June 1950, when the Security Council at the initiative of President Truman resolved to furnish such assistance "to the Republic of Korea as may be necessary to repel the armed attack" by North Korea and "to restore international peace and security in the area," world opinion stood behind it. The Communist bloc was of course opposed. But the forty-odd nations approved. India's views represented perhaps the common denominator of thinking in all capitals, for she stated that she was "opposed to any attempt to settle international disputes by resort to aggression."[12]

This indeed was a new principle of international law which had been forged by experience. It is embodied in the Charter of the United Nations: "To take effective collective measures for the prevention and removal of threats to the peace, and for the suppression of acts of aggression or other breaches of the peace." The U.N. action in Korea was the first time the outlawry of aggression was implemented by direct, military action by the community of nations. Aggressive war had become too dangerous to the world community to be allowed; so it was denounced, and joint action was taken to bring forceful sanctions against it. This was noble, principled, responsible action that gave power and force to a newly forged tenet of international law.

We do not have in this instance the kind of question stirred in the Nuremberg and Tokyo trials—whether the law was in application *ex post facto*.[13] For the charter announced in explicit terms that aggressive war was outlawed. And the argument that the action of the Security Council was unconstitutional, by standards of the charter, because Soviet Russia absented herself was frivolous. The argument turned on whether the charter required both the presence *and* concurrence of permanent members of the Security Council to validate U.N. action, or whether it required only concurrence *if* present and participating. Accepted canons of interpretation point toward the latter interpretation, not least because it is the one which gives vitality to the United Nations as an effective organization.[14]

The aftermath confused the simple, clear-cut issue before the Security Council. The Soviets soon denounced the U.N. police action in Korea as "war"—a "war" that the United States inspired and conducted under the cloak of the United Nations. Eisenhower, in his campaign speech of 4 September 1952 gave ammunition to the Soviets. He, too, called the police action in Korea a "war." The expediency of American politics caused the vital distinction between U.N. "police action" and "war" to become blurred and confused. We stepped backwards, retreating temporarily from the principal decision that "aggressive war" called for world action against the aggressor.

Since those days we have regained some of the lost ground. On 2 November 1956 the General Assembly voted 64 to 5 for a ceasefire on the actions undertaken against Egypt. Later that month it created an international command force of the United Nations to supervise the cessation of hostilities; and in a matter of a few days hostilities ceased.

When the Republic of the Congo asked for help from the United Nations to maintain its government from the machinations of a foreign power, and when, in response, the Security Council on 13 July 1960 resolved to extend that aid, the principle of the independence of nations was strengthened. Protection of a nation against aggression from without was extended to protection against any form of intervention by a foreign power. The action of the United Nations in the Congo plus the defeat of Soviet efforts to sabotage it and capitalize on the disorder and chaos have brought United Nations prestige to a new high. There is warrant for the optimism that its growing achievements presage a new period of growth for effective international law. And this will remain so, whatever happens in the Congo. The United Nations has played an essential role there. What is at stake now is the effect of a long stay of outside forces in a nation that cannot find its leaders, the purity of motives of all participants, and the continued faith of the majority of the nations in the U.N. personnel. But the principle that the United Nations stands ready to protect a people in their right to run their own affairs and that the troops sent there are engaged in "police action" in the cause of peace rather than in "war" has promise of becoming a sturdy one in international law.

An even broader advance in international law is needed. It was broached by President Eisenhower in his address to the United Nations Assembly on 22 September 1960. Referring to the African situation in particular, he emphasized five points:

> Non-interference in the African countries' internal affairs . . . Help in assuring their security without wasteful and dangerous competition in armaments . . . Emergency aid in Congo . . . International assistance in shaping long term African development programs . . . United Nations aid for education.

As the world is evolving, there are few, if any, nations that can go it alone. None is an isolated, insulated unit. Sovereignty may in theory be entirely in local hands, yet the very need for raw materials or food or loans or technicians from abroad creates a dependency on other nations. There are not many examples of self-sufficiency, as our own economy illustrates.

The dependency of nations on each other is developing international collectivism in myriad forms. This is a healthy growth of collectivism of which the free world is a part. It is, indeed, one of the aims of the United Nations as expressed in article I, "to achieve international cooperation in solving international problems of an economic, social, cultural, or humanitarian character." The development of supranational institutions of an administrative character will in time result in the emergence of patterns or codes of administrative procedure.

The list of agencies through which cooperative or collective action is taken by a group of nations is constantly increasing. The specialized agencies of the United Nations alone make a formidable list—International Labor Organization, Food and Agriculture Organization, United Nations Educational, Scientific and Cultural Organization, World Health Organization, International Monetary Fund, International Bank for Reconstruction and Development, International Finance Corporation, International Civil Aviation Organization, Universal Postal Union, International Telecommunication Union, World Meteorological Organization, Inter-Governmental Maritime Consultative Organization, International Trade Organization, and International Atomic Energy Agency.

Each of these is in a sense a government unto itself. In some a majority vote controls. The constitution of the ILO, for example, provides that while a member government may object to the inclusion of any item on the agenda, a two-thirds vote of the delegates present can put it there (art. 16).

It is commonly provided that any question or dispute concerning the constitution of one of these agencies or any international convention adopted pursuant to it shall be referred for determination to an appropriate international court or arbitral tribunal.[15] The Articles of Agreement of the International Bank provide for arbitration of certain disputes between member nations and the bank. The arbitrators are three in number—one named by the bank, one by the nation involved, and the third by the president of the International Court of Justice or by any other authority prescribed in the regulations of the bank (art. IX). A similar provision for arbitration of disputes is contained in the UPU convention (art. 31) and in the ITU convention (art. 25).

The Constitution of the ILO provides for the enforcement of conventions which member states have ratified. A procedure is providing for filing of complaints and the appointment of a Commission of Enquiry to make a report (arts. 26-28). If the report of that commission is not adopted by the governments concerned, the complaint may be referred to the International Court of Justice (art. 29) which has power to make a "final" decision (art. 31).

The United Nations and the ILO have agreed that the ILO will furnish the International Court of Justice any information the Court desires (art. IX), and the ILO is authorized to request advisory opinions from the International Court of Justice. An agreement between the United Nations and the FAO places the FAO in the same position vis-à-vis the International Court of Justice. The same is true of UNESCO (art. XI), WHO (art. X), and ITU (art. VIII).

Each of these agencies of the United Nations operates under a regime of international law. And the contracts, engagements, assignments, and undertakings that they assume set precedents and practices that may in time become firmly imbedded in international law.

The recent achievement of the International Bank of Reconstruction and Development, headed by Eugene Black, in setting the Indus River dispute between Pakistan and India is international law in operation. The process was not adjudication or legislation, the procedures we normally identify with "law." This was mediation and conciliation at a high level, procedures that have been constituent parts of our own domestic legal system for years. Whenever nations work together through a common agency, they submit to a regime of international law. The European countries and the South American countries that have established common markets work conspicuously in the role of supranational groups. When the Inner Six and Outer Seven conduct business, a rule of law that is international in character moves into operation.

There is a rather unusual international agency that was established in 1954 and known as the International Control Commission. It was created by the Geneva Conference at which France and the People's Army of Vietnam agreed on a cessation of hostilities. The International Control Commission was composed of members from Canada, India, and Poland. It served an important function in supervising the end of the war in Vietnam. It—or another agency like it—could be asked to mediate an end to other civil wars. Its usefulness in situations such as Laos presented in the winter of 1960 was obvious. Laos, closer to China than Cuba is to us, is an inflammatory situation. If it is anything other than a neutral nation, it will create endless friction. Canada, England, and India were anxious for the International Control Commission to mediate the Laos situation in the fall of 1960. Eisenhower's State Department and Pentagon were against it. Millions were poured into Laos in an effort to make it a pro-West beachhead. Power politics were again substituted for a rule of law.

Not all agencies applying or enforcing international law are international agencies. It was accurately stated by Mr. Justice Gray, speaking for the United States Supreme Court in 1900, that "International law is part of our law and must be ascertained and administered by the courts of justice of appropriate jurisdiction."[16] Our courts, like courts of other nations, have long construed, applied, and even formulated international law in a myriad of situations. The construction of treaties[17] and the construction of property settlements or assignments incident to recognition of one nation by another[18] have been grist in the mill. International law as expressed in conventions agreed to by several nations is enforced. As stated in *Ex parte Quirin*,[19] "the law of war" enforced by our courts includes "that part of the law of nations which prescribes, for the conduct of war, the status, rights and duties of enemy nations as well as of enemy individuals." Questions as to when one nation may be summoned before tribunals of another nation—questions subsumed under the head of sovereign immunity—raise questions of similar character.[20] Claims to off-shore lands may involve international law.[21] The rights of aliens may be founded in international custom,[22] as well as in treaties. Maritime controversies involve the law of the sea.[23] Control of citizens while abroad,[24] like problems of nationali-ty,[25] dual citizenship,[26] and enemy aliens,[27] touch on the inter-national field, as do some patent cases[28] and, of course, interna-tional copyright or patent treaties.[29] National courts have sat as prize courts in many cases, applying international law.[30] Much of the fabric of our law is in truth international law. The more international the activities of a nation and its people, the more they weave a web of international practice, custom, and law.

There are of course many tribunals of an international character that apply a rule of law in a supranational manner. The Court of Justice of the European Coal and Steel Community is one of many. This court was set up "to ensure the rule of law" in interpreting and applying the treaty. It has been an extremely active court: "[I]n the short period of its existence the Court has been called upon to review decisions of the High Authority in practically all the major fields of its activities under the treaty: defining prohib-ited discriminatory practices and enforcing the prohibition of such practices; fixing maximum prices under conditions specified in the treaty; helping non-competitive producers to achieve com-petitive levels; applying the anti-monopoly provisions of the trea-ty."[31] It has even considered a complaint of Luxembourgian producers charging that a local monopoly set up by their own government was illegal under the treaty.[32]

Ad hoc arbitral tribunals have been commonly used.[33] The activities of these tribunals have been numerous since the mid-seventeenth century.[34] The United Nations in 1958 proposed a Convention on the Recognition and Enforcement of Foreign Arbi-tral Awards. Though the United States has not joined it, the convention became effective on 7 June 1959, Israel, Morocco, and the United Arab Republic having ratified it. Arbitration is not mediation or conciliation but a determination according to law. As stated by Judge Joseph C. Hutcheson in *Ryan* v. *United States,*[35] sitting as arbitrator of a claim against the United States, "In this proceeding, therefore, the function and duties of the Arbitrator are those of the judge, not those of the mediator; the methods and processes of decision judicial, not mediatorial. The scope and sweep of the inquiry and search, into the facts and the law, must therefore be as wide and as free as, but no wider nor freer than, judicial methods and processes permit and enjoin." This comports with the notion of arbitration under collective bargaining agreements in the federal field. The arbitrator interprets and applies the collective agreement; "he does not sit to dispense his own brand of industrial justice."[36] "[H]owever informal, an arbitration is a kind of trial" and requires judicial disinterestedness.[37] Congress has reflected the growing faith in the ability of arbitrators to perform judicial functions by permitting provision for arbitration in transactions which are maritime or involve interstate commerce.[38] The United States has extended this fostering of private arbitration into the international sphere by a series of treaties entered into since 1946. Typically, such a treaty provides that both agreements to arbitrate and arbitration awards will be "accorded full faith and credit."[39] Such treaties are now in effect with Germany, Greece, Ireland, Israel, Japan, and China.

Conflicts between one nation and foreign investors are recurring ones. The fact that courts of one nation do not sit in judgment on the validity of the acts of another nation done within its own territory[40] is not the end but only the beginning of the problem. Arbitration clauses in investment agreements have been urged.[41] The United Nations and its various agencies, including an International Law Commission, have a variety of projects under way in an effort to put this controversial subject under a rule of law.[42] We now have special procedures prescribed for the settlement of controversies between states in this hemisphere. Sending the marines to the Caribbean or Central America was once the solution. Today we are closer to a rule of law in the management of troublesome problems in this area. The Charter of the Organization of American States (2 U.S.T. 2394), which became effective 13 December 1951, provides that all international disputes between the American states shall be submitted to certain "peaceful procedures" before being referred to the Security Council of the United Nations. The procedures designated are "direct negotiations, good offices, mediation, investigation and conciliation, judicial settlement, arbitration, and those which the parties to the dispute may especially agree upon at any time" (art. 21). We promise in that charter not to go it alone in several respects. Thus article 16 provides, "No State may use or encourage the use of coercive measures of an economic or political character in order to force the sovereign will of another State and obtain from it advantages of any kind." The charter provides a broad framework for cooperative action among the American states. Article 4 not only proclaims the prevention of disputes among the American states, their peaceful settlement, and common action against "aggression"; it goes further and announces that cooperative action is desired in solving "political, juridical and economic problems" arising among the American states and in promoting, "by cooperative action, their economic, social, and cultural development."

The European Convention for the Protection of Human Rights and Fundamental Freedoms creates a more selective administrative and juridical system. It came into force in 1953; fourteen out of fifteen countries that are members of the Council of Europe have ratified it.[43] The convention establishes a bill of rights for nationals of the member nations. It protects a wide range of human rights:

"No one shall be subject to torture or to inhuman or degrading treatment or punishment." "No one shall be held in slavery or servitude." "Everyone has the right to liberty and security of person." Everyone arrested "shall be informed promptly, in a language which he understands, of the reasons for his arrest and of any charge against him." Everyone arrested "shall be brought promptly" before a magistrate; one who is arrested or detained is entitled to have the lawfulness of the arrest or detention decided "speedily by a court"; the victim of an unlawful arrest or detention has "an enforceable right to compensation." One charged with a crime is presumed innocent until proved guilty according to law. Punishment under *ex post facto* laws is barred. One charged with crime can have a lawyer of his own choosing, or, if he is impecunious, legal representation is to be given free "when the interests of justice so require."

"Everyone has the right to respect for his private and family life, his home and his correspondence." "Everyone has the right to freedom of thought, conscience and religion." "Everyone has the right to freedom of expression." "Everyone has the right to freedom of peaceful assembly and the freedom of association with others, including the right to form and to join trade unions for the protection of his interests." Some of these rights are qualified but none may be denied on the ground of sex, race, color, language, religion, political, or other opinion.

The convention establishes a Commission of Human Rights which may receive complaints from individuals or groups or from member nations. It deals with complaints only "after all domestic remedies have been exhausted." It makes an investigation and seeks to secure "a friendly settlement" on the basis of the rights defined in the convention. If it is unable to effect a settlement, it reports the matter to the Committee of Ministers.

In that event the matter can be submitted to the European Court of Human Rights created by the convention. The commission can submit it, or the member state whose national is alleged to be the victim, or the member state that referred the case to the commission, or the member state against which the complaint is lodged. The court is empowered to decide its jurisdiction should that be challenged. Its rulings on the merits involve construction of the provisions of the convention. Its judgments are final.

The European Court of Human Rights has had few cases to date. The commission, however, has been extremely busy.[44] Some complaints are from individuals who protect the action that their own government has taken against them; others are by aliens against another government. The most publicized have been those by the German Communist Party and by German Communists detained by West Germany or convicted by its courts.[45] And perhaps the most common ground for rejection of the complaints is a failure to exhaust "domestic remedies" that were available.

This convention, designed to enforce human rights as between nations having "a common heritage of political traditions, ideals, freedom, and the rule of law," places a new and important field under international management. The agencies involved have naturally moved cautiously. The care they have exercised promises to lay solid foundations for the growth of this new administrative and juridical system.

The International Court of Justice, created by the United Nations, also has a permanent status; but it has a different kind of jurisdiction from that of the European Court of Human Rights. It decides actual controversies; and, unlike the United States Supreme Court, it has the authority to render advisory opinions. Yet only states (not individuals) may be parties before the International Court of Justice. This includes the United Nations itself, which was permitted to bring an action before the court in 1949. The disputes with which the court deals concern the interpretation of treaties, any question of international law, and the breach of an international obligation, together with the nature and extent of the reparation to be made for such a breach. The aim is to have such a court "that in the body as a whole the representation of the main forms of civilization and of the principal legal systems of the world should be assured" (stat. of the court, art. 9). Enforcement of the decrees of the court is entrusted to the Security Council by article 94 (2) of the Charter of the United Nations.

Yet in spite of the easy availability of the International Court and its eminent qualifications, it had last year only six cases to adjudicate. Low as this number is, it is the highest number the court has had before it in any one year in a decade. Most nations give only qualified acceptances to its jurisdiction.[46] In 1946, by adoption of the Connally Amendment, we accepted compulsory jurisdiction except as to "matters which are essentially within the domestic jurisdiction of the United States of America *as determined by the United States of America*."[47] The amendment was attacked as a dangerous precedent to a country seeking to sponsor the rule of law. Senator Wayne Morse said: "It is, in effect, a political veto on questions of a judicial character, and it will be instantly recognized as such by all the other countries. . . . [I]n our support of the United Nations, we are committing ourselves to a very large degree to the principle that it is better to entrust these international questions to responsible international institutions. . . . If history teaches us anything, it is that if States are left to decide these questions on the basis of immediate political expediency the result is power politics and ultimately war."[48]

Then too this "political veto" cuts both ways: the United States can accept or reject any decision against it; on the basis of reciprocity a state which the United States wants to sue can claim in return that the International Court has no jurisdiction. In the case concerning *Norwegian Loans*,[49] bonds had been issued by Norwegian state-owned banks and sold on the French bond market. These bonds contained "gold clauses," and France and Norway had had long but futile discussions on a diplomatic level as to the effect of these clauses. France finally sought to submit the dispute to the International Court of Justice. Norway objected to the jurisdiction of the court because, in its opinion, the bonds presented a matter of municipal, and not international, law. The court stated:

"France has limited her acceptance of the compulsory jurisdiction of the Court by excluding beforehand disputes 'relating to matters which are essentially within the national jurisdiction as understood by the Government of the French Republic.' In accordance with the condition of reciprocity to which acceptance of the compulsory jurisdiction is made subject in both Declarations and which is provided for in Article 36, paragraph 3, of the Statute, Norway, equally with France, is entitled to except from the compulsory jurisdiction of the Court disputes understood by Norway to be essentially within its national jurisdiction."

As Professor Louis B. Sohn recently observed: "... the narrowness of the United States' jurisdictional declaration constitutes an important obstacle to effective protection of American trade and business abroad. As matters pertaining to the treatment of American investments in foreign countries can be easily considered as being essentially within the jurisdiction of those countries, any claims brought by the United States on behalf of injured American investors are likely to founder on a rock of our own making."[50]

This optional clause, as Jessup states in *The Use of International Law*, stands in the way of the United States' exerting "its best diplomatic efforts toward the establishment of a rule of law which we invoke so religiously." This was the theme of President Eisenhower's talk to the American Bar Association on 29 August 1960. "Are we seeking a world of law or are we seeking to find ways in which we can cater to our own views and ideas in the legal field?" he asked. Yet while the president and the attorney general have taken positions against the Connally Amendment, the State Department invoked it in the *Interhandel* case.[51]

A treaty stands of course no higher than an Act of Congress under our system of government. As stated by the Court in the *Chinese Exclusion Case*: "The treaties were of no greater legal obligation than the act of Congress. By the Constitution, laws made in pursuance thereof and treaties made under the authority of the United States are both declared to be the supreme law of the land,

and no paramount authority is given to one over the other. A treaty, it is true, is in its nature a contract between nations and is often merely promissory in its character, requiring legislation to carry its stipulations into effect. Such legislation will be open to future repeal or amendment. If the treaty operates by its own force, and relates to a subject within the power of Congress, it can be deemed in that particular only the equivalent of a legislative act, to be repealed or modified at the pleasure of Congress. In either case the last expression of the sovereign will must control."

What Congress grants, Congress can take away. Every treat while it lasts of course limits the freedom of action of the contracting parties. Yet a willingness on the part of all to limit their freedom is the only way we can have a world where orderly procedures take the place of the anarchy of self-help and where we are saved from the fate of having each continent turned into an incinerator. As Corwin says in *The Constitution and World Organization*, the limitations on our power in practical effect "derive their force and effect exclusively from the principles of international justice, honor, and goodwill, *and from that species of political wisdom which prefers the long view to the short view.*"

The tools with which we can evolve a "rule of law" into a more mature system are at hand. There is only the will to use them. Why do nations hold back? Why are we not willing to take the lead in inaugurating a truly golden age for international law? We could, I think, do it, if we asserted the moral leadership of which we so often boast. We need more commitment and less lip service. World opinion is ready to be marshaled. Small nations quiver on the sidelines as they watch giant rivals spar, threaten, and shake their nuclear fists. The world is filled with such a sense of insecurity that for the first time in history solid foundations for a "rule of law" can be laid.

Khrushchev employs the classical techniques which Communists have-been taught to use when participating in parliamentary proceedings. On 2 August 1920 the Second Comintern Congress sent instructions to Communist party members on how to destroy parliamentarianism by using as an "auxiliary centre" of the "mass struggle" the "rostrum of the bourgeois parliament." This directive of 2 August 1920 also stated: "Demonstrative legislative proposals should be regularly submitted on the instructions of the party and its central committee, not with the idea that they will be accepted by the bourgeois majority, but for purposes of propaganda, agitation, and organization." The activity recommended was "chiefly in revolutionary agitation from the parliamentary tribune, in exposing enemies, in the ideological mobilization of the masses." Pounding a lectern with one's shoe at the United Nations is in the same category as maintaining a chant in the manner of Communists in the French Assembly.

Whether Khrushchev was doing more than making a play to the Communist galleries in the world, we do not know. Some think he wants to destroy the United Nations. Yet a nuclear holocaust would be destructive of all peoples, Communists included. Even for Communists the cult of force is fast becoming obsolete. Khrushchev knows it, as evident from his Bucharest speech in June 1960, in which he concluded that war with non-Communist nations was not "inevitable." Moreover, world opinion on the side of a "rule of law" is powerful. Those who were forced to vote against it would lose in prestige and influence. This force of world opinion must be mobilized.

There are of course great gulfs between the law, customs, and mores which we of the West accept as normal and which other parts of the world practice. One of our major errors, as we emerged from a century and a half of isolationism, was to think of the world as if it were made in our image; at times we even thought that the nonconformists should be remade in our image. The advanced form of democracy which we enjoy, which Europe for the most part represents, which flourishes in Canada, Australia, New Zealand, and which is taking sturdy hold in India and Israel, is largely unknown in the world. Many societies developed along family lines, not community lines. Familial, not democratic, regimes have shaped the affairs of many Asian countries for centuries. As recently stated, "All these non-Western native societies are family-centered and tribal-centered rather than nation-centered and contractually guided in their binding social organization and in their moral and religious loyalties. Not only is the family and the tribe the basic locus and transmitter of moral, political and even religious authority and value, but within the family the rule of the elder, as determined by biological birth, often constitutes the good."[52] It is a familial, not a democratic, type of regime that governs Formosa today. Pakistan is making modest advances toward a democratic society. Turkey has great promise. Indonesia is holding most political experiments in abeyance. Tribal government controls the lives of men and women in some African nations. In at least one African nation which is a member of the United Nations trial by fire—which India practiced long centuries ago and which was practiced in England until A.D. 1262—is still practiced among the tribes.[53]

African tribes hold much of the land in trust for the people. "The community (for the most part) takes care of the indigent, and everybody belongs to somebody."[54] Yet tribal life is breaking up; about 40 million have left their tribes and sought new lives in villages and cities. These transitions promise turmoil and unrest. Chaos may indeed mount in the Congo.

Africa apart, there are great diversities among nations. The dictatorships of the Communist world as opposed to the democracies of the West mark only some of the differences. There are absolute monarchies, dictatorships that have been long and enduring, military regimes that may be short interregnums, and democracies at various stages of development. Capitalism, socialism, communism, compete for followers. The goals and ideals are many and diverse.

Much of the world is illiterate. Across the Middle East and in Asia illiteracy is the rule. Ethiopia is 98 percent illiterate. Liberia—which we often think of as an American stepchild—has a literacy rate no higher than 10 percent. That represents the African average. Leaders in these countries must make bricks without straws. The question is not, will democracy be saved? It is, will democracy ever be born? If democracy emerges in the hinterland, it will be in the distant future.

The vast gulfs that exist between various world cultures mean that the common ground for world law will be narrow and selective. It starts, of course, with the rule against aggressive war; and it proceeds from there to all the stuff that treaties, contracts, commercial engagements, investments, travel, communication, and the like shape up into controversies. There are only limited areas where today we can rightfully say common ground can be found. Yet they are important, indeed critical, ones; and they will expand as the peoples of the world work with their newly emerging institutions of law and gain confidence in them.

We are at an impasse at a global level which every nation in its history has experienced at local levels. In the Civil War, Missouri was a military department governed by the army. It was torn with factionalism; bandits prowled the highways; guerrillas raided. Lincoln, in the words of Carl Sandburg, "voiced a faith in humanity not easy to apply in Missouri at that hour."[55] Lincoln wrote to the military governor of Missouri about the "destruction of life and property" in that area and the formula for ending it: "A large majority in every locality must feel alike upon this subject; and if so, they only need to reach an understanding, one with another. Each leaving all others alone solves the problem; and surely each would do this but for his apprehension that others will not leave him alone. Cannot this mischievous distrust be removed?

"Let neighborhood meetings be everywhere called and held, of all entertaining a sincere purpose for mutual security in the future whatever they may heretofore have thought, said, or done about the war, or about anything else. Let all such meet, and, waiving all else, pledge each to cease harassing others, and to make common cause against whoever persists in making, aiding, or encouraging further disturbance."

The problems of the world in the 1960s are those of Missouri in the 1860s—magnified manyfold. And the philosophy of the United Nations toward world affairs is that of Lincoln toward the regional conflicts and clashes of his day.

Some have the lingering notion that wars without nuclear weapons can be fought—if only nuclear weapons are abolished. That is dangerous thinking. Now that the art of making them is known, they could be quickly manufactured even though all were destroyed. They are so strategically important that they would tempt any participant. Once war broke out, a frantic race would be on to manufacture again the outlawed nuclear weapons. The side that won that race would have the opponent at its mercy. We know now that nuclear war risks all life on each continent that is involved, and perhaps all other life as well. That means that the central problem of this day is the *prevention* of war.

The Charter of the United Nations contains a resolve on the part of the people "to save succeeding generations from the scourge of war, which twice in our lifetime has brought untold sorrow to mankind." Effective prevention of war means disarmament. Partial disarmament is a sham except insofar as it leads to the establishment of procedures which can be extended to full disarmament. The danger of partial disarmament is that each side aims to keep the weapon—or weapons—that best suits its strategic position. Russia, for example, would gladly trade atomic bombs for tanks, since with tanks she could still dominate the land mass of which she is the center. Pursuit of peace at this stage means making the search for foolproof disarmament the first item on the international agenda. Walter Millis in his challenging work, *A World Without War*,[56] shows that a viable world could easily exist if war were actually abolished and never again became an instrument of national power.

The arrival of disarmament and the end of war would not of course mean the advent of peace in the sense that there would be a disappearance of conflict. Great antagonisms would persist. Disputes would continue; nations would press their claims for justice. Clash and conflict are present in every community. They exist in virulent form at the world level and will continue. War from time out of mind has been one of the remedies for real or fancied wrongs. Now that it is obsolete, the rule of law remains as the only alternative. This is not an expression of hope alone. We have in truth the sturdy roots of a rule of law, including a few of the procedures which human inguenuity has devised for resolving disputes, e.g., conciliation and mediation, arbitration, administrative settlement, and judicial determination. The rule of law is versatile and creative. It can devise new remedies to fit international needs as they may arise. The rule of law has at long last become indispensable for men as well as for nations. Now that the instruments of destruction have become so awesome that war can no longer be tolerated, the rule of law is our only alternative to mass destruction.

We need to return to the philosophy of our Declaration of Independence, which was summed up by Carl Becker as follows: "At its best it preached toleration in place of persecution, good-will in place of hate, peace in place of war. It taught that beneath all local and temporary diversity, beneath the superficial traits and talents that distinguish men and nations, all men are equal in the possession of a common humanity; and to the end that concord might prevail on the earth instead of strife, it invited men to promote in themselves the humanity which bound them to their fellows, and to shape their conduct and their institutions in harmony with it."[57]

If we ourselves and other members of the democratic world community once more embrace that view of world affairs, we will be on a high road to a rule of law in international matters. Those Communist groups who want "coexistence" may in time fall into line. There does not, indeed, seem anywhere else to go—whoever the people are and whatever their political creed.

There is no reason for us to get tangled up in legalisms that march inexorably to the conclusion that total and complete sovereignty must be retained. For we now know that when that claim is pressed by all nations, everyone faces extinction in a nuclear holocaust. We believe as a people that we have an "unalienable" right to "life, liberty and the pursuit of happiness"; and it is increasingly apparent that our governing agencies must have sufficient freedom in policy-making and in action to assure us that right.

Notes

1. "The Legality of the Nuremberg Trials," 58 *Juridical Rev.* 1, 9.
2. Lerner, *The Mind and Faith of Justice Holmes*, 1943, 19-20.
3. Center for the Study of Democratic Institutions.
4. J. A. B. Van Buitenen in *Tales of Ancient India* tells of the Four Brothers each of whom mastered a specialty:
   "I have mastered a science," said the first, "which makes it possible for me, if I have nothing but a piece of bone of some creature, to create straightaway the flesh that goes with it."
   "I," said the second, "know how to grow that creature's skin and hair if there is flesh on its bones."
   The third said, "I am able to create its limbs if I have the flesh, the skin, and the hair."
   "And I," concluded the fourth, "know how to give life to that creature if its form is complete with limbs."
   Thereupon the four brothers went into the jungle to find a piece of bone so that they could demonstrate their specialties. As fate would have it, the bone they found was a lion's, but they did not know and picked up the bone. One added flesh to the bone, the second grew hide and hair, the third completed it with matching limbs, and the fourth gave the lion life. Shaking its heavy mane, the ferocious beast arose with its menacing mouth, sharp teeth, and merciless claws and jumped on his creators. He killed them all and vanished contentedly into the jungle.
5. Kahn, *On Thermonuclear War*, 1960
6. See Moraes, *The Revolt in Tibet*, 1960.
7. 1 Moore, *International Law*, 107.
8. Lauterpacht, "Recognition of States in International Law," 53 *Yale Law Journal*, 385.
9. 1 Hyde, *International Law*, 161.
10. Jessup, *A Modern Law of Nations*, 1948, 57.

11. 1 *Oppenheimer's International Law*, 8th ed., 1955, 133.
12. *Yearbook, United Nations, 1950*, 224.
13. See Ireland, "Ex Post Facto From Rome to Tokyo," 21 *Temple Law Quarterly* 26; Goodhart, *op. cit.*
14. See McDougal and Gardner, "The Veto and the Charter," 60 *Yale Law Journal* 258; McDougal, "International Law, Power and Policy," *Academy of International Law*, 1953, 137, 155-157.
15. FAO Constitution, Article 17; UNESCO Constitution, Article 14.
16. *The Paquette Habana*, 175 U. S. 677, 700. *The Paquette Habana* and the *Lola* were two Spanish fishing smacks seized during the Spanish-American War. A proceeding was commenced to condemn the ships as prizes of war, but it was held that such fishing vessels were exempt from capture as prizes "[b]y an ancient usage among civilized nations, beginning centuries ago, and gradually ripening into a rule of international law." *Id.*, 686.
17. *Clark* v. *Allen*, 331 U. S. 503. In this case a California resident had left property by will to German nationals. A dispute arose over this property between the Attorney General of the United States, claiming to represent the German heirs, and relatives of the decedent living in California, who claimed the property on the theory that the will, bequeathing property to German nationals, was void under California law. The validity of this California law in turn depended on the vitality of an American-German Treaty of 1923, and it was to the interpretation of this theory that the Court addressed itself.
18. *United States* v. *Pink*, 315 U. S. 203. This famous case involved a construction of the assignment of Russian property in the United States made incident to this country's recognition of Soviet Russia. This assignment, called the Litvinov Assignment, was held effective to give to the United States a valid claim to assets, in this country, of a nationalized Russian company, over the claims of the State of New York that the assignment was void because the assets were expropriated ones.
19. 317 U.S. 1, 27-28. Quirin and seven others were German nationals, landed in civilian disguise on our coast by submarine and planning to sabotage the national war effort. They were captured, and they sought in American courts to avoid trial by a Military Commission. The Supreme Court held that the President and Congress had acted constitutionally in providing for a military trial, in part relying on the provisions of the Hague Convention, to which this country was a party.
20. See *Schooner Exchange*, 7 Cranch 116, and *National Bank* v. *Republic of China*, 348 U. S. 356. *The Schooner Exchange* involved an effort by one McFaddon to retrieve an armed French vessel, which he claimed was in reality his own schooner, *The Exchange*, unlawfully seized by the French. Chief Justice Marshall upheld the dismissal of the libel on the ground that, by the settled rule of international law, sovereigns did not waive their immunity from suit as to armed vessels in their own service. In *National Bank* v. *Republic of China*, the Supreme Court upheld jurisdiction in the particular case over the claims of sovereign immunity put forward by the Republic of China.
21. See *United States* v. *California*, 332 U. S. 19, 32.
22. *Hines* v. *Davidowitz*, 312 U. S. 52, 65. "[A]part from treaty obligations, there has grown up in the field of international relations a body of customs defining with more or less certainty the duties owing by all nations to alien residents —duties which our State Department has often successfully insisted foreign nations must recognize as to our nationals abroad. In general, both treaties and international practices have been aimed at preventing injurious discriminations against aliens."

23. *The Lottawanna,* 21 Wall. 558, 572.
24. *Blackmer* v. *United States,* 284 U. S. 421.
25. *Perkins* v. *Elg,* 307 U. S. 325.
26. *Kawakita* v. *United States,* 343 U.S. 717, 720-736.
27. See *Johnson* v. *Eisentrager,* 339 U. S. 763, 771-775. Twenty-one German nationals were charged with carrying on the war, in aid of Japan, after the surrender of Germany and convicted on these charges by a United States Military Commission sitting in Nanking. Transported to Germany, they sought to invoke the aid of the courts of the United States, claiming that their trials were unconstitutional. A majority of the Court denied them access to American courts, relying on a body of international law establishing their status as "enemy aliens."
28. *Brown* v. *Duchesne,* 19 How. 183, 198-199.
29. See Convention for the Protection of Industrial Property, proclaimed October 28, 1938, 53 Stat. 1748.
30. See *The Peterhoff,* 5 Wall. 28.
31. Stein, "The Court of Justice, 1954-1957," 51 *American Journal of International Law* 821, 829.
32. *Groupement des Ind. Sid. Lux.* v. *The High Authority,* Official Gazette, 5th Year, No. 16 (July 10, 1956), 190.
33. See Hudson, *International Tribunals, Past and Future,* 1944, 5-6.
34. Sohn, "International Tribunals: Past, Present and Future," 46 *American Bar Journal* 23. "The history of modern arbitration starts usually with the American-British arbitrations under the Jay Treaty of 1794, one of which resulted in more than 500 awards in favor of private claimants. More than 100 claims were settled by another American-British arbitral commission under the London Treaty of 1853. A United States-Mexican Commission established by a Convention of 1868 dealt with more than 2,000 mutual claims of which, however, almost 1,700 were dismissed. The claims made by the United States against Great Britain on account of alleged violations of neutrality led to the so-called Alabama Claims Arbitration under the Washington Treaty of 1871; a tribunal including eminent jurists from Italy, Switzerland and Brazil awarded $15,500,000 to the United States. Another accumulation of American-British claims was decided by a tribunal established under the Washington Agreement of 1910; while the amounts claimed exceeded $8,000,000, the tribunal awarded only $84,000 to the American claimants and only $240,000 to the British claimants. The cases decided included the claim of the Cayuga Indians against New York State and the case of the British schooner *Lord Nelson* in which the tribunal awarded interest from 1819 to 1912. In this case the claimant's ship was seized in 1812 and it took his heirs a hundred years to recover compensation for his loss.

"All previous claims commissions were overshadowed by the more than forty Mixed Arbitral Tribunals created after World War I to deal with claims of Allied nationals against the Central Powers. Three of the tribunals with Germany handled, for instance, over 60,000 cases altogether. The separate American-German Mixed Commission had to consider some 13,000 cases. The new feature of this group of tribunals was that individual claimants were given direct access to them, their national governments exercising only minimal controls over the proceedings.

"Apart from these special tribunals established to deal with private claims, there have been many international tribunals created over the last hundred and fifty years to deal with other disputes between governments, relating to almost every problem of international law; they decided disputes about boundaries, violations of laws of neutrality, fisheries, international waterways, interstate loans and the interpretation of various international treaties.

"The procedure for the settlement of international disputes was codified by the Hague Conferences of 1899 and 1907, which also established the Permanent Court of Arbitration. While this Court was merely a panel from which parties to a dispute could select judges by agreement, many important cases were decided within its framework. It exists still, and its members have the additional function of making nominations for judges of the International Court of Justice."

35. 32 *American Journal of International Law* 593, 595.
36. *Steelworkers* v. *Enterprise Corp.*, 363 U. S. 59, 597.
37. *Hyman* v. *Pottsberg's Ex'rs*, 101 F.2d 262, 265.
38. 9 U. S. C. §§ 1-15.
39. Treaty with China, Nov. 4, 1946, Art. VI (4), 63 Stat. 1299, 1306.
40. *Ricaud* v. *American Metal Co.*, 246 U. S. 304, 309.
41. See Haight, "American Foreign Trade and Investment Disputes," 14 *Arbitration Journal* (n. s. 1959) 73.
42. See Schachter, "Private Foreign Investment and International Organization," 45 *Cornell Law Quarterly* 415 (1960).
43. 50 *American Journal of International Law* 949; *British Yearbook of International Law 1958*, 356.
44. See *European Commission of Human Rights, Documents and Decisions,* 1959, vi, 132.
45. *Id.*, 219-226.
46. See Lissitzyn, *The International Court of Justice*, 1951, 61-68.
47. Declaration by the President, August 14, 1946. 61 Stat. 1218.
48. 92 *Congressional Record* 10684 (1946).
49. *I. C. J. Rep.* 1957, 9.   50. Sohn, *op. cit.*, 23, 25.
51. See *Switzerland* v. *United States*, 1959, *I. C. J. Rep.* 6; Briggs, "Interhandel: The Court's Judgment on March 21, 1959," 53 *American Journal of International Law* 547. In this case, Switzerland attempted to gain relief under international law on behalf of a Swiss corporation, Interhandel. At the outbreak of the second World War, the U. S. seized assets of Interhandel in this country (principally, these consist of a $100 million investment in General Aniline and Film Co.). The seizure was justified on the grounds that, through Swiss intermediaries, control of Interhandel was retained by I. G. Farbenindustrie, a German company. Since 1948, Interhandel has been trying in American courts to regain its assets. That action is still going on. The International Court, in the report referred to above, held that the case was not a proper one for adjudication under international law as long as the American court action was pending. Our invoking of the Connally Amendment was therefore unnecessary.
52. Northrop, *Philosophical Anthropology and Practical Politics*, 1960, 214.
53. See Warner, *Seven Days to Lomaland*, 1954, chs. 3, 13.
54. Gunther, *Inside Africa*, 1953, 890.
55. *Abraham Lincoln: The War Years*, Vol. IV, 100.
56. Center for the Study of Democratic Institutions.
57. *The Declaration of Independence*, 1942, 278.

International Due
Process and the Law

By William J. Brennan, Jr.*

FAITH in fundamental human rights, and the dignity and worth of the human person, is the inspiration and the guiding spirit of the movement for a world rule of law. We would create a world rule of law, in the words of the consensus of San José, "to the end that the rule of law will govern all men and all nations and any man can then walk any place on the face of the earth, or travel through endless space, in freedom, in dignity and in peace."[1]

But our time has known in full measure the tragedy suffered by countless human beings over the face of the globe who, deprived of their liberty without accusation, without trial, upon nothing but the arbitrary fiat of a sovereign government, have been helpless to challenge their detention in a world forum. Yes, the world community has declared in ringing words its moral condemnation of such detentions. It is in the Universal Declaration of Human Rights of the Charter of the United Nations. Article IX of that declaration, among other things, reads that: "No one shall be subject to arbitrary arrest, detention or exile." But this is and must remain empty rhetoric until implemented by some international structure and procedure for enforcing compliance by an offending signatory state

---

*Associate justice, United States Supreme Court. B.S., 1928, University of Pennsylvania; LL.B., 1931, Harvard University; D.J.S., 1956, Boston University. Member, New Jersey Bar.

with the great principles it guarantees. Concepts of personal and territorial supremacy—national sovereignty—leave each member state free to grant its nationals only that measure of due process provided by its own laws, however far short that measure is of the standard contemplated by the Universal Declaration.

Some have conceived that world peace through the rule of law can be achieved only with the creation of a full-fledged super state in which all nations are merged—a supranational organization that has political and military control over all of its units. My own view accepts Roscoe Pound's premise that "all states need not be merged in a great world state, in which their personality is lost, in order that their conduct may be inquired into and ordered by authority of a world legal order."[2] The all important—indeed the *most* important—end of a world rule of law, the securing of individual liberty, can be attained without the creation of a world state.

All that seems necessary is that the U.N. signatories ordain by a simple treaty-statute a structure and scheme for securing international due process of the nature of the national due process familiar to every American: a prompt and speedy trial; legal assistance, including assistance for the indigent; prohibition of any kind of undue coercion or influence; freedom to conduct one's defense; the right to a public trial and written proceedings; the presumption of innocence and the burden upon the state to prove guilt beyond a reasonable doubt; and security against cruel and unusual punishments. These standards of due process, and thus of effective justice, only words now in the Universal Declaration of Human Rights, have their counterparts in our own U.S. Constitution. The vital difference, however, is that our nation has vitalized them for our people through a national forum and a national procedure for their enforcement.

We are a nation of fifty states—each not of course so sovereign as a sovereign nation, but nevertheless sovereign in important respects. But a state which prosecutes and imprisons an individual under procedures which violate the fundamental principles of liberty and justice embodied in the guarantees of due process in the federal constitution may be called upon by the individual to answer for its conduct in a federal forum. Almost a century ago the Congress extended the ancient writ of habeas corpus—that most important writ known to the constitutional law of England, affording as it does a swift and imperative remedy in all cases of illegal restraint or confinement—to any person claiming to be held in state custody in violation of the Constitution or laws or treaties of the United States.[3] The individual may petition a federal court to hear his claim that his detention is in violation of federal constitutional guarantees. It avails the state nothing that the detention does no violence to state law or the state constitution. The guarantees of the federal constitution are the higher law. It is true that the federal court will not hear a state prisoner who has not first exhausted any available state remedies for decision of his federal claim. For upon the state courts equally with the federal courts rests the obligation to guard, enforce and to protect every right granted or secured by the Constitution of the United States. However, the state prisoner is not concluded by any determination of the courts of the state that his federal claim has no merit. The prisoner may seek review of that holding in the federal courts including the Supreme Court of the United States. Since he asserts a federal claim the last word as to its merits is for the decision of federal and not state tribunals.

Here then in our own country is almost one hundred years of experience with the feasibility of a suprastate procedure for realizing the concepts of decency and fairness which are the foundation of our free society. And a most important corollary effect of the existence of this suprastate remedy has been its influence toward keeping the separate states on the path directed to securing those who run afoul of state laws against invasion of the procedural rights guaranteed them by the basic law of the land.

Why should we not internationalize the writ of habeas corpus along these lines to enforce the guarantees of the Universal Declaration of Human Rights? The research of Professor Luis Kutner and others has demonstrated that it can be done. Professor Kutner has performed an invaluable service for the world in blueprinting a plan for world habeas corpus including a judicial structure and a procedure.[4] He proposes doing this within the present United Nations' structure through a treaty-statute. It is a concrete program whereby the now only morally binding Universal Declaration of Human Rights would be made, by the voluntary consent of the nations of the world, a legally binding commitment enforceable in an international court of habeas corpus which would function through appropriately accessible regional courts. Regional world attorneys general would either prosecute or resist application for the writ. Of perhaps equal or greater importance, in the reflection of what happens in our states under the regime of federal habeas corpus, the sovereign nations would commit themselves to enforce the guarantees of the declaration in their own tribunals, authorizing review of their decisions by the international court of habeas corpus. Thus individuals would have relief in the international tribunal only upon a proper showing either that relief was wrongly denied under available remedies in the courts of the member state, or that that state provided no such remedies.

I do not say that this plan for world habeas corpus following the outlines of the structure of our federal habeas corpus is the only or the best plan. That is not important for our purposes. What is important is the obvious utility of world habeas corpus as a tool for the avoidance of the dangers of the police state, and its great promise as a contribution toward preserving and furthering world peace by repudiating, through an enforceable international rule of law, systematic and deliberate denial of human rights. The plan requires no surrender of national sovereignty to a supranational state and there is more than a feeble hope that the nations of the world would perceive that this plan would indeed serve their national interests. For as Professor Kutner has said:

> If there are any denials of human rights which all nations might in principle agree violate standards of fairness, certainly arbitrary arrest (i.e., a wrongful custody without color of legal justification) is one. If individuals may be arrested or incarcerated without cause, or for causes which clearly violate fundamental human rights, they do not have the most elementary fundamental freedom.[5]

Indeed a beginning has already been made in the creation in 1953 by the fifteen countries of the Council of Europe of the European Court of Human Rights, and a Commission of Human Rights which may receive complaints from individuals or groups, or from member nations, of alleged violations of a wide range of human rights established by the Convention as a Bill of Rights. The conference of lawyers from the twenty-three nations of the Americas who convened in San José, Costa Rica, last June also made the creation of a world court of human rights a specific goal. No nation should be ahead of our own in furthering the goal. Objections once expressed by the Department of State that "with the many deep seated political and ideological differences which exist among the various nations, it would not appear to be practical to seek meaningful agreement upon a statute for such a court on the part of most countries,"[6] if they still obtain, must surely be subject to reexamination. At all events American lawyers cannot in good conscience fail wholeheartedly and completely to devote themselves to the achievement of the goal. That they feel so is implicit in their joinder in the consensus at San José that "the need for a legal, definitive writ through appropriate machinery in order to exercise collective and individual protection of human rights is not only regarded as essential and necessary but as moral and right."[7]

[The text of this paper was originally presented in an address by Mr. Justice Brennan before the Law and Layman Conference of the American Bar Association at its eighty-fifth meeting, in San Francisco, California, on 7 August 1962, then published in *Virginia Law Review* 48, no. 7, 1962.]

Notes

1. American Conference on World Peace Through the Rule of Law, Consensus of San José (1961).
2. Roscoe Pound, "Toward a New Jus Gentium," *Ideological Differences and World Order* 7 (Northrop ed. 1949).
3. See 14 Stat. 385 (1867).
4. Kutner, *World Habeas Corpus* (1962).
5. Kutner, *World Habeas Corpus: A Legal Absolute for Survival*, 39 U. Det. L.J.279, 317 (1962).
6. Letter From Department of State Listing Objections to H.R. Res. No. 318, 85th Cong., 2d sess. (1958), quoted in Kutner, op. cit., supra n. 4, at 154.
7. American Conference on World Peace Through the Rule of Law. See supra n. 1.

A Practicable Measure
for Human Rights

By Myres S. McDougal*

IN MANY contemporary national communities the writ of habeas corpus, or some equivalent, serves both as a substantive guarantor of that most basic of all human rights—personal liberty—and as an economic procedural strategy for the protection of this right.[1] In a letter recently published in the American Bar Association Journal, Ambassador Goldberg has developed the theme that the "idea of worldwide habeas corpus, internationally recognized and enforceable in an appropriate international court, can only be applauded by those who are dedicated to the rule of law and the attainment of lasting world peace."[2]

As widespread as is this understanding of the inescapable interdependence of the protection of human rights and the conditons of peace, it is not generally expected that the proposed comprehensive new covenants on civil and political rights and on economic, social, and cultural rights[3] will obtain the immediate acceptance of many of the major states of the world. The effective elites in our national communities are still too much the captives of syndromes of parochialism and expectations of violence.

* Professor at Yale Law School, former president of the American Society of International Law, chairman of Appointments, and former president of the American Law School Association; author, with others, of *Studies in World Public Order, Law and Public Order in Space, Law and Minimum World Public Order, The Public Order of the Oceans*, and others, and numerous law journal articles.

Fortunately, however, the relatively limited prospects for the immediate implementation on a global scale of many of the more important substantive human rights may not be entirely paralleled on the procedural level. The policies implicit in the writ of habeas corpus are, for example, so fundamental to a decent human existence, and so universally demanded in diverse legal systems, that a concerted effort to institutionalize the process on a transnational scale could be regarded as more in the nature of consolidation than of innovation. Several factors would appear to contribute to the practicability of contemporary endeavors to move in this direction.

First, and most important, is the fact, already emphasized, that the basic policy which habeas corpus is intended to serve is already widely accepted about the world: the right to personal liberty is commonly recognized, not merely in national constitutive prescription but also in authoritative international formulation, as the most basic and fundamental of all human rights. Thus, the much invoked Universal Declaration of Human Rights, adopted by the General Assembly of the United Nations in 1948, provides:

> Everyone has the right to life, liberty and security of person (art. 3);
> Everyone has the right to an effective remedy by the competent national tribunals for acts violating the fundamental rights granted him by the constitution or by law (art. 8); and
> No one shall be subjected to arbitrary arrest, detention or exile (art. 9).[4]

Similarly, the proposed new International Covenant on Civil and Political Rights, drafted after many years of deliberation by the representatives of many different peoples, prescribes that "Everyone has the right to liberty and security of person. No one shall be subjected to arbitrary arrest or detention. No one shall be deprived of his liberty except on such ground and in accordance with such procedures as are established by law" (art. 9, S.1).[5]

Secondly, the agencies—courts or other institutions—to which competence might be accorded with respect to habeas corpus, or its equivalents, could be made as diverse as the realities of the contemporary world process of effective power may require. Provision could be made for international, regional, and national agencies, and states could be encouraged to accept responsibility to whatever agencies their internal power processes may permit. Any degree of acceptance of inclusive responsibility would be an advance over the present conditions of absolute irresponsibility. Happily, the United

States offers, as Justice Brennan has documented, "almost one hundred years of experience with the feasibility of a suprastate procedure" in the administration of habeas corpus.[6]

Thirdly, the standards against which the lawfulness of detention is measured could be left as various, and open-ended, as states might demand. The long-term aspiration would of course be for the development and maintenance of standards approximating those of the bills of rights in the constitutions of mature national communities or of the Universal Declaration of Human Rights.[7] Again, however, any degree of acceptance of inclusive international standards would be an advance over continued assertion of unilateral irresponsibility.

Fourthly, the procedures by which hearing and release are sought could easily be accommodated, in their detailed modalities, to all the relevant diversities in contemporary world culture. Just as equivalencies have been developed in states having common law between the older and newer states. The important outcomes and civil law traditions, so also equivalencies could be developed between the older and newer states. The important outcomes sought are those of hearing and, if merited, release; institutional practices require honor only as they may serve these ends.

Fifth, and finally, the sanctions of public opinion would appear to be peculiarly efficacious for the enforcement of any commitments which states might make toward internationalizing habeas corpus. It had been demonstrated in a number of instances in recent years that even the most ruthless totalitarian communities do not relish being spotlighted at the focus of world attention as deprivers of the most fundamental of all human rights.

It was appropriately urged by the late Judge Hersch Lauterpacht that until "an effective right of petition—which means a right of petition with the right to have it investigated with the view to such action being taken upon it as is necessary—is granted to individuals concerned or to bodies acting on their behalf, any international remedy that may be provided will be deficient in its vital aspect."[8] The provision in the Optional Protocol to the proposed Covenant on Civil and Political Rights[9] for a limited right of individual petition, though a step in the right direction, is but a timid, halting measure, hemmed in by many restrictions. For the larger community of mankind genuinely aspiring toward improved implementation of human rights the proposal for internationalizing habeas corpus would appear to offer plausible hope for remedying the greatest defect in its present armory of institutional practices. Certainly the United States could have nothing to lose, save its reputation for indifference to the human rights program, by vigorous and positive action in exploration and promotion of the potentialities that inhere in the habeas corpus proposal.[10]

Notes

1. Documentation of the widespread use of the writ or equivalents is offered in Kutner and Carl, *An International Writ of Habeas Corpus: Protection of Personal Liberty in a World of Diverse Systems of Public Order,* 22 U. of Pitt. L. Rev. 469 (1961).

   A cogent statement of the importance of the writ appears in Chafee, *The Most Important Human Right in the Constitution,* 32 Boston U. L. Rev. 143 (1952).
2. 53 *Am. B.A.J.* 586 (1967).
3. 4 *U.N. Monthly Chronicle* 38 (1967).
4. See Schwelb, *Human Rights and the International Community* (1964) at 81.
5. The remaining sections of article 9 amplify the prescription in this tenor:

   2. Anyone who is arrested shall be informed, at the time of arrest, of the reasons for his arrest and shall be promptly informed of any charges against him.

   3. Anyone arrested or detained on a criminal charge shall be brought promptly before a judge or other officer authorized by law to exercise judicial power and shall be entitled to trial within a reasonable time or to release. It shall not be the general rule that persons awaiting trial shall be detained in custody, but release may be subject to guarantees to appear for trial, at any other stage of the judicial proceedings, and, should occasion arise, for execution of the judgment.

   4. Anyone who is deprived of his liberty by arrest or detention shall be entitled to take proceedings before a court, in order that that court may decide without delay on the lawfulness of his detention and order his release if the detention is now lawful.

   5. Anyone who has been the victim of unlawful arrest or detention shall have an enforceable right to compensation.
6. Remarks of William J. Brennan, Jr., on "International Due Process and the Law," Law and Layman Conference, San Francisco, California, 7 August 1962.
7. Alternatives among possible standards are indicated in Kutner, "The Case For An International Writ of Habeas Corpus: A Reply," 37 *U. of Det. L. J.* 605 (1960).
8. Lauterpacht, *International Law and Human Rights* (1950) 287.
9. 4 *U.N. Monthly Chronicle* 69 (1967).
10. A case for still more ambitious leadership by the United States in the whole human rights program is stated in McDougal and Leighton, "The Rights of Man in the World Community: Constitutional Illusions versus Rational Action," 59 *Yale L. J.* 60 (1949); reprinted in McDougal and Associates, *Studies in World Public Order* (1960) 335.

The Bond between Prescriptive Content and Procedure

By Harold D. Lasswell*

THE COMPLEX task of building motivation and muscle for the rights of man once more draws attention to the fundamental components of an authoritative and controlling legal norm. It is not enough to obtain widespread concurrence on overriding goals or on more particularized standards to be applied. Unless there are clear expectations about the identity of those who are authorized to decide, the modalities to be followed in the resolution of a controversy, and the sanctions appropriate to the impermissible deviator from the prescribed norms, the legal situation remains incomplete. It is the peculiar merit of the discussion of the writ of habeas corpus that it brings into the open any incompleteness in the implementation of a fundamental human right, and aids in the evolution of shared expectations about the relevant prescriptions.

When examined in minute detail the "conventional" arrange-

* Ph.D., LL.D., professor of Law and Political Sciences, Yale Law School and University; author of numerous books and articles; selected on 5 May 1967 as one of twenty-six of the world's outstanding scholars by the University of Chicago and awarded the degree of Doctor of Law.

ments called habeas corpus (or an equivalent designation) differ from one jurisdiction to another. Since we are here concerned with the discovery of equivalencies in various systems of public order, and must therefore employ valid categories of "functional" comparison, it is appropriate to outline some equivalent dimensions among the prescriptions that limit official arbitrariness in the detention of individuals.

The issues can be conveniently explicated if we consider the three components of a legal prescription: norm, contingency, sanction. The norm is the standard of conduct to be adhered to by participants in the social process. International law norms obviously apply universally or generally throughout the world community. The norms are divisible in two broad categories: goal, instrumentation. The goal norms are the most general expectations concerning the state of affairs to be realized or maintained by public authority and control. Instrumental norms are less generalized than the former category, partly because they refer to strategies by which the goals can be brought into social reality and are therefore more vulnerable to reconsideration. In regard to writs of habeas corpus (or equivalent) the overriding goal is the realization of a worldwide system of public order in which public authority, when exercised toward an individual, is free from arbitrariness. This is part of the more universal goal of human dignity. Instrumentally, the norm calls upon authority to provide a means whereby an individual who suffers detention can permissibly challenge and obtain an immediate decision about the permissibility of the detention.

The contingency component of a prescription relates to the factual circumstances to which the norm is applicable. In deciding any controversy that comes before him, the authorized decision maker must settle to his satisfaction whether the factual circumstances alleged by the parties were those referred to in the contingency components of the prescription. Without focusing unduly on this dimension of the problem it may nevertheless be pointed out that an act of "detention" is required; and, further, the body politic is required to have arranged facilities in advance for the object of the deprivation (detention) to obtain access to the counsel required to make his challenge. Implied further is that the body politic has arranged an access facility to a decision maker competent to act promptly and effectively. If the decision maker is to act as a curb on arbitrariness it is evident that the facilities arranged for the claimant must meet the following minimum specifications: (1) enjoy a sufficient measure of independence from the detaining authority to arrive at a decision without fear of severe retaliation; (2) enjoy a sufficient degree of motivation to exercise the authority to curb arbitrariness; (3) enjoy a sufficient measure of skill and knowledge to perceive and resolve the legal problem involved. The implication is that the procedures utilized by the body politic in training, selecting, and making conveniently accessible the decision makers required are adequate to the task. Further, it is implied that the procedures employed by the decision maker to make up his mind are appropriate and adequate. These procedures include obtaining evidence regarding the factual context and interpreting relevant prescriptive norms and contingency components.

The third component of a prescription covers sanctions, or the value indulgences, deprivations, and institutional practices, designed to obtain conduct in conformity with norms. The decision maker who hears the claim of the allegedly deprived party responds by (1) denying the claim or (2) directing the detaining authority to release the detainee. If the detaining authority disregards the directive, he is presumably open to deprivational sanction. In theory, the conforming authority may be open to an affirmative sanction, a value indulgence, perhaps in the form of a citation that enters the record. We may note other complications that may occur: Is the detainee to receive compensation (in terms of money or any other value) for the values lost to him by unduly long or otherwise impermissible detention?

As matters stand at present in the world community the rising intensity of demand for human dignity, including freedom from arbitrariness, is bringing all these issues into ever-widening controversy. In the context of a comprehensive legal system a writ of habeas corpus is chiefly to be understood as a procedural practice through whose application the passage can be expedited between highly generalized statements of norm and contingency and effective action in appropriate circumstances. It is opportune to promote the cause of human rights by calling for international action in two fronts: (1) a world conclave to add weight and precision to the prescriptions to be applied by each nation state and transnational organization; and (2) a world conclave—perhaps the same one—to agree upon the design of new transnational institutions specialized to the writ of habeas corpus (or equivalent procedures). Whatever action is taken it cannot fail to contribute to the clarifying of the indissoluble bond between the several components of authoritative and controlling prescriptions pertaining to human rights.

Islam: Concept, Law, and Habeas Corpus

By M. Cherif Bassiouni[*]

Foreword

THE PROCEDURE of the writ of habeas corpus was adopted and developed in England as one of several devices designed to restrict the exercise of the royal prerogative in the interest of the liberty of the subject. In theory the king's power and authority were not subject to any check or restraint, except such as his own good sense might impose. He was the source of all authority in every sphere of governance and administration.

One of the earliest checks imposed on the absolute authority of the monarch was that embodied in Magna Carta (1215). The process then started by the barons in the meadows of Runnymede continued through seven centuries till the devolution of authority from the crown to the freely chosen representatives of the people was completed.

In Islam the concept of sovereignty is entirely different. Absolute sovereignty pertains to Allah alone (3.27): the Lord of mankind, the King of mankind, the God of mankind (114.2-4).

In matters of administration, authority proceeds from the people and vests, by Allah's command, in those to whom it is entrusted by the people. It is designated a trust and must be discharged as such.

*Associate professor of law, De Paul University; College of the Holy Family, Cairo; Licence en Droit. Cairo University; LL.M., The John Marshall Law School; chairman, American Institute of Criminology; author of *Cases and Materials on Criminal Law* (1965); chairman of the board, The Islamic Center of Chicago.

The people are admonished to commit it into the hands of those best fitted to discharge it; and those to whom it is committed are commanded to discharge it with justice. "Allah commands you to entrust authority to those most capable, and that when you are called upon to judge between the people, or to exercise authority over them, you do it with justice. Excellent is that with which Allah admonishes you. Allah is All-Hearing, All-Seeing" (4.59). Seeking counsel with the representatives of the people is made obligatory (3.160; 42.39).

The office of judge is the highest office in the state, next to the head of state. Except in matters of state, the head of state is subject to the jurisdiction of the courts.

The authority of the head of state is controlled and circumscribed by the *Shariah*, that is to say, the whole body of law. The interpretation and administration of the law is the function of the judiciary.

Islam grants no privilege and tolerates none. The only badge of honor is the righteousness of a person's life. "O mankind, we have created you from a male and a female; and we have divided you into nations and tribes for greater facility of intercourse. The most honorable among you in the sight of Allah is he who is the most righteous among you. Surely, Allah is All-Knowing, All-Aware" (49.14).

Islam seeks to set up a universal brotherhood on the basis of equality and justice, and recognizes no distinction based on race, color or blood.

The Prophet of Islam (on whom be peace) concluded his famous Farewell Address with the words: "You are all brethren, one of another. An Arab has no preference over a non-Arab, nor a non-Arab over an Arab; nor is a white man to be preferred to a black, or a black to a white."

Islam fully safeguards the dignity and worth of the human person. The safeguards set out above, and many more, were prescribed and became the norm of the Muslim state and society six hundred years before the barons forced a reluctant King John to subscribe to the Magna Carta.

Muslim rulers have not uniformly given full effect to the safeguards designed to secure the dignity and worth of the human person, with which Islamic jurisprudence abounds; and Muslim society has had to endure tyranny at the hands of rulers who usurped and exercised authority for selfish ends. But the consciousness of the prescribed values has always in the end helped to restore their primacy.

The writ of habeas corpus is a procedure designed to make effective what has latterly come to be known as the rule of law, as a contrast to the arbitrary exercise of executive authority. The rule of law is firmly rooted in Islamic jurisprudence. In his excellent article Dr. Cherif Bassiouni has demonstrated that the purpose of the writ of habeas corpus is in conformity with the norms of Islamic jurisprudence, and that there is nothing in the concept and procedure of the writ that needs create any problem or difficulty for an Islamic state. The whole trend of Muslim juristic thinking lends strong support to the maintenance of effective safeguards for human freedom. I offer my sincere felicitations to Dr. Bassiouni on his very valuable dissertation.

Chaudhri Sir Muhammed Zafrulla Khan*

THE PURPOSE of this paper is to outline and suggest the acceptability of World Habeas Corpus by an Islamic state.[1] It is intended to demonstrate the potential of Islam in spirit, theory, and practice (in the Muslim states) in the field of international relations and human rights, in which the concept of World Habeas Corpus holds a place of distinction. Mr. Justice Jackson stated it eloquently in these terms:

> Greater barriers have discouraged any general interest in Islamic law.
> Though our debt to Islamic culture is exhibited in the custumary enumeration of our astonishing output of law reports, we long held the impression that the Muslim world had nothing to contribute to what was inside covers. Islamic law was regarded as of speculative rather than of practical interest and received attention from a relatively few specialists and scholars. But a review of the reasons we have deemed such knowledge too alien but useful to us show the reasons why we should abandon the smug belief that the Muslim experience has nothing to teach us.[2]

---

* Hon. Chaudhri Sir Muhammed Zafrulla Khan has been permanent representative of Pakistan at the United Nations since 1961; president of the United Nations General Assembly, 1962; minister of foreign affairs and Commonwealth relations of Pakistan (1947–1954); member of the International Court of Justice (1954–1973). Publications: *Indian Cases*; the *Criminal Law Journal of India*; reprints of *Punjab Criminal Rulings* 4; *Fifteen Years' Digest*; *Islam: Its Meaning for Modern Man*.

The conceptual basis of World Habeas Corpus rests largely in the Judeo-Christian and Anglo-Saxon tradition of the idea of man.[3] Luis Kutner, the father of World Habeas Corpus, retraces the origins of his concept to the natural law school of Aristotle and Aquinas and progressively crosses the path of the Magna Carta, ending with the "due process of law"[4] of the U.S. Constitution. World Habeas Corpus is intended, however, as a universal remedy and not solely as a self-perpetuating Christian-Western ideal. To the end that the goal of universality be accomplished, we must first strip World Habeas Corpus of any parochialism and truly enlarge it to the place of an accepted common denominator for the world. This article is the beginning of an enlarging process designed to enrich World Habeas Corpus and gain for it wider acceptance.

There are numerous Islamic conceptual characteristics to buttress authority in the Islamic legislative process for adherence to the World Habeas Corpus treaty-statute, administered by an Islamic circuit.

The limitations imposed by World Habeas Corpus on the absolute powers of the ruler for the maintenance of the inalienable rights of man as endowed by his Creator are wholly in communion with Islam.[5] Law in Islam is that which answers the following query: "What should the conduct of man be in his individual and collective life,"[6] in his relationship to God, to others, and to himself in a universal community of mankind for the fulfillment of man's dual purpose: life on earth and life in the hereafter.

Islamic law is said to be moral and ethical in spirit, and the expression of this conclusion is found in the *Qur'ānic* principle of *Hudud-Allah,* the divine limits. These limits constitute the checks and balances placed on man in his human endeavors to afford maximum personal freedom and to tolerate only those limited restrictions which distinguish anarchism from organized society. Hudud-Allah are the limitations placed on freedom to secure "a scheme of ordered liberty" and to prevent arbitrary and despotic limitations of human freedom.[7]

The limitations of personal rights operate as limitations against personal abuse of the rights of others. The concern of World Habeas Corpus is the protection of the individual through the due process of law. Islam afforded this protection and guaranteed due process and individual justice over thirteen hundred years ago. To that end that the personal rights of individuals to life, liberty, and property shall not be abridged without due process of law and that the rulers shall be subject to the rule of law which shall prevent their tyranny, World Habeas Corpus finds itself in full accord with Islamic principles.[8]

Islam introduced a social revolution. Its cornerstone was individual and collective morality. These principles of morality providing the basis for a society's spiritual values are enunciated (among others) in terms of equality, justice, freedom, brotherhood, mercy, and compassion. Unlike other sources of law, the *Qur'ān* emphasizes duties rather than rights. It insists on the fulfillment of individual obligations before the individual can claim his privileges. The individual is neither apart nor separate from society, and his rights are neither different from nor conflicting with those of the community. He is part and parcel of society, and the fulfillment of his obligations and those of the other members of the society constitutes the reservoir of social rights which are then shared by all.[9]

A fundamental tenet of World Habeas Corpus is justice through a fair trial affording due process. How more eloquently can it be phrased than by the few and direct words of the Qur'ān: "Lo! Allah enjoineth justice and kindness . . ."[10] Elevating justice to the level of a duty-obligation incumbent upon all, it continues: "Deal justly, that is nearer to your duty . . ."[11] To the modern query, Is man his brother's keeper? Islam replied thirteen centuries ago:

> O Mankind, be careful of your duty to your Lord who created you from a single soul and from it created its mate and from them twain hath spread abroad a multitude of men and women. Be careful of your duty toward Allah in whom ye claim [your rights] of one another.[12]

How else can it be when equality of mankind was so clearly enunciated:

> O Mankind! Lo! We have created you male and female and have made you nations and tribes that ye may know one another. Lo! The noblest of you in the sight of Allah is the best in conduct.[13]

The relation between the state and the individual has always been troublesome and confusing to the Western thinker. While certain authors deplore the lack of specific individual guarantees in

Islamic law and impute the weakness to the *Shariah* itself, they fail to realize that the basis of the Shariah is the principle of *original freedom*, for only free men can be free to choose Islam. The inalienability of life, liberty, and property is indispensable to the general order and well-being of the community and needs no specific statement.

The right to life, liberty, and property, the right to petition for redress of wrongs and grievance, the requirement of a fair and impartial trial without distinction of color, creed, or origin are fundamental in Islamic law. Protection against unreasonable deprivation of any such right is subject to judicial scrutiny, and prompt legal determination is commanded. This is essential not only as a human right but as a political right indispensable for the maintenance of a scheme of ordered liberty and fundamental freedom.[14]

The search for individual justice presupposes equality before the law, while the goal of a trial is to reveal the truth. Individual justice in Islam is sought to be accomplished on an individual basis notwithstanding the form, and not through a series of general edicts which would result in justice by form. To emphasize the sanctity of a legal due process concept to guarantee life, liberty, property, and honor, the Prophet, in his farewell pilgrimage speech, commanded: "Your lives, your property, and your honor are as sacred as this day."[15] [The day of *Haj*, or pilgrimage.]

Continuing further with his speech, the Prophet described that even if life, liberty, and honor are demanded by law, they must be realized in accordance with the prescribed process of the law. The practice and tradition of the Prophet are replete with examples where personal freedom has been upheld and its violations by the police powers of the state condemned. Not because of the belief that the state seeks to suppress the individual, but because, in the face of the power of the state, the individual needs guarantees to protect himself.[16] The criminal process through which oppression is most likely to occur requires a valid accusation to be made in the face of the defendant who, therefore, will confront his accusors and have a right to interrogate them, cross-examine them, and ask them to take the oath.[17] The burden of proving the charge is always on the accusors, and an accusation in and of itself is inconclusive proof.

Imam Khattabbi explained that there are only two kinds of detention under law: (1) detention under the order of the court,

which is mainly when a person has been sentenced by a court; and
(2) a detention prior to sentencing during the court's investigation
of a criminal violation. He concludes that there can be no other
ground for deprivation of a person's freedom.[18] It must be noted
here that this in no way contemplates deprivation of freedom for
what may be termed loosely as political crimes but only for specific
common crimes validly prohibited by law.[19]

Statutory criminal violations wihch are not part of the Qur'-
ānic precepts but which are validly legislated will depend for
their constitutionality on their adherence to the Qur'ānic precepts
and their guarantee of the individual rights stated therein. The
practice of the Prophet and the tradition requires that mere accusation in the absence of tangible proof is insufficient and that an
accusor who is an interested party cannot be the sole evidence
sufficient to sustain a criminal conviction. The moving plaintiff
must appear personally and be accompanied by two witnesses who
shall testify to the commission of the crime.[20] Omar, the second
calif after the death of the Prophet, is reported in a famous case to
have decided: *"In Islam no one can be imprisoned without due
course of justice."*[21] [Emphasis added.]

The presence of such a guarantee is indispensable for the maintenance of freedom of opinion and belief and to uphold the rights
of the individuals composing the Islamic nation as a whole and
maintaining its political integrity. At an early stage of the Islamic
nation in the days of Aly, the fourth calif, a certain group known
as the *Kharijite* revolted against his regime. This group was often
labeled as anarchists who defied the state openly and denied the
need for its existence. It is reported that Aly sent them the following message: "You may live wherever you like, the only condition
between us being that you will not indulge in blooshed and you
will not practice cruel methods."[22] On another occasion he addressed them thus: "As long as you do not indulge in any actual
disruption and disorder, we will not wage war against you."[23]
From these instances draws Maududi the logical conclusion that
even an organized group opposed to the form of government may
entertain its political opposition as long as it is not done in a
disorderly fashion and does not call for the destruction of the state
by forceful means or violence.[24] The right to dissent and to be
free from governmental compulsion or duress is thus secured.

In addition to the individual rights stated, a constitution should also guarantee that:

> No citizen of the state shall be deprived of the fundamental rights without his guilt being judicially established in an open court of law according to the common law of the land.
> Without this guarantee nobody can feel secure against the high-handedness of the executive, and the feeling of constant insecurity cannot but breed discontent and even hatred against the Government itself. This, in its turn, will be most dangerous and harmful for the larger interest of national solidarity and sincere cooperation between the Government and the people.[25]

To further insure the individual against the abuses of the executive branch, Maududi maintains that the most effective remedy is habeas corpus.

> ... The Executive should in no circumstances be allowed to possess the power of suspending either the fundamental rights or the writ of *Habeas Corpus.* The maximum allowance that can be made in this respect is that in case of actual war, rebellious persons who are charged with high treason, conspiracy against the State or armed revolt may be tried *in camera.* But the power of detention without judicial trial or of suspension of fundamental rights or of the writ of *Habeas Corpus,* should in no case be granted to the Executive. And let it be known at this very moment that if any such attempt is made in our Constitution we are determined to resist it with all the force at our command.[26]

Maududi, a great Muslim scholar, was not alone in professing those thoughts. Between 11 and 18 January 1953 a special convention of Ulemas representing all schools of Islamic thought gathered to discuss the 1952 proposed constitution of Pakistan. The convention submitted a unanimous report on the Constitutional Commission's report submitted in 1952. It called for an immediate amendment of the following provision of section 3 of the Constitution: "Except in the case of an external or internal threat to the security of the state or other grave emergency," the right to habeas corpus can be suspended by executive decree. The committee reports that Islamic Shariah does not allow in any circumstances whatsoever that any Muslim or non-Muslim citizen be deprived of his right to move to the highest court for redress against unwarranted detention.

While restrictions imposed on individual freedom must be conceded to the state, they must be at all times "reasonable restrictions" and must always be subject to the right of the individual to petition a court of justice for redress in case of abuse or unreasonableness.[27] Those contemporary Islamic scholars were quick to respond and assert the principles of the Shariah to protect against potential threats to individual rights by abuse of the criminal process. The remedy of habeas corpus was singled out as the most important safeguard and became the counterpart of the tenth-century *Mazalin* tribunal, also allowing for an extraordinary remedy by which to petition for immediate redress of wrongs.[28]

There is no question as to the existence of human rights within the Islamic states. While there are no problems insofar as relations between Muslim political subdivisions or states, since the same rights exist for all Muslims regardless of where they are located, the question arises as to the protection of minorities within the Muslim states by treaty and the relationship of the Muslim states and other states with reference to human rights.

The protection of minorities in the Muslim states is purely a problem of internal law. Modern international law, however, seeks to cover human rights within a state itself. An examination of a Commission of Human Rights' report discloses international criteria for equality: "The principle of equality or nondiscrimination implies the following two consequences. In the first place, the members of the minority have the right to the nationality of the state that exercises sovereignty over the territory in which they reside. In a modern state, the possession of nationality implies equal rights for all those possessing it. Secondly, discrimination *de facto* or *de jure* against minority elements is forbidden."[29] The report further attempts to identify what is meant by equality— "equality of all. persons before the law, equal treatment *de facto* and *de jure*."[30]

While the United Nations seeks to establish the guarantee of those rights by international obligation, one author commented: "The general protection of fundamental human rights which Oppenheim hoped to have enacted as part of municipal laws conceivably 'through the indisputably binding obligations under the aegis of the United Nations' after the generally admitted ineffectiveness of the League of Nations were more than thirteen cen-

turies ago both introduced and sanctioned as part of the fundamental laws of Islam."[31]

Notwithstanding the truth of that statement, a Muslim state can
enter into an international treaty to sanction human rights. An
examination of the following human rights treaties signed or ratified by the Muslim states shows that, if the need for securing
human rights by international obligation arises, these states can
and do take part in it.

Selected international human rights conventions:[32]

1. International Covenant on Economic, Social and Cultural
    Rights (not yet in force).
2. International Covenant on Civil and Political Rights (not yet
    in force).
3. Optional Protocol to the International Covenants on Civil and
    Political Rights (not yet in force).
4. Convention on the Prevention and Punishment of the Crime
    of Genocide (in force since 12/1/51).
5. International Convention on the Elimination of All Forms of
    Racial Discrimination (not yet in force).
6. Convention relating to the Status of Refugees (in force since
    22/4/54).
7. Convention relating to the Status of Stateless Persons (in force
    since 6/6/60).
8   Convention on the Reduction of Statelessness (not yet in
    force).
9. Convention on Political Rights of Women (in force since
    7/7/54).
10. Convention on the Nationality of Married Women (in force
    since 11/8/58).
11. Convention on Consent to Marriage, Minimum Age for Mar-
    riage and Registration of Marriages (in force since 9/12/64).
12. Convention on the International Right of Correction (in force
    since 24/8/62).
13. Protocol amending the Slavery Convention signed at Geneva
    on 25 September 1926 (in force since 7/12/53).
14. Slavery Convention of 25 September 1926 as amended (in
    force since 7/7/1955).
15. Supplementary Convention on the Abolition of Slavery, the

Slave Trade, Institutions and Practices similar to Slavery (in force since 30/4/57).

16 UNESCO Convention against Discrimination in Education— 1960.

17. ILO (29) Forced Labor—1930.

18. ILO (105) Abolition of Forced Labor—1957.

19. ILO (87) Freedom of Association and Protection of the Rights to Organize—1948.

20 ILO (98) Right to Organize and Collective Bargaining—1949.

21 ILO (100) Equal Remuneration—1951.

22. ILO (111) Discrimination (Employment and Occupation) — 1958.

23. ILO (117) Social Policy (Basic Aims and Standards) —1962.

The number before each convention named above represents the convention itself in the table that follows, each having been either signed or ratified by the corresponding listed state:

United Arab Republic: 4 - 5 - 12 - 13 - 14 - 15 - 16 - 17 - 18 - 19 - 20 - 21 - 22

Jordan: 4 - 14 - 15 - 17 - 18 - 21 - 22 - 23

Kuwait: 14 - 15 - 16 - 18 - 19 - 22 - 23

Lebanon: 4 - 9 - 14 - 16

Morocco: 3 - 5 - 13 - 14 - 15 - 17 - 18 - 20 - 22

Pakistan: 4 - 5 - 8 - 9 - 14 - 15 - 17 - 18 - 19 - 20 - 23

Saudi Arabia: 4

Sudan: 14 - 15 - 17 -20

Syria: 13 - 14 - 15 - 17 - 18 - 19 - 20 - 21 - 22 - 23

Tunisia: 4 - 5 - 6 - 14 - 15 - 17 - 18 - 19 - 20 - 21 - 23

Turkey: 4 - 6 - 9 - 13 - 14 - 15 - 18 - 20

Afghanistan: 4 - 9 - 13 - 14 - 15 - 18

Algeria: 4 - 5 - 6 - 7 - 14 - 15 - 17 - 19 - 20 - 21

Indonesia: 9 - 16 - 17 - 20 - 21

Iran: 4 - 5 - 15 - 17 - 18 - 22

Iraq: 4 - 13 - 14 - 15 - 17 - 18 - 20 - 21 - 22

The relevance of Islamic concepts of international law is more imperative today than it used to be, in light of the existence of the United Nations and the International Court of Justice.[33] The International Court of Justice notes that the court will apply "the general principles of law recognized by civilized nations."[34] Wherefore, the importance of perceiving and understanding the

Islamic concepts of human rights since they will be part of those general principles which the court will have to apply.[35]

Greater significance must be attributed to the fact that all Muslim states are signatories of the Charter of the United Nations, which says in its preamble: "We, the peoples of the United Nations, determine to ... reaffirm faith in the fundamental human rights, in the dignity and worth of the human person, and in the equal rights of men and women." Not only there is no impediment to the Muslim states today, or the Islamic state if it existed in its ideal theoretical form, to enter international treaties for human rights and the proposed treaty-statute of World Habeas Corpus but the necessary elements for the establishment of a world habeas corpus tribunal exist in the Islamic legal and philosophical concept.

This last general statement requires, however, a qualification, and that is that such a tribunal operate under principles not in violation of Islamic law and be composed of Muslim judges who would also apply "general principles" of Shariah law. The right to redress of wrongs, the right to habeas corpus, the right to go above a ruler of a state to a judicial body organized under an international court aegis applying principles compatible with Islamic law are indeed welcome steps in the development of Muslim law as they are in the development of human rights. To the Islamic concept it is more than a question of human rights; it is the establishment of a guarantee against dictatorship and oppression and will serve to uphold one of the most basic and fundamental Islamic concepts: fredom of thought, freedom of opinion, freedom of religious practices, and other individual rights from the arbitrary power of any ruler.

AN ANALYSIS OF WORLD HABEAS CORPUS WITH REFERENCE TO ISLAMIC LAW

1. World Habeas Corpus constitutes a collective summary remedy designed to protect and guarantee individual rights. To comply with Islamic law, it would have to enlarge upon its fundamental tenets of natural law source as its exclusive source. Specific references made to the Bible and the creation of man in the image of God[36] will have to be altered to take cognizance of the Qur'ān and Islam. The statement that the "state is for men and not men for the state"[37] does not exactly comply with the ideals of the

Islamic state, where the state is for man what man is for the state.[38]

2. To recognize that man has certain inalienable and fundamental rights which must be secured and protected against the overbearing power of a government overstepping its boundaries is in conformity with Islamic principles. The concept of the inherent dignity of man as enunciated in the U.N. Charter, the Universal Declaration of Human Rights, the Nuremberg principles, the Genocide Convention, and other human rights conventions are indeed acceptable to the ideal Islamic state and to most Muslim states.

3. The "absolute primacy"[39] of human rights as being "immutable, inflexible, yielding to no pressure of convenience, expediency, or the so-called judicial instrument"[40] has to be amended to consider that there is no absolute primacy of individual rights in Islam in the absolute sense. All individual and human rights are subject to the purpose and objectives of a given society with respect to its purposes. The limitation is that life, liberty, and property cannot be impaired except through the operation of the due process of law. Reference to absolutism is incompatible with Islamic relativism in individual rights with the exception of the primacy of certain rights enunciated in the Qur'ān with which no authority can tamper. Islamic tradition agrees with Chief Justice Marshall that "when in doubt of the construction of a constitution, the courts will favor personal liberty."[41]

4. The doctrine that an individual may also be a subject of the law of nations and may be "endowed directly with rights and burdened with obligations under international law"[42] is not incompatible with Islam if those rights and obligations emanating from the international law are not in conflict with Islamic law. Under Islamic law, however, principles of Islamic international law are part of general law and, therefore, obligations arising under international law are as equally enforceable and applicable as those of national law.

5. The summary remedy shall be "prosecuted by world attorney generals that will stand against any winds of tyranny that blow as a haven of refuge for those who might otherwise suffer because they are helplessly weak, outnumbered, or because they are nonconforming victims of prejudice or public excitement."[43] To provide the shield of the due process of law to individuals is also established

by Islamic law. Its exercise and application, however, must be by an Islamic circuit[44] which would take into account the specifics of Islamic morality.

6. Nothing prevents an ideal Islamic state or a Muslim state from becoming a signatory to the treaty-statute imposing specific limitations on its government, provided it will not impair the national sovereignty but will guarantee certain inalienable rights to the people, such as: "Freedom of speech, press, religion, and assembly; the right to trial by jury; the right to be secure against unreasonable searches and seizures; the right not to be compelled to be a witness against oneself; the right not to be deprived of life, liberty, or property without due process of law; the right to speedy and public trial; the right to confront witnesses against oneself; the right to counsel; the right to be secured against excessive bail and cruel and unusual punishment."[45]

The rights enunciated above are acceptable if their objective is to insure a fair trial. The specific standards of application will have to be adjusted, however, to a system of justice different from the Anglo-Saxon and American tradition. The Islamic system of law is not the only one which differs with that tradition; so does the civil system in most Western European countries, Africa, and Asia. The specific guarantees stated above are intended to protect the freedom of an individual from duress and to insure equality before the law and fairness of trial. This can be achieved by other means and standards than those stated. To recognize the value of the human being, his inherent rights, the inalienability of certain divinely endowed rights, and their protection is certainly in conformity with the spirit and the letter of Islam.

7. The means to implement such rights by the establishment of a specified tribunal operating under the proposed treaty-statute cannot, for instance, afford any greater guarantees to minorities than are available to the majority in the area in which the court will have jurisdiction. Most of the Muslim states have recently emerged from colonialism, and the memory of capitulations and privileges is still vivid. The proposed treaty-statute, when affording greater rights to individuals than the local constitution or judicial system allows, will necessitate constitutional amendments. The general purposes enunciated by World Habeas Corpus are fortunately compatible with some constitutions of the Muslim states and certainly in keeping with the spirit of the ideal theoretical Islamic state. The

question arises as to the standards of application for the enforcement of those specific guarantees as enunciated above, which emante from the Bill of Rights of the U.S. Constitution. Because they are familiar to the Anglo-American jurist, they must not be construed as necessary or indispensable for the whole world. Other systems of law have operated just as effectively and provided justice and equality.

8. The procedure or *modus operandi* of the court as described[46] can be found in the history of the Islamic judicial system. Individuals have the right to invoke the jurisdiction and require the court to intervene on their behalf to scrutinize the validity of their detention.[47] In theory, governmental authorities do not have the right to prevent a person from petitioning the court or to deny him the right to appear in court in his behalf. The right of the state to intervene before the circuit court and the requirement that the state produce the person detained, give him the right to confrontation, to cross-examination, to be heard, and to hear the testimony and evidence presented against him are generally compatible with most legal systems of the world, including the Islamic system. The right of a legally constituted court, having proper jurisdiction, to order the release of a prisoner at once in the event that the detention is found to be illegal or improper is valid under Islamic law.[48] However, to establish a system by which a "procedural defect" can be the basis for the release of a person who otherwise would not be released is to substitute the rule of the form for the rule of the substance and would ultimately detract from the search for truth and individualized justice. Under the Islamic criminal concept, the search for justice is the search for the truth and veracity of the facts and matters stated and not for that portion of truth which certain rules of form may allow or disallow. Errors of form and defects of form are best left for the judges, who will determine the extent of their effect on the truth, veracity of the matter, and credibility of the evidence presented, rather than constitute an absolute bar to its admissability. In this respect, both the Islamic and the civil laws concepts differ from the American tradition. The English legal system also differs in that violations of certain rules of form are not treated as an absolute bar to the admissibility of such evidence but are left for the determination of the judge guided by the judge's handbook on evidence.

9. To allow a petitioner to appeal a decision of the proposed circuit court to a higher court is acceptable, but it must be noted that the right to petition a court of law already exists at the national level and the individual may have exhausted several remedies at the national level before reaching the circuit court of World Habeas Corpus. In this respect, an additional appeal to a supreme court sitting above the circuit court of World Habeas Corpus would duplicate an existing remedy. With some restrictions of that process in the treaty-statute, however, there is no impediment to such an additional recourse.

10. World Habeas Corpus may indeed function as a "ligament for world order," offering a summary remedy for individual rights, taking into account certain personal guarantees accepted by societies of the world and recognizing universally accepted concepts of human dignity. This is indeed a substantial accomplishment. It must be understood, however, that such a system operating against governmental action will constitute an impediment to the sovereignty of governments.[49] While it is true that upholding individuals' rights would in effect tend to become a check against arbitrary governmental action, it does not necessarily follow that the purpose of World Habeas Corpus is to be a limitation upon valid governmental action. The concept of sovereignty has been criticized by Luis Kutner and other authors.[50] The concept of sovereignty narrowly conceived and construed often operates as an impediment to the development of world legal order. It is equally true, however, that the object of World Habeas Corpus is not world government or world citizenry and that, therefore, the place of sovereignty and its respect are quite important even when subject to the limitations of the proposed world habeas corpus treaty-statute. The protection of human rights and guarantees of individual freedom cannot lead to the imposition of restrictions on governmental power and sovereignty beyond the limited purposes of World Habeas Corpus.

11. Luis Kutner concludes that "Implicit in World Habeas Corpus is the recognition of the existence of an international community."[51] Yet, it must be explicitly clear that the recognition of an international community is not the destruction of the individual units (the nations) that comprise that community. Just as individuals have rights that must be protected, collectivities (nations) must also have the undisturbed right to pursue their national

objectives and internal policies. Guarantees of individual rights cannot serve as an impediment to the attainment of national objectives. The recognition of the universality of mankind is not a limitation upon the recognition of the right of some members of mankind to concentrate in certain areas with objectives that may differ from others. National rights must be given equal protection as individual rights. To that extent World Habeas Corpus must be amended to recognize the equal importance of the collective and social rights of a given community. The treaty-statute, I suggest, should, therefore, also grant the signatory states the right to petition the "circuit" to deliver the body of a person seeking asylum in a foreign state after having committed a crime in the petitioning state. World Habeas Corpus is a summary remedy to extradite the body of a detained individual who is so detained in violation of his rights. Similarly, the states and governments must have the right to request the extradition of the body of a person who may seek asylum in a foreign state and try to avoid the legal due process of law. To render more effective the maintenance and upholding of individual rights and to induce states to recognize the supremacy of such a court over its local courts, World Habeas Corpus must also grant the signatory states a concomitant right. It should, therefore, afford a procedure for the states to request extradition in the event that individuals commit common crimes against said states and manage to flee with impunity. In recognition of individual rights to persons as members of an international community, it cannot be ignored that with those rights there also arise certain obligations and duties. Citizens of one state cannot be made to escape these by avoiding the sovereignty and jurisdiction of that state, yet at the same time benefiting from all the advantages of a summary remedy such as World Habeas Corpus.

The sifting of the decision-making process from a national court to the circuit court of world habeas corpus will, in fact, eliminate internal political pressures on the judiciary as may occur in certain instances. Similarly, it will give governments that depend for their existence upon precarious political balance the opportunity to shift the blame or credit, as the case may be, to an international impartial legal organ without any reflection on their political course and its continuity.

CONCLUSION

The above exposé of Islam, from a philosophic concept to specific World Habeas Corpus application, was designed to show that World Habeas Corpus can be made applicable to Muslim states and, with certain changes, to the ideal Islamic state. I would be derelict if I concluded without paying tribute to Luis Kutner, the father of the concept, and to those persons he has motivated or who have joined him in this practical idealistic vision of the future of world order. In an age when the "world is convulsed by events that threaten its existence and the dignity and survival of entire peoples are challenged,"[52] it is with gratification that we witness such efforts. They are the architects of mankind's hopes and the builders of the rule of law.

Justice through law is the difference between tyranny and freedom; it is in fact the measuring cup of civilization. The lawyer is the recipient of the highest essence of human responsibility: the maintenance of the rule of law as a servant of freedom and as the vehicle of justice.[53]

Notes

1. Throughout this article "Muslim state" means a state in which there is a Muslim majority or a government representing a Muslim majority, while "Islamic state" refers to a form of government where in the conduct of all aspects of human endeavor and law is subject to Islamic law.
2. Justice Jackson's "Foreword" to *Law in the Middle East*, Middle East Institute, Khadduri, ed., (1955).
3. Luis Kutner, "World Habeas Corpus, Human Rights and World Community," XVII De Paul L. Rev. I (1967), p. 12.
4. Ibid., pp. 12-16.
5. Kutner, *World Habeas Corpus* (1962), the basic text on World Habeas Corpus; and subsequently, Kutner, "World Habeas Corpus: The Legal Ultimate for the Unity of Mankind," 40 Notre Dame Law. 520 (1965).
6. Maududi, *Islamic Law and Constitution* (Lahore, 3d ed., 1967), p. 46.
7. Ibid., p. 151, n. 26; see also Watt, *Free Will and Predestination in Early Islam* (London, 1948).
8. Brennan, "International Due Process and the Law," Law and Layman Conference, American Bar Association, 7 August 1962; and Kutner, "World Habeas Corpus for International Man: A Credo for International Due Process of Law," 36 U. Det. L. J. 235 (1959); and supra, n. 5.
9. T. W. Arnold, *The Preaching of Islam* (2d ed., 1913); Roberts, *The Social Laws of the Quran* (London, 1925).
10. Q. 16:90. 11. Q. 5:8. 12. Q. 4:1. 13. Q. 49:13.
14. H. A. R. Gibb, *Mohammedanism* (1962), p. 167. Here Gibb refers to the creation of special tribunals called *Mazalim*, or courts for the redress of wrongs.

15. Maududi, supra, n. 6, p. 267.   16. Ibid.
17. Baroody, *Shariah, The Law of Islam*, Case and Comment, vol. 72-2 (1967).
18. M'Alim Al Sunnah, cited in Maududi, supra, n. 6, p. 267.
19. See A. Ouda, *Islamic Criminal Legislation.*
20. See Anderson, *The Malki Law of Homicide* (Nigeria).
21. Imam Malik, *Kitab Ahkam Al Khilafat.*
22. Shaukani, *Nail Al-Awtar*, vol. VIII, p. 139.
23. Ibid.   24. Maududi, supra, n. 6, p. 268.
25. Ibid., pp. 339-340.   26. Ibid., p. 341.   27. Ibid., p. 385.   28. Gibb, supra, n. 14.
29. U.N. Commission on Human Rights, Subcommission on Prevention of Discrimination and Protection of Minorities, document prepared for the First Session (24 Nov. to 6 Dec. 1947). UN Doc. /E/CN. 4/SUB 216, 7 Nov. 1947, p. 14.
30. Ibid., p. 15.
31. Ramadan, *Islamic Law, Its Scope and Equity* (London, 1961), p. 159, citing Oppenheim, *International Law*, pp. 713-716.
32. The sources of the ratification table are: International Conventions of Human Rights, U.N. Office of Public Information, Reference Paper No. 6, June 1967, *Status of International Conventions on Human Rights*, as of 15 May 1967; and International Labor Conventions, *Chart of Ratifications*, 1 June 1967.
33. Rabbath, *Pour Une Theorie du Droit International Musulman*, Revue Egyptienne de Droit International, vol. VI, 1950.
34. Article 38-1B of the state of the court.
35. See McNair, *The General Principles Recognized by Civilized Nations*, 33 Brit. Y.B.Int.L. 1 (1957); and Friedman, *The Use of "General Principles" in the Development of International Law*, 57 A.J.I.L. (1963).
36. Kutner, supra, n. 3, p. 5.   37. Ibid.   38. See text, p. 00.
39. Kutner, supra, n. 3, p. 6.   40. Ibid.
41. *Ex parte Burford*, 7 U.S. (3 Cranch) 448 (1806).
42. Kutner, supra, n. 3, p. 6.   43. Ibid., p. 8.   44. Ibid., p. 17.
45. Ibid., p. 8.   46. Ibid., p. 14.   47. See supra, n. 14.   48. Ibid.
49. Kutner, supra, n. 3, p. 28.   50. Ibid.   51. Ibid., p. 34.
52. Bassiouni, *The Summons*, vol. 1, no. 3, December 1967.
53. Ibid.

The United Nations
and the Protection of
Personal Liberty

By Egon Schwelb*

In his contribution to this symposium[1] Professor
McDougal presents, and comments upon, the provisions of the
Universal Declaration of Human Rights[2] and of the International Covenant on Civil and Political Rights,[3] which purport to
protect everyone's right to liberty and security of person and re-
spectively provide that no one shall be subjected to arbitrary arrest
or detention and that no one shall be deprived of his liberty except
on such grounds and in accordance with such procedure as are
established by law. In the present essay, it is proposed to draw
attention to a project that is aimed specifically at the strengthening
of individual freedom. It is independent from and additional to
the International Bill of Rights, which was completed in 1966 by
the adoption of the International Covenants on Human Rights
and the Optional Protocol to the International Covenant on Civil
and Political Rights. The project concerned, the "Draft Principles
on Freedom from Arbitrary Arrest and Detention," has been dor-

* LL.D., Prague (1922); LL.B. London (1945); senior legal officer of the U.N.
War Crimes Commission in London (1945-1947); deputy director of the Division
of Human Rights, U.N. Secretariat (1947-1962); Yale Law School since 1962 to the
present; consultant to the U.N. Secretariat, International Law; author of numerous articles in law journals published worldwide.

mant for several years. This, however, is an additional ground why attention should be drawn to it in the framework of a symposium on World Habeas Corpus.

Mainly on U.S. initiative, the Commission on Human Rights decided in 1956 to undertake studies of specific rights and groups of rights and to stress in these studies general developments, progress achieved, and measures taken to safeguard human liberty, with such recommendations of an objective and general character as may be necessary. The commission further decided to select as its first subject of study the right of everyone to be free from arbitrary arrest, detention, and exile.[4] The commission's parent body, the Economic and Social Council, noted the undertaking by the commission of worldwide studies of specific rights and approved as the first subject for special study the one which the commission had selected.[5]

THE RIGHT TO BE FREE FROM ARBITRARY ARREST, DETENTION, AND EXILE

The study of the right of everyone to be free from arbitrary arrest, detention, and exile was prepared by a committee of four members of the Commission on Human Rights. It was submitted to the commission in 1961[6] and revised by the committee in 1962 in the light of observations received from governments. The revised version[7] includes, at the commission's request, "draft principles on freedom from arbitrary arrest and detention." It is not possible to summarize here the study, which is based on information concerning the situation in more than ninety countries. Nor is it possible to go into details of the forty-one articles that form the draft principles prepared for approval by the General Assembly.[8] The General Assembly, in agreeing upon the articles, would state that law and practice should conform to them. Only the most important provisions proposed by the committee will be briefly summarized in the paragraphs that follow.

Arrest or detention, draft article 1 provides, is arbitrary if it is (a) on grounds or in accordance with procedures other than those established by law or (b) under the provisions of a law the purpose of which is incompatible with respect for the right to liberty and security of person. In the chapter dealing with the arrest and detention of persons suspected or accused of a criminal offence it is provided that the arrest or detention of a suspected or accused person shall be regarded as an exceptional measure (art. 3). Arrest or detention before sentence is not a penalty and shall never be employed to accomplish ends that legitimately fall within the province of penal sanctions (art. 4). No one shall be arrested or detained unless there is reasonable cause to believe that he has committed a serious offence for which a penalty involving loss of liberty is prescribed by law, and unless, furthermore, there are grounds to fear that if not taken into custody he would evade the processes of the law or prejudice the results of the investigation (art. 5). An arrest can be made only upon the authority of a written warrant or order of arrest issued by a judge or other official authorized by law to exercise judicial power (art. 6). The requirement of a written warrant or order of arrest can be dispensed with only in cases where the suspect is found *in flagrante delicto* or in urgent cases when the arrest cannot be safely delayed (art. 7). A person who is arrested shall be brought promptly, and in any case not later than twenty-four hours from the time of his arrest, before a judge or other officer authorized by law to exercise judicial powers (art. 10). After the expiration of the specified time limit the detention becomes illegal and the arrested person shall be released forthwith (art. 11). The judge or other officer before whom the arrested person is brought shall decide within twenty-four hours whether to release him or order his continued custody (art. 12).

The period of detention shall not exceed four weeks. For good cause the order of detention may be renewed for a further period not to exceed four weeks. Thereafter no further extension may be granted except for serious reasons and upon the written order of a higher judicial authority. The period of detention shall in no case exceed one-half of the minimum term of imprisonment prescribed by the law for the offence with which the detained person is charged (art. 14). There shall be a review *ex officio* at regular intervals not exceeding four weeks, or at any time upon the application of the detainee or by someone on his behalf, of the necessity for his detention (art. 15). The arrested person shall be given an opportunity to obtain his provisional release, with or without financial security or other conditions (art. 16). The economic discrimination inherent in the bail system raises, the committee has stated, a serious human-rights problem. For this reason it has thought it necessary to stress that forms of provisional release other than upon financial security should be provided.

The authority arresting or detaining a person shall immediately notify his family, legal representative, or other person of his confidence of his arrest and of the place where he is kept in custody (art. 18). The arrested or detained person may not be held *incommunicado, mise au secret,* or in solitary confinement (art. 19). From the moment of his arrest the arrested person shall have the right to be assisted by legal counsel of his own choice; he shall be immediately informed of this right. If he is unable to obtain counsel the court or competent authority shall provide him with counsel (art. 20). The arrested person and his counsel shall always be allowed adequate opportunity for consultations (art. 21). No examination of the arrested or detained person or of witnesses or experts shall take place in the absence of his counsel (art. 22). No arrested or detained person shall be subjected to physical or mental compulsion, torture, violence, threats, or inducements of any kind, deceit, trickery, misleading suggestions, protracted questioning, hypnosis, administration of drugs, or any other means which tend to impair or weaken his freedom of action or decision, his memory, or his judgment (art. 24).

Where the trial and punishment of persons charged with very minor infractions may be entrusted to administrative authorities, the accused person shall be accorded adequate guarantees for his defense and decisions and orders of such authorities shall be subject to judicial review (art. 28). The draft principles also provide for safeguards in case of arrest and detention on grounds unconnected with criminal law, such as deportation proceedings, the detention of persons of unsound mind, alcoholics, or drug addicts, or the detention of persons for the prevention of the spread of serious infectious diseases (arts. 29 to 33). They also attempt to regulate and therefore to limit arrest and detention under emergency powers (arts. 34 to 37).

For the purposes of the present symposium the chapter dealing with remedies and sanctions (arts. 38 to 40) is of particular interest. Anyone who is arrested or detained contrary to the provisions set forth in the draft articles, or is in imminent danger thereof, or who is denied any of the basic rights and guarantees set forth in these articles shall be entitled to take proceedings immediately before a judicial authority in order to challenge the legality of his arrest or detention and obtain his release without delay if it is unlawful, or to prevent the threatened injury, or to enforce his rights. The proceedings shall be simple, expeditious, and free of charge. The aggrieved party, if in custody, must be produced without delay. The onus shall be on the detaining official or other person to establish affirmatively the legality of his act. The proceedings may be instituted by any person in the interest of the aggrieved party (art. 38). The draft principles also provide for penal sanctions, disciplinary measures, and an enforceable right to compensation in cases of arrest or detention in contravention of the draft articles (arts. 39 and 40).

Having received the committee's report and the draft principles at its 1962 session, the Commission on Human Rights decided to transmit the draft principles to states members of the United Nations and of the specialized agencies and requested them to submit comments thereon.[9] At its 1963 session, noting the comments by thirty-one governments, the commission invited governments that had not yet sent in their comments to do it as soon as possible.[10] In introducing the draft resolution to this effect, it was said on behalf of its sponsors that it was obvious from the comments which had been received by then that the laws and practices of countries relating to matters of arrest and detention differed greatly, and that it might be advisable at a later stage to consider the setting up of an expert committee which might prepare, in the light of the comments of governments, a shorter and more general draft of the principles relating to freedom from arbitrary arrest and detention, with recommendations as to the form in which these principles should be adopted.[11] At the sessions of the Commission on Human Rights held in 1964, 1965, 1966, and 1967, the commission, due to lack of time, postponed each time to the next session the consideration of the question. Its consideration is also on the provisional agenda of the 1968 session of the commission as item nineteen.[12] No action on the proposed draft principles has been taken at the time of this writing.

The draft principles as prepared by the committee do not provide for the establishment of international machinery for the enforcement of the rights and guarantees which they set forth. As drafted, they have the form of a draft resolution to be adopted by the General Assembly. The resolutions of the 1963 session of the commission (se n. 11) indicate, however, that "the form in which these principles should be adopted" is still an open question. This implies that the alternative of casting them in the form of an international treaty is also a possibility. Even if the eventual result should be a mere recommendation of the General Assembly embodied in a resolutuon, its adoption might be an event of considerable impact.

THE QUESTION OF U.N. MACHINERY OF IMPLEMENTATION

In 1947 the Commission on Human Rights stated in a well-known passage that it "recognizes that it has no power to take any action in regard to any complaints concerning human rights."[13] This statement was promptly approved by the Economic and Social Council,[14] maintained in spite of repeated attempts to reverse it, and reenacted in 1959.[15] In 1966/67, however, an important inroad was made into the self-denying ordinance of 1947. Acting on the initiative of the Special Committee (of twenty-four) on the situation with regard to the implementation of the anti-colonial declaration of 1960, the Economic and Social Council invited the Commission on Human Rights to consider as a matter of urgency the question of the violation of human rights and fundamental freedoms, including policies of racial discrimination and apartheid in all countries.[16] Later in 1966 the General Assembly invited the council and the commission to give urgent consideration to ways and means of improving the capacity of the United Nations to put a stop to violations of human rights *wherever they might occur*.[17] The outcome was a resolution of the Economic and Social Council adopted in 1967 in which it, *inter alia*, welcomed the decision of the commission to give annual consideration to the question of the violation of human rights and authorized the Commission on Human Rights and the Subcommission on Prevention of Discrimination and Protection of Minorities to examine information relevant to gross violations of human rights and fundamental freedoms contained in communications from private persons. It also decided that the commission may, in appropriate cases and after careful consideration of the information thus made available to it, make a thorough study of situations revealing a consistent pattern of violations of human rights.[18] While these decisions were primarily motivated by the situation existing in the southern part of the African Continent, both the General and the council were careful to make it clear that their scope covered violations of human rights wherever they might occur and that it "included" and, one would add, was therefore not limited to racial discrimination, segregation, and apartheid in southern Africa.

The Subcommission on Prevention of Discrimination and Protection of Minorities, one of the grantees of the authority delegated by the council by that resolution, interpreted its mandate to this effect. At its session in September/October 1967 the subcommission noted that flagrant violations of human rights are still being committed in South Africa, South West Africa, Southern Rhodesia, and in Portuguese territories in Africa. In addition, it drew attention to two "particularly glaring examples of situations which reveal consistent patterns of violations of human rights." These situations are of particular relevance for the present symposium. They are:

"(a) the situation in Greece, resulting from the *arbitrary arrest, detention and ill-treatment of political prisoners,* and the denials of human rights involved, for example, in censorship and prohibitions on the rights of assembly and free speech, since the *coup d'état* of 21 April 1947; and (b) the situation in Haiti, resulting from *the arbitrary arrest and detention of political prisoners.*"[19]

The subcommission also recommended that the Commission on Human Rights establish a special committee of experts similar to the working group that was established by the commission to investigate charges of torture and ill-treatment of prisoners, detainees, or persons in police custody in South Africa, and that it authorize the special committee of experts to consider the situations to which it was drawing attention.

The Working Group of Experts to which the subcommission referred had been established by the commission some months earlier and had been directed to investigate charges of torture and ill-treatment of prisoners, detainees, or persons in police custody in South Africa; to receive communications and hear witnesses and to use such modalities of procedure as it may deem appropriate and recommend action to be taken in concrete cases.[20] The Economic and Social Council welcomed the establishment of the working group.[21] These decisions were, of course, directed against one member state which is in particularly bad grace with the U.N. membership. As a reversal of the rule that the Commission on Human Rights has no power to take action they were certainly remarkable. That they created an important precedent was proved by the fact that only a few months afterwards the subcommission recommended that a similar investigating body should be created to consider, *inter alia,* the situations in Greece and Haiti where the problems of colonialism, racial discrimination, segregation, and apartheid do not enter the picture at all.

CONCLUDING OBSERVATIONS

The draft principles on freedom from arbitrary arrest and detention submitted by the committee to the Commission on Human Rights in 1961 and 1962 represent, as the perusal of the summary given in this essay shows, a more than satisfactory basis for the establishment on the international plane of a compreshensive code on the question with which they deal. Such a code, in whichever form it eventually appears, will be of great value.

It will carry persuasive authority with the organs, the Human Rights Committee and the ad hoc conciliation commission, that will apply the International Covenant on Civil and Political Rights on the international plane when that covenant enters into force. It will be recalled that in article 2 (3) of the covenant each state party undertakes:

(a) To ensure that any person whose rights or freedoms as herein recognized are violated shall have an effective remedy, notwithstanding that the violation has been committed by persons acting in an official capacity;

(b) to ensure that any person claiming such a remedy shall have his right thereto determined by competent judicial, administrative, or legislative authorities, or by any other competent authority provided for by the legal system of the state, and to develop the possibilities of judicial remedy; and

(c) to ensure that the competent authorities shall enforce such remedies when granted

The draft principles are more detailed than the substantive provisions on the right to liberty and security of the person as set forth in article 9 of the covenant[22] and the provisions of its article 10, pursuant to which all persons deprived of their liberty shall be treated with humanity and with respect for the inherent dignity of the human person, and which also provides that accused persons shall, save in exceptional circumstances, be segregated from convicted persons and shall be subject to separate treatment appropriate to their status as unconvicted persons. The international machinery which the covenant and the Optional Protocol create does not aim at judicial or quasi-judicial decisions but leads, if an amicable settlement is not achieved, to the international organ, the Human Rights Committee, forwarding "its views to the State Party and to the [complaining] individual." These are the "views" that ought to be, and will be, influenced if the General Assembly approves, with or without changes, the draft principles.

Once they are approved, these principles will be of still greater value for the machinery of implementation which is being built under the Economic and Social Council resolutions of 6 June 1967.[23] These principles will stand whenever the U.N. organs concerned will be expected to act on allegations that a consistent pattern of gross violations of the right to liberty and security of person exists. This machinery is, as already stated, not based on a new international treaty, but will be operating by virtue of the powers vested in the United Nations by the charter. These arrangements have great potentialities but they, too, stop far short of creating an international judicial remedy as that contemplated by the advocates of World Habeas Corpus. [This article was completed in February 1968.]

Notes

1. Myres S. McDougal, "A Practicable Measure for Human Rights," page 000 above.
2. General Assembly resolution 217A (III), December 10, 1948.
3. Annex to General Assembly resolution 2200 (XXI) of December 16, 1966; reprinted in 61 American Journal of International Law 870 (1967).
4. Commission on Human Rights. Report of the 12th session (1956) Economic and Social Council Official Records: 22nd session, supplement no. 3 (E/2844), para. 49 (Resolution II).
5. Resolutions 624 B I and II (XXII) of the Economic and Social Council, August 1, 1956.
6. U.N. Doc. E/CN.4/813; Commission on Human Rights, Report of the 17th session (1961), Economic and Social Council Official Records: 32nd session, supplement no. 8 (E/3456), paragraphs 34 to 50.
7. Study of the right of everyone to be free from arbitrary arrest, detention and exile, E/CN.4/826/Rev. 1, United Nations Publication Sales No. 65. XIV.2.
8. Ibid., pages 205-217.
9. Commission on Human Rights, Report of the 18th session (1962). Economic and Social Council Official Records: 34th session supplement no. 8 (E/3616/ Rev. 1), resolution 2 (XVIII).
10. Commission on Human Rights, Report of the 19th session (1963), Economic and Social Council Official Records: 36th session, supplement no. 8 (E/3743), resolution 2 (XIX). Eventually a total number of forty-two Government replies were received. They are reproduced in U.N. Doc. E/CN.4/835 and Addenda 1 to 11.

11. Ibid., (E/3743), paragraph 26.
12. U.N. Doc. E/CN.4/957, January 2, 1968 and Addendum 1, January 25, 1968.
13. Economic and Social Council Official Records, 4th session, supplement no. 3 (E/259), Report of the Commission on Human Rights, January/February 1947, para. 22.
14. Resolution of the Economic and Social Council 75 (V) of August 5, 1947.
15. Resolution of the Economic and Social Council 728 F (XXVIII) of July 30, 1959.
16. Resolution of the Economic and Social Council 1102 (XL) of March 4, 1966. For the follow-up see resolution 2 (XXII), part B, of the Commission on Human Rights, 22nd session, Economic and Social Council Official Records, 41st session, supplement no. 8 (E/4184), paragraph 222 and resolution of the Economic and Social Council 1164 (XLI) of August 5, 1966.
17. General Assembly resolution 2144 (XXI) of October 26, 1966. For the follow-up see Commission on Human Rights, Report of the 23rd session, Economic and Social Council Official Records, 42nd session, supplement no. 6 (E/4322), resolutions 8 (XXIII) and 9 (XXIII) (1967).
18. Resolution of the Economic and Social Council 1235 (XLII) of June 6, 1967.
19. Report of the 20th session of the Sub-Commission on Prevention of Discrimination and Protection of Minorities, September/October, 1967 U.N. Doc. E/CN.4/947. Paragraph 95, resolution 3 (XX). (Italics added.)
20. Resolution 2 (XXIII) of the Commission on Human Rights, in Report of the 23rd session (note 17 above), paragraph 268.
21. Resolution of the Economic and Social Council 1236 (XLII) of June 6, 1967. The comprehensive first report of the Ad Hoc Working Group is contained in document E/CN.4/950 of October 27, 1967.
22. Quoted by Professor McDougal, op. cit., note 1 above.
23. Notes 18 and 21 above.

The Struggle for International Rule of Law

By Tran Tam*

For a millennium and more states have guarded monopolistic authority comprehensively termed "powers of the state." They have used this concept to condemn the individual considered to have violated the law or disturbed public order, even when the offense was minor or as a result of arbitrary interpretation of the law. Concurrently, the state has reserved unto itself the right and power to exercise the self-same acts for which it would adjudge an individual in violation of the law.

State contempt for the law by which it would regulate the individual reaches an apex in the field of international relations, i.e., relations between sections of the community of peoples. Here, the state deliberately disregards such basic of law as morality, justice, and honesty—areas which the individual is expected to respect, observe, and honor unquestioningly.

* Former legal advisor for the Ministry of Pacification, Saigon; former chargé de mission of the Department of Justice; former director general of Information and Press; former secretary general of the Asian Peoples' Anti-Communist League (1954-1961), a nongovernmental organization founded by the peoples of twenty-three nations in Asia and the Middle East; former editor and publisher of two popular reviews, Free Front and Front de la Liberté; secretary general of the International Association of Criminology; author of many books.

Such development in practice is the consequence of the prevailing characteristic of so-called "public power," long defined legalistically as "sovereignty of state." In reality, as the twentieth century moves along in its second half, state sovereignty undergoes profound modifications both in doctrine and practice which are tending to render that dogma no more than an anachronism. We continue to hear calls to state sovereignty as the term is deeply ingrained in our language, but its import and impact no longer carry universally the weight of a half-century past.

In fact, the concept now emerges as anti-legal on two counts. First, there is a contradiction of terms in claiming that the formulator of law for all is sovereign—because of his power to create law—"out of reach" or above this very law. No resolution is possible for this basic contradiction. Rather, sovereignty, or the rulers of the state, only possess competence subordinate to the overall structure of the state, manifested through the role of servant of the state and that of social representative of the state, not supreme arbiter of the "true law."

A literal interpretation of sovereignty conflicts with the rationale of fact. Interationally speaking, every state sovereignty, with its basis of supremacy, would run up against every other equal state sovereignty. According to the most widely accepted doctrine, state is to be considered the juridical form of the nation, its formal structure as it were. State represents to the world and to its individuals a nation or assembly of nations in their judicial organization. In public functioning, the state, a corporate individual, must act through the medium of physical beings who are constitutionally endowed with that power necessary to do its will, as individuals or collectively. Such individuals, such physical beings, act on behalf of and for the state as its representatives, its embodiment for an occasion. They go forth as emissaries of the civilized community, the state, of which they are part, not as embodiments of God on earth greater than that of which they are a part nor as interpreters of a "divinely essential universal order." Stripped to the essential truth, rulers are no more and no less than human beings living in a human society.

In theory, the problems come to a simple, common sense resolution, as we have seen. In reality, they are more enduring and complex. Trampling of human rights is not typical of primitive societies; we find strong individual rights in the Eskimo community structure, for instance. Rather, social sophistication breeds disregard for the individual, with contemporary regimes, structured by self-aggrandizing men, filled with personal ambition, intent upon material and political profit abounding. As one extreme of political and social development, the sovereign state represents an extreme limit of social integration. It would have us believe that man's happiness begins and ends with the furthering of that state's interest. The state is God on earth!

It is ironic that even as man has made impressive strides in science and the humanities, man's inhumanity to man, terror, violence, and disregard of human rights have developed at even a greater pace. Herein lies the greatest threat to the present and future of humanity. This is the consequence of arbitrary interpretation of so-called international crimes, a term used to camouflage varied and sundry affronts to the sovereign state.

Judicial science and political science unquestionably have differing natures because their original intents were quite different. In practice, today they are converging because political policies must be in conformity with the precepts of the rule of law if they are to serve the people instead of endangering them.

We might view the science of politics and the science of law as having the complementary relationship of poetry and music. Though the latter are quite separate vehicles of art, combined they furnish us with opera and the oratorio, tributes to this relationship.

The search for spheres of cooperation and coordination between law and politics, to the benefit of national and international activities, can be most beneficial to world civilization as a whole. That government which is conceived to serve the people of a nation cannot do other than adopt the principles of the rule of law as basic if it is to achieve this purpose. International and national policy must be in harmony with law if we are to gain a cessation of world holocausts and personal misery, all too well known to each of us.

"It is better to light a candle than curse the darkness." If this author can but place the first shovel of fill in the abyss, created by contradiction and mistrust, existing on our planet today, his reward will be great. Rule of law for all nations and habeas corpus for mankind as a whole, regardless of political leanings of the individual and the composition of political regimes, must come to pass "as the day the night." Whatever the regime under which he lives, man has a right to absolute security guaranteed by a world legal system secured through natural and international law.

New international law and World Habeas Corpus constitute a complex, dynamic field of study full of change. It is fitting that they are emerging in today's world as this is freeing itself of old restrictions and unworkable traditions, entering the "space age." To neglect the building of a *new public order* of human dignity at such an auspicious moment would be unthinkable.

If the present crisis of international law must be viewed as merely "growing pains," as affirmed by some authors, the problem of World Habeas Corpus remains in a state of "gestation!"[1] The present writer should make it clear from the outset that he has a feeling of profound sorrow that, so far, the great powers as well as newly independent countries, the Communist bloc included, have paid special need to military armament but only lip service to building for man a legal statute worthy of the name.[2]

Were we to compare the budgets for defense and munitions in general with that reserved for the setting up of a legal statute, we would see several billions of any given national currency coming up against ten's of thousands of the same currency—and this intended only to soothe the national conscience. Admittedly, danger of war and especially thermonuclear war grows rather than diminishes, but human dignity also continues to be trampled upon and wallow under a veritable "law of the jungle." We *know* such conditions exist under prevailing tyrannical and totalitarian regimes.[3] Theoretically, taking into account the present stage of evolution, man ought to be enjoying an ever greater protection under law guaranteed by the Universal Declaration, but, instead, he continues to suffer persecution. The threat of nuclear war is often used as an apologia for harsh government. Can it not be seen that a "rule of law" might dissipate the friction and resolve the confrontations that are prolonging the spectre of a nuclear war? Einstein reveals just such thinking in his "Spiritual Testament." Regretfully, the emergence of a World Habeas Corpus is the only positive step taken by humanity of late toward the desired goal.[4]

Jurists and internationalists urgently call for those men who are achieving such success in the exploration and conquest of space to consider the concept of World Habeas Corpus with its jurisdiction to be accomplished by the end of the twentieth century. Lawyers and criminologists are being confronted with facts and figures contrary to their own aims as they work for industry. They see billions going into the arms race, even as their quest of modest sums dedicated to the study and research of the science of law and human rights is rejected. It would seem that the arrival of man on the moon is a more predictable prospect than the realization of a world legal statute for the protection of inalienable rights of all members of the human family.

There are very compelling cases for support of scientific research: research for improved defensive potential and research for the fulfillment of human needs from a humanitarian standpoint. Equitable division of effort and funds would assure the pursuance of all these ends and, more important, their recognition. Man has a spiritual and politic nature worthy of study for betterment. This nature deserves study as we continue the more publicized research programs.

The world is today divided roughly into three parts, as Caesar's Gaul: advanced nations, emerging countries, and the Communist states. This is indisputable. Just as there is a three-way division of nations, so does a tripartite condition obtain regarding international law and its claim to universality. Some observers have carried the thesis to the conclusion that there are three extant systems of human rights. In reality there could be no more than two, for the Soviet Union and its hegemony function without consideration of the problem of habeas corpus and the development and application of international law. Throughout the world of communism, lawyers exercise little influence on government policy, almost never being listed among those considered top policy figures and part of the party hierarchy. To avoid oversimplification, we will refrain from saying flatly that every utterance of Communist jurists is dictated by the government,[5] but there is just enough truth in the statement to merit consideration.

As for the newly independent and less developed nations, human rights remain a problem to be resolved with all the others present at the birth of a state. For example, the Republic of South Africa falls into this grouping, but in order to keep minority rule it maintains Draconian laws which are indistinguishable from Communist law in their severity. Haiti, mature in years yet underdeveloped as a state born yesterday, resorts to similar disregard of human rights, not because of racial unrest but due to the megalo· mania of one man. Need more be said on either of these shameful situations?

Let it be understood that we recognize that differences in race, geography, culture, and political tint will call for variances in the legal systems of human rights so that they will be compatible to different regimes.[6] No one with understanding would consider one interpretation of government to be applicable to all peoples.

There are some countries that have confused *Dura Lex, Sed Lex* and violence with coercion. According to the popular interpreta- tion, coercion and violence are measures of despotism that result from the rule of man. Dictatorship is so couched in legalities as to distort fundamental norms of law. Political sorcery mesmerizes a populace into believing the interpretation convenient to those in power, and *Dura Lex, Sed Lex* molders.[7]

Dictatorships today have such sophisticated legal mechanisms that they are able to publicly justify the overthrow of very elemen- tal notions of law. Semantic treachery has turned honored terms as "rule of law" and "justice" into political instruments directed to conceal violence and terror. This situation leads the legal anarchy of a considerable portion of mankind from bad to worse. These anomalous phenomena impose on those of us who love freedom and justice a responsibility, to wit: adopt a firm stand to confront legal anarchy and the *summun jus, summa injuria* of the world today.

To draw a simile, the rapport between human rights (*jus natu- rale*) and sovereignty of state (domestic law) is much like a rubber band, and like that rubber band cannot be stretched ad infinitum lest it break. Strictly speaking, each political regime is entitled to a legal system appropriate to the individual national situation, but this legal system must respect the fundamental principles stated in the Universal Declaration of Human Rights, unanimously consid- ered as a desirable common standard of treatment for all peoples and nations.[8]

There may exist many shades of political thinking in the world today, schools of law varying in individual legal interpretations and differing applications of democracy. All these give a different aspect to human rights across the world, but all must converge when man's sacred and basic rights, already stated in the jus naturale and international law, are defined. Men, no matter of what race or nationality, regardless of ruling political regime, are human beings and deserve no less as a result of this endowment.

World leaders of many professions recognize the merit of this struggle for man's basic rights. Following is what Pope John XXIII has said about World Habeas Corpus:

> Any human society, if it is to be well ordered and productive, must lay down as a foundation this principle, namely, that every human being is a person. That is, his nature is endowed with intelligence and free will. By virtue of this, he has rights and duties of his own, flowing directly and simultaneously from his very nature, which are, therefore, universal, inviolable, and inalienable. If we look upon the dignity of the human person in the light of divinely revealed truth, we cannot help but esteem it far more highly.[9]

The late secretary general of the United Nations, Dr. Dag Hammarskjold, also dealt with the issue, to wit: "The universal expression in the field of human rights of the aims of our world today, a world where the memory is still fresh of some of the worst infringements of human rights ever experienced in history and a world which is also facing the problems of human rights in new and increasingly complicated form, is the significance of the Declaration of Human Rights."[10]

All this leads us to the conclusion that World Habeas Corpus, a legal alignment for political diversity, or more precisely, the legal ultimate for the unity of mankind, can be playing a growing role in molding our destiny. The movement, conceived and guided into actuality by Luis Kutner, chairman, Commission for International Due Process of Law and the World Habeas Corpus Committee, World Peace through Law Center, Washington, is vital to the enduring problems of today's divided world.

If present-day news recognizes as heroes the precursors of travel in space, Glenn, Carpenter, Armstrong, Scott, Collins, Conrad, and Gordon, then we should also demand attention for the pioneers of World Habeas Corpus: Quincy Wright and Charles S. Rhyne, U.S.; Hersch Lauterpacht, United Kingdom; H. Donndedieu de Vabres and Renè Cassin, France; A. Sottile, Italy; Jean Graven, Switzerland; and Luis Kutner.

Kutner forwarded his authored cause of World Habeas Corpus at the Washington World Conference on World Peace through

Law, held 12 to 18 September 1965, when he proclaimed as follows:

World Habeas Corpus is concerned with the collective sovereign responsibility for individual security without impairment of sovereignty. Based on a treaty-statute, premised on civilized concepts, the International Bill of Rights could be judicially, competently implemented by regional international courts of habeas corpus.

A world in devious disarray must resolve competitive political idealogies and diversities by creating one worthy, indomitable world process suggesting a world conscience that will robustly structuralize the eternal truth of individual liberty and justice . . .

. . . The explicit terms of the concept of World Habeas Corpus are meaningful and realistic. It suggests a minimal dialogue tribunal communication between all sovereignties and a faith and mutual trust that no person shall be arbitrarily detained or wrongfully imprisoned anywhere on the face of the globe. As an international tribunal, it can deal promptly and effectively in correcting the suppression of individual rights and fundamental freedoms, including the exploitation, mass deportations, and exiling of individuals. It can extinguish partial or total tyranny.[11]

In dealing with individual prerogative as a major counter to the supremacy of sovereignty, the author of World Habeas Corpus declares:

The United States Supreme Court recognized in 1856 the language of "due process of law" as conveying the same meaning as the phrase "law of the land," Magna Carta, chapter 39.[12] In 1921, Chief Justice Taft added this further thought: "That due process, having its origins in Magna Carta, overlaps to an extent that equal protection in the sense that due process give a required minimum of protection for everyone's right to life, liberty and property . . .[13]

The basic concept of jurisdiction of the International Courts of Habeas Corpus in judicially processing World Habeas Corpus is that any imprisonment without due process of law is an absolute nullity. While the exhausting of available state remedies is adjudicated, an allegation of extraordinary emergency that the jailer-state does not have any available remedy similar to Habeas Corpus or *amparo* or any corrective procedure for arbitrary detention, will enable the International Court of Habeas Corpus to act summarily on the application. The allegation of "unclean hands" of a jailer-state can also invoke summary relief.

World Habeas Corpus proclaims no general theory of government. Instead, it merely concerns itself with the practical problem of a summary remedy for wrongful imprisonment. *It demands that a government shall be a government of laws and not of man.* It is the absolute rule of law by which a free world can live because it defies and overcomes tyranny and bad government.

In probing banal clichés and the conventional dogmas of tyrannical governments, World Habeas Corpus produces a competent awareness of the inadequate standards of due process of law, making individual freedom and legal necessity consistent and inseparable. It creates the convergence of the tributaries of diverse competing political systems into the mainstream of authoritative and accepted International Bill of Rights, rejecting all static, quantitive, abstract symbols (so consciously practical to tyranny) ; and it can shape the domain of human liberty for eternity.

It may well determine the destiny of man, who lives in a world of hazards. Ever since early recorded history, man has propitiated the powers of his environs and his compelling quest for security. The crude methods of supplication, sacrifice, ceremonial rite, and magical cult have given way to ever growing attitudes of reverence and devotion to the rule of law.[14]

The macroscopic features of World Habeas Corpus are characteristic of the progress of scientific history from Galileo and Newton to Michaelson and Einstein, about which there is no disagreement.[15] A process of change in the chronology of history exhibits a dynamic continuity of a self-expanding and self-correcting history. The ultimate reality of World Habeas Corpus is as inevitable as a mathematically logical system in science. Because planets go round in circles is, however, no reason why human beings should.[16] It exemplifies "the right to be let alone."[17]

Facing the problem of world law for diverse peoples, the pioneer of World Habeas Corpus has declared:

In making the world safe for diversity, there must be recognition of a united objective, a somewhat worthwhile goal of evocative significance to all human beings and political systems, if the act of legal cooperation is to be creative in fact. International organizations, international arbitral machinery, the international character of the International Court of Justice and the European Court of Human Rights offer the sovereign states of the world the grand opportunity of freeing themselves from national embarrassment in resisting the providing of legal remedies for wrongs committed against person and property. Obsolescent fears of those who are still laboring under the delusion of invasion or surrender of sovereignty will be abdicated in favor of formative, simple, and fair legal procedures furnished by international treaty-statute. The concept that individuals should have an equal capacity to act on the international level with that of international organizations is today a *"fait accompli."*

World Habeas Corpus is clearly a magnificent initiative, one to which the whole of mankind should be indebted, as well as to its distinguished author. It is not surprising that since World Habeas Corpus has come into being, it has been earnestly welcomed by eminent jurists, statesmen, politicians, and publicists. Such men accord a prominent place to World Habeas Corpus in global considerations. Due to the sheer volume of comments, we can only present a sampling from world opinion:[18]

Justice Kotaro Tanaka, of the International Court of Justice and former chief justice of the Supreme Court of Japan, noted: "I am pleased to participate in the significant movement for World Habeas Corpus. I believe the rule of law should cover all the world and, in particular, there must be no vacuum in the protection of fundamental human rights. I think it is a primary requirement in the national and international societies. From the viewpoint of such belief of mine, I quite agree with the inspiring movement for the international court of habeas corpus."

Justice Silvio Tavolaro, president of the Supreme Court of Cassation of Italy: "I trust that the actuation of World Habeas Corpus, through the institution of a World Court system, will be the most important task of our civilization and the main achievement of human progress."

Chief Justice Cesar Bengzon of the Supreme Court of the Philippines: "I am pleased to state my belief that the acceptance or establishment of World Habeas Corpus would effectively contribute to the cause of world peace. As presiding officer of the highest court of this land, and as president of the Philippines Section of the International Commission of Jurists and of Civil Liberties Foundation, Inc. (Philippines), I heartily endorse the movement and support the creation of regional internation courts of habeas corpus."

Chief Justice K. M. Baye, Supreme Court of the Republic of Senegal: "It is a real pleasure for me to make known that I do accept and join in the sponsorship of the concept of World Habeas Corpus and the Regional international courts of habeas corpus."

Chief Justice J. R. Blagden, High Court of Zambia, concludes: "I would like to be associated with expanding the sponsorship of World Habeas Corpus and the ultimate institution of regional international courts of habeas corpus ... The need for the implementation of the principles underlying the idea of a World Habeas Corpus in any and every civilized state admits of no question."

It is clear that the time for the adoption of World Habeas

Corpus has come since its organic structure and statute alone can remedy the divisions in human society in both political and legal fields, as well as respond to the growing crescendo of vocal aspirations from humanity.[19]

INDIVIDUAL AND STATE

"The individual, the human being," said Donnedieu de Vabres, "is the origin of law, and, above all, subject to law ... Solidarity, which nature has created amongst all men, gives each individual the right and the power to fight for the repression of injustice."[20] And from Pieter N. Drost we quote: "What is justice? The question is as old as the world. Since the beginning of time man has tried, sometimes with more, sometimes with less success, to answer this question. This quest will probably never end, for perfect justice appears to be an ideal which can never be achieved. As Maurice Hauriou, the great French lawyer, noted, we must resign ourselves to the fact that an established social order virtually always contains a certain measure of justice which is incorporated into it, but in practice, also, it is always in conflict with a new measure of justice which is not yet incorporated. After one reform, there always remains another to be brought in."[21]

On this basis, it is Utopian to conceive of a world where all injustice would be abolished for all time. Yet, injustice exists in degrees, and all injustices are not immutable. For instance, wage-price controls that did not take into account daily fluctuations in the price control index could theoretically be held to be unjust, but what thinking citizen would vocalize a complaint. Nor would be expand this one instance into a charge that justice no longer reigned in the land. The average citizen knows, of course, that there will always be somewhat of a time lag between change and the promulgation of laws to take into account this change. That is inevitable in a continuously evolving society, and through understanding man can reconcile himself to the inevitable.

It is very different, however, when the law of the land constricts what the citizen considers to be his most elemental and sacred rights. This situation is intolerable. No man will ever freely and willingly agree to be at the whim and mercy of an authority which has unilaterally declared itself total and absolute. Where arbitrary rule replaces justice, when torture and the concentration camp become the disciplinary modus operandi of a nation, then men will tend to revolt at the first opportunity with an innate feeling that they are exercising right. There are certain basic and personal rights which every law, every public authority, must respect. These are known, according to the local vernacular, variously as human rights or habeas corpus.

Individual human rights in international law must take ultimate precedence over those of the state and its political subdivisions. The state rights stand supreme in organizational questions pertaining to legislative, administrative, and judicial systems.

Both acts and omissions may constitute a violation of human rights. The existence of contrary conditions under the legal system and in the administrative and judicial branches of the state constitute violations of human rights by the state itself. Official negligence, the condoning of breaches of obligations, or connivance to secure same are just as much wrongs upon human rights as crimes by individuals against others.[22]

"The relationships, vis-a-vis human rights," A. Buckly declares, "between the individual and the state, which formerly were considered to be problems of domestic law have now become matters of international concern. The international community, organized by the United Nations, has taken up the task of safeguarding these human rights under a higher system of law, i.e., in international law and by international machinery."[23]

Buckly further asserts: "As long as the sovereignty of states rules supreme in international relations, the protection of human rights will remain defective. Absence of vision and imagination, want of courage and conviction, lack of intelligence and common sense, unviable and obsolete traditions, old school ideas and time-worn concepts—for all this and much more, the rulers, civil servants, diplomats, and delegates of many countries have been blamed. It seems that this public reproach is not entirely misdirected. The peoples of the world are surely prepared to see the rights of sovereignty surrendered by their human rights whereby the international community may eventually grow into a family of peoples instead of remaining a precarious association of overbearing states."[24]

No one would pretend that all is well, if human rights are enjoyed anywhere, as long as freedom remains denied, be it by extremes of the Right or of the Left, as displayed in self-seeking personal rule or in those small but stubborn areas in some otherwise democratic countries where authoritarianism holds out. In parallel reasoning, criminal law is recognized as an indispensable weapon of social defense against violation of human rights. It is also true that under the banner of criminal justice, the most atrocious violations of the "inherent dignity" and of the equal and inalienable rights of all members of the human family have taken place down through history. Can it be denied that, under the guise of a bona-fide penal system, the "atheist world" has outrageously furthered its disregard and contempt for human rights, and further outraged the conscience of mankind?[25]

In order to fill in the picture completely, let us expose the following traditional truths as stated by Aroneanu:

"When law sanctions murder, the murderous assault constitutes a crime which is subject to common law. The guilty party undergoes the penalty he deserves. When the sovereign or the rulers kill their own people by 'Illegal Rights' or 'Legal Wrongs' under repressive rule—true murder not excepted—suppression of justice is clear. The same masters of rule escape thus in the cited instance from sanction, and henceforth law is perverted so that murder of any type is in open season and the 'victim' is no longer a sacrifice to the law that has been violated and instituted to protect life but a sacrifice to the absence of law—a result of the suppression of human rights and justice."[26]

We come to the overwhelming conclusion that such conditions lead directly to crimes against humanity, i.e., crimes under international law in which the public force becomes an accomplice of the "crime" by executing the criminal order of the state.

Let us mark carefully that states cannot confer upon man fundamental rights, as the state itself is a human creation. We must be sure, therefore, not to confuse protection of a law with its creation, nor hold that a law, even unpublicized or suppressed, ceases to exist. It is erroneous to think that such judicial order is proscribed by internal positive law as well as by the "sovereignty of state" and could exclude international consideration in defense of human rights considered as essential to human welfare.[27]

Let us further remark that dedication to the key points of democracy, through which sovereignty of the state acknowledges an obligation and capacity to protect and leave human rights unfettered, is applicable to all classes in society.

Without fear of contradiction, we can say that protection for human rights can be fully activated only after states capitulate to positive international law by a compulsory submission to its world-wide enforcement.

Human rights afford protection of liberty against the state and assistance in maintaining personal security by the state. The guarantees offered by the state in respect of its moral obligation are, presently, entirely inadequate. National law and domestic practice have amply demonstrated this insufficiency. Moreover, the individual and the state become opposite poles in the theories of right and duty subordinate, but not always complementary, to law. We see the law of human rights emerging, where the state would be in the role of defendant, with the individual as prosecutor. Criminal law casts the two in reverse order.

Or so it would seem to the layman. Actually, professionals, viewing law as protection and not as a weapon, see that in the law of human rights, the individual and the state constitute the two opposing subjects of rights and duties, both equally subordinate to the law. In criminal law, the individual is subordinate to the state. The law of human rights is directed against the state; the criminal law is directed against the individual. In the law of human rights, the state is responsible versus the individual. In criminal law, the individual offender is responsible versus the state. The law of human rights lays down public duties of the state; criminal law defines public duties of the individual.

We expand the thesis to declare that international law forbids violation or suppression of human rights by the state or other states through acts endangering world peace and the security of mankind.

Man, the subject of rights and duties outlined in international law, must have his individual security guaranteed by international criminal machinery. This organ will reinforce the "supremacy of international law" in protecting the absolute right of justice for mankind.

The New International Penal Law and its Functions in Protecting the World Habeas Corpus

"A civilian process," wrote the scholarly French professor H. Donnedieu de Vabres, "most often regards only pecuniary interests. On the contrary, in a criminal process, it is the freedom, life, and honor of man that are at stake." Therefore, if we agree on the gravity of concerned interests, we must regard penal law as the most important branch of law.[28]

Penal law is not only first among the many laws, it embodies the foundations of our very civilization. While it is important to proclaim the constitutional right to life, greater insight into the state is gained through its legal treatment of the crime of murder. The most enlightened of laws are only dead words if the extent of repressive law annuls them. In treatment of the crime of murder, there is, implicitly a proclamation of the right to life. Therefore, the extent or limit of penal law contains the frankest declaration of human rights in a given state.

Greeks and Romans of antiquity recognized human rights, and their penal code confirmed them. The French Revolution recognized that these rights predated it, and only claimed to be recalling the "forgotten," "ignored," and "despised." Rights do not cease to exist simply because constitutions and practice in fact do not take them into account. Today, the human being is often protected most completely in certain countries without constitutions in effect. International law is, above all, international penal law.

When we give consideration to the international field, we find the constitutional proclamations of the U.N. Charter and the Universal Declaration of Human Rights representing a broadening of basic individual yearnings to the international scale. Prior to being implicitly inscribed in these documents, the yearnings were variously carried in national laws and less tangibly in rights of man. The points therein have stood the tests of time and trial. Indicated to us now is the necessity to turn to the Nuremberg Charter and the 1945 San Francisco Conference as bases for the reign of international rule of law.

Human rights can be assured by a veritable judicial "troika": the constitution proclaims solemnly the rights of the individual and the structure and duties of the state. It forbids powers in state sovereignty from endangering the life and freedom of the individual. The penal code proclaims clearly the right to life and freedom. And, finally, international law, or more precisely, international penal law, plays the prime role, i.e., a superior legal judge to shelter man against crime.

Contemporary civilization is the civilization of human rights. Humanity has an obligation to protect that civilization by an international penal law with jurisdiction, and not by armed might, nuclear power, prisons or concentration camps.

Penal law, that embodíment of rules to safeguard order, reigns in all societies. It includes:
1. Common law or penal law,
2. national political penal law,
3. international penal law (classical and modern).

Corresponding to these three categories of penal law are the three fields of crime to be handled: Crime under common law, crime for political consideration, and crime of an international nature.

Common law: This covers rules designed for the repression of acts disturbing the peace, security, and order in every civilized nation. It follows that there can be no social organization if the members are not bound to respect human life, personal freedom, and the right of property, individual or collective.

Murder, wanton destruction, theft, and fraud are examples of crimes subject to punishment regardless of the nation involved. The subject of inadmissability attached to these crimes does not vary from one country to another.

That there exists crime when the common right is threatened is a universally accepted concept. Safeguards are called for by elementary social morality. Consequently, he who offends the common law is not only in violation of his individual nation's law but is a threat to the general and prevailing international social life.[29]

It can now be asserted by proponents of the penal doctrine that there is a dominant current of thought which considers infractions of the common law as supranational, not merely simple violations of national law. These infractions are acts of an anti-social nature which offend universal morality and call for general repression by all countries with equal punishment.[30]

Political national penal law: Here consideration is given to the control of illicit acts directed against the form of government and the political order of a given country. In general, such repression concerns only the country in question. This concept post-dates the French Revolution. Before this time, the political criminal accused of *crimen majestatis* was severly punished.

In most cases, the author of political crime aims only at giving his country another political structure. To achieve this end, he seeks a takeover of power in order to impose a new political doctrine.

According to the classical theory, political crimes do not have the same criminal intent as crimes against the common law. These crimes are not those of an individual but collective in the name of the entire political affiliation of the individual. In the perpetration of such acts, the individual plays only the role of an instrument rather than an agent.[31]

The Communist system has provided mankind with numerous contemporary examples of the political crime. Acting uniformly in any country where it has interests, the Communist machinery runs the gamut of so-called political crime: terrorism, genocide, crime against peace, crime of aggression, crime against humanity—the disastrous consequences of which are unpredictable. Now, classic doctrine holds that other countries do not have the right of interference in internal conflicts of a political nature in a given country, even if these conflicts generate crimes regarded as against humanity as a whole.

The whole idea raises complicated problems beyond the scope of this present study, so it cannot be regarded in detail.

International penal law: Let us deal initially with the classic interpretation of this legal code. Penal law on the international level too often cannot be reduced in scale to cover crimes against the common law. For this reason, certain countries have grouped at the interstate level to control criminal acts, even though these may be committed abroad, if they are offensive to the nations involved. Protection of a whole set of interests is involved in what is a most varied and complicated action.

Every country, therefore, is called on to determine the competence of its own penal jurisdiction vis-à-vis foreign jurisdictions and the applications of its criminal laws—laws of essence and laws of form—with regard to the place and persons it rules and the authority in its territory as well as the foreign judgment of control.

Such is the definition of the classical international penal law given by Professor H. Donnedieu de Vabres.[32]

While acknowledging that the terms of international penal law are based on long-standing custom, we must admit that the legal discipline as stated above is in reality a part of international law.

New international penal law: In 1924 Professor V. V. Pella, the knowledgeable creator of international penal law and pioneer of a

draft "Code of Crimes Against Peace and the Security of Mankind," raised the thesis of international criminal jurisdiction before
the Inter-Parliamentary Conference held in Berne, Switzerland.
Professor Pella has further raised the question of the creation of a
new legal discipline, an international penal law endowed with the
mission of guaranteeing effective the peaceful relations among
nations.[33]

Professor Pella declares that wars of aggression committed during past centuries may be regarded as manifestations of collective
criminality, when evidence is properly weighed, if they are conceived according to the new science of international criminology.[34]

The point of view of Professor Pella was upheld by the Legal
Commission of the Parliamentary Union in session in Paris, April
1925, and at the Washington Inter-Parliamentary Conference held
in October of the same year. The latter meeting adopted a resolution admitting on the one hand, "the responsibility of a collective
criminality of States," and on the other hand that "this criminality
must be studied in the scientific point of view" in order to determine the natural laws which administer it and to establish the
means destined to prevent and repress it.[35]

This resolution has the advantage of identifying the new international penal law as a force to cope with criminality, different[36]
in many aspects from the criminality of the common law as well as
from generally recognized international criminality.

While avoiding the hasty generalizations that could be founded
on a parallel between the means of protection of the social order
within nations and the means of defending the international order,
it is advisable not to neglect lessons of history which give evidence
of the function and peacemaking assets of the penal law within
social organizations. Why, then, could the force and example attributes of penal sanctions be effective on the international level?
There is no logical reason why the proven existence of the deterrent force of penal sanctions as a counter to evil cannot be transferred to use in international relations through international application.

The same idea has been expressed, albeit phrased differently, in a
report prepared by United States Supreme Court Justice Jackson to
his president and presented on 19 October 1946. Referring to the
status and decisions of the Nuremberg "war criminals" trials, Justice Jackson affirmed, "Of course, it would be extravagant to claim

that agreements of trials of this character can make aggressive war or persecution of minorities impossible, just as it would be extravagant to claim that our Federal laws make Federal crime impossible. But we cannot doubt that they strengthen the bulwarks of peace and tolerance. The four nations, through their representatives on the Tribunal, have enunciated standards of conduct which bring new hope to men of good will and from which future statesmen will not lightly depart."[37]

Numerous declarations similarly phrased may be found. One need only recall the point of view expressed by Dr. Spiropoulos at the International Law Commission. This commission has the task of releasing the principles of the Charter of Nuremberg and proclaiming them the declared warnings to would-be aggressors.[38]

According to the definition of Professor Pella, the International Law Commission findings are a promulgation of measures of control already stated by international criminologists in the field of positive international law. Professor Pella also gave another definition of international penal law and its nature: "International Penal Law is the embodiment of rules of essence and form which preside over the use of repression against acts committed by the State or Inter-States, or individuals to disturb public international order and the harmony existing among peoples; and finally, this legal discipline is just like the branch of International Law which determines the infractions, establishes punishment and fixes the conditions of the international penal responsiblities of the State, or Inter-States and individuals."[39]

The role of international penal law in the international field is similar to that of the national penal law in the internal affairs of a state. Just as the internal penal law has the mission of safeguarding, by penal sanctions, the superior interests as guaranteed in national law, the international penal law exists to safeguard those superior interests whose protection lies in the competency of international law.

Clearly, there is much common ground between international penal law and the national penal law, particularly the principles administering the domain of penal responsibility. These are wellnigh the same in international penal law and national penal law.

To the contrary, however, influenced by its very nature, international penal law separates from its national counterpart at a given point. We know that international penal law covers the same ground as international law, of which it is, in fact, a part. Actually, as international law, international penal law stems from custom and is not a tangible written or codified system. The rules under which it operates originate in international custom and conventional law. This relationship with international law explains the divergence between international and national penal law. Not being a codified law, the international penal law has no body charged with interpreting and extending its legal system. To its benefit, it is not limited by the frontiers of any state, and does not depend on the arbitrary will of a state. As international law, it represents a power superior to the will of the state.[40]

We recognize that international penal law is still in the formative state. If, therefore, international law, of which it is a subsection, is still understandably considered imperfect, international penal law is, in its present state, even more in a condition of flux. Born as a result of need for a social rule based on man's conscience, it is still finding its place in international law. It is furthered, nevertheless, by an impressive heritage from international law, and this steadily enriches and adds stature to international penal law.

Until recently, the responsibility for a *chef-d'omission* in international law was of a civil nature, concerning damages. Now, the principles of penal responsbility in international law is recognized. This recognition is the foundation of new international penal law; therefore, nothing stands in the way of admission of penal responsibility for the chef-d'omission. Such responsibility must, understandably, be applied to violations committed in the name and for the benefit of the state as well as to individuals themselves.

That criminal responsibility for the chef-d'omission exists has now become a well established rule in positive international law. Article 7 of the Charter of the Nuremberg Tribunal lays down the fundamental principles for international competacny in the field. It states: "The official position of defendants, whether as Head of State or responsible officials in government departments, shall not be considered as freeing them from responsibility or mitigating punishment." The authors of these acts cannot invoke their official rank to avoid the usual procedure or escape punishment. Existence of that statute and jurisprudence spelled out by the Nuremberg and Tokyo Tribunals has the intent that law, especially the new international penal law, regulates not only the behavior of ordinary people, i.e., the governed, but also covered top officials and leaders of the state. An analogous formula specifies that extreme punishment can be called for the guilty, be they minor noncommissioned officers in the army or chiefs of state.[41]

For this reason, authors of the draft Code of Offenses Against the Peace and Security of Mankind have foreseen certain cases of infraction of law by omission which involve penal responsibility. These are the so-called infractions of "state," which can only be committed by the authorities of a state.

Accordingly, the draft code reads: "The fact that a person acted as Head of State or as responsible government official does not relieve him of responsibility for committing any of the offenses defined in this Code (art. 3). . . . The fact that a person charged with an offense defined in this Code acted pursuant to an order of his government or of a superior does not relieve him of responsibility in International Law if, in the circumstances at the time, it was possible for him not to comply with that order (art. 4)." Unfortunately, this draft code has remained in the draft stage until now. That is to say, this meritorious concept may never get beyond that stage in this century because of contradictions and conflicting interpretations as to the definition of "crime of aggression" which persist in the many political theories present in the world today.[42]

More optimistically, the scope of international penal law increases little by little, day by day. For example, we should regard hopefully the humanitarian conventions of Geneva, dating from 1949. These expound on "grave infractions" of human rights and reinterpret the definitive meaning of "infraction." There has already been a convention charged with the protection of cultural welfare in case of armed conflict, held in 1954, from which came a new concept concerning "infractions," in penal orders, as covered in its article 28. Simultaneously, principles of international penal law are entering the legal structure of nations. One example is the Constitutional Law of the Federal Republic of Germany, adopted in 1949, which specifies the principle that duties of the individual in regard to international law supersede those imposed on him by domestic law (art. 25). Recently, German law was extended to cover the legal status of members of its armed forces (Soldatengesetz). The action, taken in March 1956, adopted principles renouncing excuse from crime of any accused who has acted through hierarchical order.[43]

We must not omit mention of a serious obstacle that continues to paralyze, or at least hinder, the development and reinforcement of international law and international criminal law. This obstacle is the age-old dogma of "sovereignty of state." Through its domination of present action, one can see that nations are still unable to reconcile themselves to the idea that members of their governments and other functionaries can be held criminally responsible for "acts of state" as judged by a supranational body.

The prevailing hope is that such dogma, archaic and meaningless today as the world grows closer, will fade away as a result of the new reality. This reality teaches that if independence of states is to be manifested by their isolation, such independence is superannuated, no longer viable in the age of the United Nations and breathtaking advances in the fields of science and technology. Nuclear physics alone has made isolated independence a phrase of no substance. Nations, be they large or small, inevitably will decline if they remain unaware of anachronisms in their structure. If, instead of looking toward the future inspired by the ideal of brotherhood, they cling to the past and an outdated nationalism—which, through dictatorship and allied totalitarianism continues arrogantly to disregard the basic precepts of law—that which is now a threat will come to pass.

The state condemns that individual who disturbs the public order, even in the case of minor offenses, through law. Yet, a state may reserve to itself the right to commit more or less the same crime for which it would condemn the individual.

In the field of international relations, specifically relations between the community of peoples, a state can disregard, with forethought, those basic rules of law, morality, justice, and honesty which it forces individuals to respect and observe.[44]

We find it necessary to bring up the blunt truth about results of twenty years of trial and tribulation in the United Nations. Wars of words, political strife, and diplomatic manuevering have constantly impeded meaningful action; on the positive side, however, they have served to pound out new international ploys to meet each individual crisis according to its political portent and the technical national vocabularies involved.

Regrettably, a draft Code of Offenses against Peace and the

Security of Mankind still remains a mere project twelve years after it was conceived. The same stagnancy prevails concerning the Convention on the Prevention and Punishment of the Crime of Genocide, which has no international organism for judging this heinous crime.[45] There are presently some one hundred other problems in a state of paralysis brought about by U.N. veto or political motivation. Undeniably, these are the anomalous phenomena of contemporary international life.

Development of the rule of law, maintenance of public and legal order, as well as the judicial competency of the United Nations are virtually at a standstill because of national political interests.

The time is now for mankind to abandon its passive consideration of international law as a law of coordination. The new international law should have a new obligation—that of a law of subordination. International law is clearly weakened by a serious fault; it not only ignores the lawmaker but also the law enforcer. In other words, the present power of international law exists only through exercise of extreme military sanctions.

The preamble of the U.N. Charter carries the following statement: "To unite our strength to maintain international peace and security and to ensure by the acceptance of principles that armed force shall not be used, save in the common interest . . ." Is it because the authors of the charter realized the impotency of international law at present without military force that they decided to bring up the question that "armed force shall not be used, save in the common interest"?

We should also deal with articles 41 and 42 of the U.N. Charter. These are of paramount importance in cases where the Security Council of that body determines that there exists a threat to world order, a breach of the peace, or an overt act of aggression. In reality, the procedures necessary to implement the provisions of these articles waste considerable time and are subject to paralysis by the rule of the "big five," more popularly known as the veto when unanimity does not exist among the world powers. Further, the deterrents contained in these articles are not purely penal in nature.

Without chance of error, it can be said that legal doctrines and political science in this nuclear age do not regard the concepts of a "victorious state" and a "vanquished state" in conflict, as tradition decreed. Today we have the legalistic justice and criminals quite apart from winner and loser in a power confrontation. Needed now is a revision of articles 41 and 42 in order to adapt them to the present evolution of mankind, with consideration of the changes in the science of international law and its penal branch.

We should, furthermore, stress the fact that threats to peace, breaches of the peace, acts of aggression, genocide, suppression of human rights, and flagrant violations of the international rule of law are now in the realm of international criminality and should be contained by penal not military controls.

To be more precise, military sanctions should be limited to those occasions where penal judgments are not fully respected, i.e., where the verdict of an international penal court is ignored. Naturally, at the beginning, world criminal law and its jurisdiction will be questioned by those nations with a tradition of defying world opinion and threatening the peace. We can proceed on the assumption that they will initially deny court competency. It is only realistic to accept that prevailing conditions will not change overnight, and those nations plagued by subversive activities will not control them upon enactment of a modern international law. Let these not, however, be regarded as insurmountable obstacles. Codification of international penal law and definition of its jurisdiction remains a possible and a compelling need.

For the sake of humanity, there is presently a clear need to reinforce the rule of law by arming international law with adequate powers to assert its supreme authority for preservation of both public order and the legal order. Such reinforcement can now be assured through the new international penal law.

In considering the competence of the new international penal law and its effectiveness through a judicial mechanism, we must be certain that no state, member or not of the United Nations, will be in a position to deny recognition of the competence of the world criminal law and the compulsory character of the international penal court. Universal international obligations apply to all states regardless of global affiliation. The principle *consensus omnium* of world criminal law and its jurisdiction is a sine qua non condition for a civilized world.

Violations of common law in general have an international character. Piracy on the high seas, traffic in narcotics, white slavery, counterfeiting—all are crimes with international implications and calling for international control armed with universal competence.

It is reasonable and logical to include war crimes, crimes of aggression, and crimes against humanity, which violate international common law, under the same system of international repression. In fact, they can be many times more damaging than other infractions of the common law.[46]

In consideration of legal discipline as dictated by international common law, acknowledgement must be given that humanity is called upon to confer upon international penal law the mission of defending not only international peace but also the fundamental and inalienable rights of all men on this globe, in other words, world democratic law. This is a mission that neither diplomacy, politics, nor the present United Nations are empowered to fulfill.

New international penal law and its jurisdiction can be considered as destined:[47]

1. To reinforce international law by conferring on it the authority and prestige essential to catalyze the law into a means for consolidating peace and assuring justice.

2. To revive such principles as have already been enunciated in the pact of the League of Nations and the Kellogg-Briand Pact and brought up to date in the Charter of the United Nations, the findings of Nuremberg, and the Universal Declaration of Human Rights.

3. To further the concept that war and violations of human rights are to be considered international crimes, thereby contributing to their control and eventual banishment from international life.

4. To constitute a solemn warning to all statesmen and rulers that, as provisional holders of supreme power of state, they do not have the right or authority to be intoxicated by this power to the point that they push humanity to the abyss of war or make of sovereignty of state an instrument for repression or violence. Power is not vested to disregard elementary principles of international law, especially the fundamentals of human rights.

5. To become an effective *verbum directum* limiting sovereignty of state, since most violations of international law come as the result of the exercise of state sovereignty or, *verbi gratia*, they are not committed in violation of international law but owing to the subordination of that law to the prejudice of certain categories of individuals due to race, nationality, religion, or political affiliation.

Limitation of state sovereignty by international law and by the judicial scope of its penal authority promises to open a new era for the furtherance of peace, justice, and human rights.

Considering the principles herein exposed, we need not question whether World Habeas Corpus will benefit by penal protection since the functions of the new International Penal Code have already provided an answer to this issue. It is evident that the international community as well as the international rule of law want to protect what will constitute the supreme judicial refuge for all their members: World Habeas Corpus.

Just as national penal law, in protection of the individual combats that which is directed against the interests of human life—personal integrity and health—and protects also the state through its institutions and political, economic and social life, international penal law must assure the peace of the international community by combatting that which would endanger the inalienable rights of all in the human family.

In summation, twenty years after the creation of a formal United Nations structure we still await a world penal code with full jurisdiction. Such a code is long overdue; it should have come into active existence following World War II. The mistakes of the past may be unpardonable—their continuance today is surely unthinkable.

So long as the world is deprived of a world penal law with jurisdiction, just so long will it have to put up with judicial anarchy, violence, and injustice, with an ever-present threat of self-destruction.

CONCLUSION

As the world considers the natural plagues of drought, flood, earthquake, and hurricane as historical enemies of mankind, it is altogether logical to qualify dictatorship and dictator, tyranny and tyrant, despot and totalitarianism, whether of the Right or Left, as artificial disasters besetting humanity. The concept gives rise to multiple forms of crimes against mankind: crimes of aggression, crimes against the peace, crimes against persons, war crimes—all of which, under different names and characteristics, are undeniably directed toward the destruction of human society.[48]

Clearly because of these artificial disasters, the world is forced to a crucial turn of unforeseeable consequences which will decide the lot of mankind as a whole. The full power of humanity must be exerted to control these disasters, with survival as the goal.

These disasters are not vague or abstract fears without justification. They are brutally real, sad facts and acts that are well beyond the realm of the theoretical.

If international law is to act significantly upon human affairs, its first task must be to establish a rule of order to deter international crime, and its second to develop principles of international justice and procedure. It must assure that these obligations are kept current in view of the changing world and it must have "teeth." Its precepts must be applied to disputes under the jurisdiction of international law, and a penal code broad enough for equitable punishment of infractions should back it. The rule of order for international law will be destined to play a prominent, perhaps dominant, role in the control and elimination of international crime through established principles of justice understood by all who would put world peace in jeopardy. Both public order and legal order remain the fundamental needs of the society of nations. Without a minimum of order, justice is powerless.[49] Peace, adjudication, and law are interdependent, and their mutual development is a sure way to a more stable, satisfactory world for the atomic age.[50]

Conscious of the necessity for safeguarding the order of an international human society now in the process of full transformation and evolution, we present this study with the hope that it will not offend the sensitivities of those schooled in "sovereignty of state." All members of the human society should bear in mind that history is dynamic not static—in this manner change will be appreciated not feared.[51]

Confronted by the terrible spectre of destruction by thermonuclear weapons, as well as by the insidious crimes of political nature against state or between states, we can take solace in the knowledge that there are those who work for a World Habeas Corpus—a universal statute complete with an international penal system designed for judicial protection of mankind, and equitable, consistent application of penalties to those who would commit crime. The worthy goal is to put love, brotherhood, and human solidarity with justice above national and political ambition. The alternative is to admit the irresistibility of politics and crime in state and inter-state affairs.

We have a clear, enviable goal envisaged for humanity that is consistent with a universal desire for world peace and human dignity assured to all peoples throughout the world. This can become a present reality for generations to come. So long as the security of the international community as well as the fundamental and inalienable rights of man depend on the capricious and change-able will of the sovereign state, they will necessarily remain unstable and unsure.[52]

Let us not be discouraged by the magnitude, difficulty, and inherent imperfections at this stage of a work of such a large scope. Let us put aside the traditions of arbitrary, confused, and violent national and international politics. Let the truth which might have been neglected or unknown in the past triumph in the future. For all those who are charged with responsibility for the fate of humanity, as well as those who have to live with it, should cling to a clear bright hope that the fate can be synonomous with the highest human yearnings—and within reach.[53]

Our civilization is greatly indebted to the works of Pythagoras, Aristotle, Ptolemy, Copernicus, Galileo, Kepler, Newton, and, recently, to Einstein for his formula of $E = MC^2$. These philosophers have enriched our lives, but simultaneously they have released a call for new planning in the realm of world controls—World Habeas Corpus, under the protection of international penal law with jurisdiction, ranks high among such plans.

The time has come for leaders of men throughout the world to take immediate steps to fulfill the maxim *Pectus est quod disertos facit*, so that the peoples of the earth may have a shelter of security through the rule of law. Only then may we venture forth confidently on exploration of the universe.

Jus est ars boni et aequi holds wide respect as the most worthy philosophy for today's civilization. Its value is everlasting, valid to regulate space exploration as it is on this planet. Such a noble spirit constitutes a sine qua non condition for the maintenance of order and for the administration of justice. No force, no violence, no nuclear weapons can change or overturn its position and role in international life. It is incumbent upon humanity to maintain this code of honor. If not, we would have no recourse, for the sake of the human family, save an urgent SOS in the days to come. We cannot falter because of erroneous policies not remedied in time.[54]

To struggle to prevent the subjugation of law by force, violence, and oppression for political gain, to combat injustice and terror, mean a sacred struggle for freedom, human dignity, honor, and justice. It is concurrently a struggle for rule of law. Such a battle should enlist all human beings, be they rulers or the ruled; this notion pervades philosophy through the generations.[55]

We must arrive at the conclusion that new international penal law is a body of paramount importance to serve man on earth. World Habeas Corpus has been conceived by man and goes to prove that the best friend of man is man. Without its guidance we will also see, as at present, that man's worst enemy, likewise, is man. Man, properly motivated, makes a fine administrator; improperly guided, a despot. We have the choice, and it will indicate the path of civilization so long as man endures on earth.

Notes

1. See Trân Tâm, The Role of Law and Human Rights in a Divided World (Geneva-Switzerland, 1964).
2. See Trân-Tâm, S.O.S. de la Démocratie en Asie (International law Review, op. cit. 1964).
3. The political systems and policies of new States can be expected to be to some extent unpredictable. The increased extent on these unpredictabilities, dependent in material degree on personalities of leadership and the lack of established national patterns of policy in international affairs, is indicated in a report of June 1960 of the Commission to study the Organization of Peace (Commission to study the Organization of Peace, Peaceful Coexistence): A new challenge to the United Nations, 12th report, New York, 1960. This report makes an empirical classification of the members of the United Nations into sixteen mature democracies, nine party (i.e. Communist) dictatorships, twelve hereditary monarchies, and the remainder as "military dictatorships and emergent democracies." Only the first two categories can be considered to have strong traditions and established institutions for dealing with world affairs. This leaves fifty to seventy-five sovereign states in categories where the personal inclinations of a few leaders or of a small leadership group can determine—admittedly in varying degrees, depending on the particular country—that country's way in foreign affair. New leadership must arise and gain experience. (Cf. Norman J. Padelford and George A. Lincoln, *The Dynamics of International Politics*, pp. 20-21).
4. Cf. Trân Tâm, S.O.S. de la Democratie.
5. In fact, disagreement among them on technical points is frequent. Even on such a seemingly important question as the continuity of the Russian empire and the Soviet state as a single subject of international law, there has been persistent disagreement among Soviet writers. Similarly, there is a continuing controversy over the question whether international Organization, in particular the United Nations, are to be regarded as subjects of international law. Disagreement on more fundamental issues, such as the proper explana-

tion of the existence of international law in terms of Marxist doctrine, has also occurred. At the height of the post-Stalin "thaw," some voices were even raised in defense of the concept of natural law and natural rights, which is usually rejected by Soviet jurists. It would be a mistake, therefore, to attribute to the Soviet government every view on international law expressed by every Soviet writer. The government, it may be surmised, seeks to retain freedom of argument, particularly on some of the more technical points of international law, by not approving or disapproving the views found in "unofficial" Soviet literature until the concrete necessity for taking a position arises. But Soviet writers are not expected to express an opinion contrary to officially adopted doctrine or policy. No Soviet jurist has admitted that USSR has ever violated international law. (Cf. Oliver J. Lissitzyn, International Conciliation, no. 542, March, 1963 (Carnegie Endowment for International Peace).

6. See Trân Tâm, The Role of Law and Human Rights.
7. When a man feels he is the victim of injustice, what does he do? He applies to the judges of his country and calls on them for a decision. Normally, if his case is well founded, he will obtain satisfaction.

   But where will he establish his rights if the judges are corrupt, or if they render *justice* with reference to the interests of the powers-that-be? This is something which has happened more than once in the course of history and still happens at the present day. What is needed is a means of testing the value of a judiciary which is both upright and independent of the political powers.

   The existence of such a judiciary is not, however, the only condition for the "rule of law". For judges may only apply the laws laid down by the political powers. Therefore, in addition, the laws of the country must be just, or at least they must not be unjust (Cf. Trân Tâm, SOS de la Democratie en Asie, op. cit.).
8. Cf. The preamble of the Universal Declaration of Human Rights.
9. Pope John XXIII, Pacem in Terris, April 1963. The Papal Encyclicals, edited by Anne Fremantle, p. 393.
10. Arthur J. Goldberg, former associate justice, Supreme Court of the United States. Congressional Record 12860 (June 11, 1965).
11. The author would like to stress that there is some difference between Luis Kutner and this writer on the World Habeas Corpus, especially on the legal technical field. Readers may compare the writer's concepts exposed in the next parts of this essay with the project of the treaty-statute of the International Court of Habeas Corpus.
12. Lessee V. Hoboken Land and Improvement Co., 18 Nov. (59 US) 272,276 (1856).
13. Truax V. Corrigan, 257 US, 312,332 (1921).
14. Dewey, Quest for Certainty 3-20 (1929); Dewey, Intelligence in Modern world, John Dewey's Philosophy 73, 1939.
15. Ibid.
16. Ibíd, p. 163.
17. Griswold, The Right to Be Let Alone, 55 N.U.L. Rev. 216 (1960).
18. Luis Kutner, Report presented to the World Conference of the Alliance Mondiale des Religions, Paris, Feb. 17, 1966.
19. Ibid.
20. See H. Donnedieu de Vabres, Introduction à l'etude du droit Pénal International, Sirey, Paris, 1922, p. 283.
21. Cf. A. Buckley, For Your Rights (Council of Europe, Strasbourg, France, op. cit).
22. See Pieter N. Drost, Human Rights as Legal Rights.

23. On December 10, 1948, the General Assembly of the United Nations approved and proclaimed the Universal Declaration of Human Rights. But faced with the impossibility of finding a common conception of these fundamental freedoms immediately agreeable to all, the United Nations was unable to create a world wide jurisdiction to safeguard democracy! (Cf. A Buckly, For Your Rights, Europe Council, no. 6, December, 1963, op. cit.)
24. Ibid, pp. 169-170.
25. Ibid.
26. See: E. Aroneanu, Le Crime Contre l'Humanité (Libr. Dallozz, Paris, 1961), pp. 15-17.
27. Cf. V. V. Pella, La Guerrè-Crimes et les Criminels de Guerrè, op. cit. See also Trân Tâm, The International Penal Law and Crimes Against Humanity, op. cit.
28. See H. Donnedieu de Vabres, Traité de droit Criminel (Sirey, Paris, 1947), p. 6.
29. See Garofalo, The Solidarity of Nations in the Struggle against Criminality. See also V. V. Pella, Proposal made to the League of Nations in view of organizing a general system calculated to eliminate dangerous criminals and habitual offenders (Revue de droit Penal, no. 2, 1952).
30. Garofalo, op. cit. p. 3.
31. See J. Reuben Clark, Proceedings of the American Society of International Law, Third Annual Meeting, 1909, p. 98.
32. See Trân Tâm, Traité de droit Criminel et de Législation Pénal comparée. Geneva, Switzerland, 1959. See also V. V. Pella, Des incapacités résultant des condamnations Pénales en droit International. Paris, 1920.
33. See V. V. Pella, Apercu de la Criminalité de la guèrre et la Création d'un droit repressif des Nations. Débat général, séance du 25 Aout Compte rendu de la 22ème Conférence interparlementaire (Berne, 1924), p. 335.
34. Even though the Science of International Criminology was dealt with by Prof. V. V. Pella since 1924, it was not until 1962, at the International Association of Criminology (IAC) fourth conference, in Geneva (September) that the criminalists and internationalists who took part in this conference gave it the following definition: "the International Criminology, a new science of international criminality is not only founded on Psychology, Sociology and Statistics, but also based on the Political Sciences, the Sciences of International Relations, especially the Democratic principles, the Universal Declarations of Human Rights and the Rights of all peoples to self-determination." On the other hand, we ought to stress that if there does exist a new international penal law, then the science of international criminology should be developed accordingly so as to adapt it to the needs of the new international penal law so that the international penal sanctions would bring fruitful result. Only international penal sanctions and *not* military sanctions can protect effectively the public and legal orders as well as serve well world peace. (Cf. IAC in Brief. Published by the International Secretariat of the IAC, Geneva, Switzerland, 1965).
35. Read the minutes of proceedings of the sessions held in Paris by the Commission of Legal Questions (sessions of April 27, 1925, p. 7, and April 28, p. 5) communicated to the members of the Interparliamentary Union by circular no. 3 of June 23, 1925.
36. Report of the 22nd Interparliamentary Conference (Washington) 1945, pp.24 and pp. 79-81, the text in the United Nations doc. A/CN 4/7 Rev. I, May 27, 1949, pp. 75-80.
37. See V. V. Pella, La criminalité collective des Etats et le droit Pénal de l'avenir (1949, Geneva, Switzerland).

38. See International law Commission, session of May 24, 1949, U.N. doc. A/CN4/SR 26, p. 4.
39. See V. V. Pella, Le Code de crime contre la paix et la Sécurité de l'humanité, Geneva, 1951, p. 35.
40. See St. Glacer, Infraction internationale (Lib. générale de droit et de jurisprudence, Paris, 1957), pp 8-10.
41. See Trân Tâm, The role of law and Human Rights in a divided world; The International Penal Law and Crimes against Humanity, op. cit.
42. Cf. L'Institution d'une Cour Pénal Internationale. Rapport et projet de Resolutions et définitifs présentés par le Prof. H.'Donnedieu de Vabres (Ed. La tribune de Genève, Dec. 1951).
43. Voir: V. Pella: *La Guerre Crime et les Criminels de guerre*, "Revenue de Droit international", Sottile, Genève, 1, 1946.
    A. Sottile: *Les Criminels de Guerre et le Nouveau Droit Pénal international, moyen efficace pour assurer la paix du monde*, 3me édition, 1946, Genève.
    A. Sottile: *Le Problème de la création d'une Cour pénale internationale permanente*, "Revue de Droit international", Genève; *The Problem of the creation of a permanent International Criminal Court*, 1951.
    A. Sottile: *Le Pape Pie XII et le Droit pénal international*, 1953, Genève.
    A. Sottile: *Le Nouveau Droit Pénal international, seul moyen efficace pour assurer la Paix du monde. Le Droit pénal interétatique et sa fonction pacificatrice*, 3me édition, 1945, Genève.
    E. Aroneanu: *La Définition de l'Agression*, Paris, Les Editions Internationales, 1958.
    R. Alearo: *Le Problème de la juridiction pénale internationale*, "Revue de Droit internationale", No. 4/1950.
    S. Glaser: *Infraction Internationale*, Paris, Libr. Générale de Droit et de Jurisprudence, 1957.
    Trân Tâm: *Les auteurs des Crimes contre la Paix et la sécurité de l'Humanité, Problèmes de Criminologie Politique collective et internationale*, 1962. "Revue de Droit international", Sottile, Genève.
44. See St. Glacer, op. cit.
45. See V. V. Pella, La Guerrè Crimes et les Criminels de Guerrè, op. cit.
46. See art. VI of the Convention on the Prevention and Punishment of the Crime of Genocide.
47. See Trân Tâm, La democratie contemporaine (Geneva, 1965), ILR.
48. See V. V. Pella, La Guerrè Crimes et les Criminels de guerrè, op. cit.
49. See Trân Tâm, SOS De la Démocratie en Asie, op. cit.
50. See Carles De Visscher, American Journal of International Law, 1956, vol. 50, pp. 574.
51. See Quincy Rights, *The Role of International Law in the Elimination of War* (Manchester University Press, 1961), pp. 86-87.
52. See Trân Tâm, The International Penal Law and Crimes against Humanity, op. cit.
53. See Jean Graven, Le nouveau droit penal international (International Law Review A. Sottile, Geneva, nos. 3 and 4, 1962).
54. See Trân Tâm, The Spectre of Thermonuclear war and its influence on the Sciencè of International Relations (APACL's Edition, 1962).
55. See Jean Graven, L'Injustice en tant que systeme ou le droit menacé. (International Law Review, no. 1, 1953).

Steps in the Realization of World Habeas Corpus

By QUINCY WRIGHT*

A WORLD ORDER which will relieve mankind of the danger of destruction by nuclear war and protect men and nations from injustice is generally considered desirable, but opinions differ on what such a world order would look like and how to achieve it. Its development seems, therefore, to require a consensus among the peoples, nations, and governments of the world of its general character; legal principles to define the rights, duties, powers, and responsibilities of the participating persons and agencies; and institutions, agencies, and procedures to maintain these principles and continually to adapt them to changing conditions.

The first is a task of imaginative insight, historical understanding, and education. What images of the world order have been prevalent in the past? In antiquity, an image of "universal empire" was generally accepted; and during the *pax Romana* of the Antonine caesars peace was generally maintained and justice generally administered by Roman law throughout the empire, guarded on its periphery by Roman legions.

In the Middle Ages an image of "universal Christianity," interpreted by the pope and the clergy, was generally accepted in

* Professor Emeritus, University of Chicago and University of Virginia; former president, American Society of International Law; author of *A Study of War* (1942), *The Study of International Relations* (1955), and *The Role of International Law in the Elimination of War* (1961).

Europe, and in the thirteenth century under the *pax ecclesiae* Christendom enjoyed relative peace through maintenance of the "peace of God" and "the truce of God" limiting private war and the crusade diverting political rivalries and public war to the Islamic lands of the Middle East. Justice as defined by feudal and cannon law was administered in secular and ecclesiastical courts.

In the modern period a world order of sovereign territorial states, each united by the sentiment of national loyalty, was accepted, at first in Europe and gradually throughout the world. During the *pax Britannica* of the nineteenth century, imperial wars to expand the state system, international wars to expand states, and civil wars to establish nations occurred. They were controlled, since universal empire was prevented through maintenance of a balance of power under the leadership of Great Britain with her predominant sea power and a corpus of international law requiring each state to respect the territory, independence, and domestic jurisdiction of the others. States observed the treaties, to which each was a party, to moderate violence by rules of war and reprisal and to maintain relations by diplomatic and consular institutions. Constitutional requirements assuring due process of law and diplomatic requirements assuring justice to aliens gradually improved the administration of justice to individuals in most parts of the world, while practices of diplomacy, conference, and arbitration contributed to the maintenance of justice to states.

None of these world orders—a universal empire, a universal ideology, or a universal system of sovereign states—maintained either perfect peace or perfect justice at the periods of their widest acceptance. All of them came to an end because of changing conditions of technology and opinion.

In the twentieth century, and especially since World War I, a new image of world order, including some features of the past, has been emerging. In the Hague Conventions, the League of Nations Covenant, the Kellogg-Briand Pact, the Nüremberg Charter, the U.N. Charter, the Universal Declaration of Human Rights, and other general treaties and declarations, a world order—less politically centralized than the Roman empire, less ideologically unified than medieval Christendom, but more politically centralized and more committed to fundamental human rights than the state system of the nineteenth century—has been formally accepted by most states. This image has not, however, been fully understood or accepted by most people, or even by most governments. They still think in terms of nation states struggling for power, of a world state like the nation state with which they are familiar, or of conversion of all people to a particular religion or ideology that teaches brotherhood and harmony. As a result, this image, although formally accepted by states, has not been adequately implemented or observed.

Statesmen and scholars, however, have generally perceived that a world order resting on a balance of military power or mutual deterrence is inadequate to maintain either peace or justice in the nuclear age. The struggle of states—all vulnerable to attack and destruction by missile borne nuclear weapons—for a power position sufficient to defend at all times their territory, independence, and other national interests will develop arms races inviting preemptive attack as well as military dictatorships capable of prompt action but destructive of justice. They also perceive that the variety of cultures, of economic conditions, and of political traditions, as well as the general demand for national self-determination, will, for a long time, prevent the establishment, by either conquest or agreement, of a world state maintained by central military power. Furthermore, they perceive that these conditions, augmented by the religious and ideological diversities of the human population, will long prevent universal acceptance of any one religion or ideology. They have, therefore, generally subscribed to the image of world order suggested by the great treaties of the twentieth century, to which nearly all states have formally committed themselves. This image of a world committed to "internationalism," different from "nationalism," "imperialism," or "cosmopolitanism," seems to them the only image yet thought of which is both reasonably desirable and relatively feasible to realize in the present period of history.

Realization of this image of world order requires, as noted, education to implant it in the understanding, consciousness, and sentiment of people everywhere; the development and clarification of the legal principles already accepted by states in the great treaties, together with improvement of the institutions, agencies, and procedures intended to assure its realization in practice.

Education is important, therefore, to qualify the sentiment of nationalism by the sentiment of mankind, the concept of the sovereign state by the concept of international organization, and to indicate the present barriers and questionable desirability of either a universal state or a universal ideology. If people are to enjoy peace and justice, they must believe in "a world safe for diversity," as suggested by President Kennedy, a world of peacefully coexisting and cooperating states, an international world, a United Nations world.

Development of the United Nations, of the International Court of Justice, of the specialized agencies, of the regional organizations, and the establishment of other institutions such as a U.N. peace force, a world court of human rights, and a world criminal court is also of great importance. Such developments have been continuously explored in the General Assembly.

This article concerns itself mainly with the legal problem, whose solution is necessary to clarify the image of an international world and to provide the basis for action by international institutions. While a balance of world power may function without law, the complicated structure of an international world requires clear substantive and procedural law. The basic problem is to integrate international law defining those rights and duties of states which, if observed, will protect their national interests in peace and security; with world law defining the rights and duties of individuals which, if observed, will protect their interests in justice; and with international organization law defining the powers and responsibilities of international agencies which, if applied, will assure the observance of both international law and world law.

International law has been based on the right of each sovereign state to territorial integrity, political independence, and exclusive jurisdiction over individuals in its territory, except insofar as rules of customary international law or treaties to which it is a party have imposed limitations, as in the case of resident diplomats, aliens, and the territorial sea. Intervention in the domestic jurisdiction of a state, defined as the residual not affected by such limitations, is therefore forbidden to other states.

These provisions of traditional international law are designed primarily to protect the sovereignty of states, including the right to deal with individuals in their territories as they see fit and to give no protection to individuals against unjust treatment by the state of residence. This has three exceptions: International law permitted states to enter diplomatic protests or even to intervene to protect their nationals abroad against any "denial of justice" after local remedies had been exhausted; to protect all individuals, even citizens of the state of residence, if victims of "barbarities which shocked the conscience of mankind"; and to take action expressly permitted by treaties such as those which formerly gave western states extraterritorial jurisdiction in eastern states. These limitations upon a state's territorial jurisdiction were exceptional. Traditional international law put the rights of states ahead of the rights of individuals and left the latter dependending for justice on the law and administration of the state where they resided.

The United Nations declares in its charter that it is based on the sovereign equality of all its members and accepts the basic principle of traditional international law giving priority to protection of the territorial integrity, political independence, and domestic jurisdiction of states. Even the United Nations itself is in general forbidden to intervene in matters essentially within the domestic jurisdiction of a state (art. 2, par. 7.). In the interest of international peace and human justice, however, it makes major innovations in the traditional law, justifying the expression "the new international law."

In the interest of peace, the United Nations is permitted to intervene in the internal affairs of a state if civil strife or other conditions constitute a threat to international peace and security (art. 2, par. 7; art. 39). States are not permitted to intervene individually in such circumstances or to resort to any threat or use of force in international relations (art. 2, par. 4) except for individual or collective self-defense against armed attack (art. 51), or in accord with a decision or recommendation of the United Nations (arts. 11, 39). Defensive action must be reported to the United Nations and is permissible only so long as the United Nations has failed to take "adequate" measures to maintain international peace and security (art. 51). The United Nations may take "provisional measures" (art. 40) such as ordering the parties to "cease fire" and sending peace-keeping forces to the area. But if these fail to stop hostilities, the United Nations is obliged to determine the aggressor and to recommend or decide upon economic, political, or military collective security action to be taken by its members (arts. 11, 39, 41, 42), obligatorily if decided by the Security Council (arts. 25, 48).

These legal principles, imposing obligations upon states in the interest of peace, developed in the twentieth century after the Hague Conference of 1899 and have modified the sovereignty of states by "outlawing aggressive war" or "war as an instrument of national policy," as explicitly declared in the Kellogg-Briand Pact and enforced by the Nüremberg Charter and trials. These obligations are codified in article 2 of the U.N. Charter, but they leave unimpaired the right of states to territorial integrity, political independence, and domestic jurisdiction.

The charter, however, includes other articles to protect the interest of individuals in justice. A basic purpose of the United Nations is "to promote and encourage respect for human rights and fundamental freedoms for all" (art. 1). The General Assembly (arts. 13, 14), the Economic and Social Council (arts. 62, 68), and the United Nations as a whole (art. 55) are given powers, and to this end the members "pledge themselves to take joint and separate action in cooperation with the organization to the same end."

The effective implementation of these provisions has, however, been hampered by the reluctance of states to submit to international procedures which would impair their exclusive jurisdiction over individuals in their territories.

The problem of reconciling the rights of states, the rights of individuals, and the powers of international agencies is the same as that which faced the United States before the Civil War and which it has continued to face for a century after in controversies over federal action to implement the 14th and 15th Amendments to protect civil rights while impairing the independence of the states.

World Habeas Corpus, which would provide an international remedy against arbitrary arrest and detention of individuals, is a fundamental requirement of human justice. Does the law of the charter permit its realization? The Universal Declaration of Human Rights, accepted by the General Assembly without dissent in 1948, by prohibiting arbitrary arrest, detention, or exile (art. 9) and demanding a fair and public hearing by an independent and impartial tribunal on all charges (ar. 10), accepts World Habeas Corpus in principle. The draft Covenant of Civil and Political Rights. approved by the General Assembly would convert this principle into a legal obligation of the ratifying states (art. 9). The problem is how to achieve general ratification of the covenant and to establish a tribunal with adequate competence to issue and enforce a writ of habeas corpus all over the world. As indicated, the traditional concept of state sovereignty, the prevailing sentiment of nationalism, the different conditions of civil order, and the different beliefs in respect to it in the different nations present difficulties to such an achievement.

Most states resist international procedures to maintain human rights on the ground that they would encroach upon matters which they consider within their domestic jurisdiction. They are inclined to put the independence of the state ahead of the international maintenance of human rights. I recall a conversation with a member of the Supreme Court of India some years ago on the "preventive detention" act in India, which had been used during the British period to imprison Ghandi and Nehru and was at the time being used to keep the Sheikh Abdullah, former prime minister of Kashmir, in prison without trial because he advocated independence for Kashmir. The justice said: "Of course the act is contrary to all principles of constitutional government, but under the conditions in India it is necessary."

There are many, perhaps a majority of states that admit the principle of habeas corpus but would resist giving an international tribunal competence to issue the writ for the benefit of an individual whom they feel it politically necessary to hold in custody without adequate legal grounds. President Lincoln felt such a necessity in suspending the writ in Indiana during the Civil War, an action subsequently found to be unconstitutional by the Supreme Court in the case of *Ex parte Milligan* (4 Wall 2, 1866).

In view of this difficulty it seems probable that progress toward realization of World Habeas Corpus must proceed step by step by establishing legal obligations and tribunals with adequate competence nationally, regionally, and finally universally, and by taking ad hoc action in the United Nations as occasions arise.

On the national front, every effort should be made by discussion in the United Nations, reports by the Human Rights Commission, reports by private groups such as the International Commission of Jurists, and the example of countries like the United States which have long implemented habeas corpus in their constitutional systems and their judicial procedures to persuade other countries to incorporate the principle in their constitutions and laws. Over thirty-one countries have in fact done so. [Luis Kutner, *World Habeas Corpus*, New York, 1962, p. 283.]

On the regional front, the Western European countries have gone far to assure the principle in their area by the Rome Conventions and the establishment of the Commission and the Court of

Human Rights. It is to be hoped that other regions, composed of states of similar culture and concepts of law, like the Organization of American States, may make similar progress.

On the universal front, the principle of habeas corpus is recognized by the Declaration and Draft Covenant, but delays may be expected in bringing the covenant, which has taken two decades to draft, into force. The United States has not ratified any of the nine U.N. treaties on human rights though some of them have been before the Senate for many years. To gain general acceptance of a tribunal with adequate jurisdiction will probably take even longer. There are different conceptions of the relations of man to the state, of the rights which all men should enjoy, and of the necessities which may require government action above the law in the interest of political stability or the maintenance of an ideology. For these reasons the governments of many states insist that the implementation of human rights, including habeas corpus, is a domestic question and resist pressures to accept international obligations and even more international jurisdiction in the field.

In basic philosophy man is prior to the state—the state is for man not man for the state—but in the imperfect world in which we live concepts of the rights of man differ, and peace depends, as the charter recognizes, upon maintenance of the rights of states that control military power.

Consequently, until there is greater consensus on the rights of man and the danger of international hostilities and of civil strife is reduced, human rights are likely to continue in jeopardy in many places, and universal acceptance of covenants to realize them and international tribunals to enforce them cannot be anticipated for some time.

Even in the absence of conditions permitting universal legal institutions to assure World Habeas Corpus, ad hoc action on a universal basis is possible through the United Nations. One of its main purposes is "to achieve cooperation ... in promoting and encouraging respect for human rights and fundamental freedoms for all without distinction as to race, sex, language, or religion" (art. 1, par. 3), and it is specified that the "United Nations shall promote this purpose with a view to the creation of conditions of stability and well-being, necessary for peaceful and friendly relations among nations based on respect for the principle of equal rights and self-determination of peoples" (art. 55). "Subject to the provisions of Article 12 (to avoid conflict with the Security Council) the General Assembly may make recommendations to implement this purpose and discharge this obligation" (art. 13, par. b). It may also "recommend measures for the peaceful adjustment of any situation regardless of origin, which it deems likely to impair the general welfare or friendly relations among nations, including situations resulting from a violation of the provisions of the present Charter setting forth the purposes and principles of the United Nations" (art. 14). The Social and Economic Council may also make recommendations to the same effect (art. 62, par. 2) and shall set up a commission for the promotion of human rights (art. 68). Furthermore, all members "pledge themselves to take joint and separate action in cooperation with the Organization to promote universal respect for and observance of human rights and fundamental freedoms."

In pursuance of these purposes and responsibilities, the General Assembly has exercised its powers and made recommendations to rectify grave violations of human rights, including illegal detention of persons. It made recommendations in 1946 concerning the maltreatment of Indians in South Africa; in 1948 concerning the detention of Soviet wives of foreign nations in the Soviet Union, resulting in a settlement; in 1948 concerning Greek children deported to Bulgaria, Hungary, and Yugoslavia; in 1950 concerning the detention of prisoners of war by the Soviet Union; in 1952 and later concerning the application of apartheid laws by South Africa; in 1952 concerning the repatriation of prisoners of war in Korea, resulting in a settlement; in 1954 concerning the preventive detention by India of the Sheikh Abdullah, former prime minister of Kashmir, resulting in his formal trial; and in 1960 concerning the kidnapping of Eichmann by Israel from Argentina, resulting in a settlement.

In addition to these General Assembly recommendations, some of which proved effective, a proposal was made in 1950 by Luis Kutner, a Chicago lawyer experienced in habeas corpus proceedings, to petition the United Nations for release of Catholic Cardinal Mindszenty, Lutheran Bishop Ordass, and Robert Vogeler, an American business man, all detained by Hungary without trial. Hungary was not then a member of the United Nations, but this action was contrary to human rights guarantees in the peace treaty with Hungary. [Kutner, Habeas Corpus, p. 99.] No action was taken nor were there any results from the General Assembly's recommendations in the previous year concerning the violation of the human rights provisions in the peace treaties by Hungary, Bulgaria, and Romania. The Assembly had requested an advisory opinion from the International Court of Justice on the applicability of the provision for arbitration in these treaties, but the court advised that the arbitral tribunal could not be constituted unless these countries appointed the arbitrators to whom they were entitled.

In 1952 Luis Kutner drafted formal petitions to the General Assembly and the Economic and Social Council for the U.N. habeas corpus proceeding in the case of William N. Oatis, an American Associated Press correspondent detained without trial by Czechoslovakia, a member of the United Nations. The United States hesitated to introduce the petition but the Dominican Republic agreed to present it to the General Assembly in 1953. [Kutner, *Habeas Corpus*, p. 263.] A resolution calling for the adoption of habeas corpus was also to be presented to the General Assembly. The resolution suggested that World Habeas Corpus was the summary remedy to implement the moral human rights principles of the charter and the Universal Declaration of Human Rights. Before action was taken, Oatis was released. It was asserted on the floor of Congress that Kutner's action and petition was the legal fagot that lit the fires for Oatis' freedom.

A similar petition for World Habeas Corpus was filed on 27 July 1967 with the U.N. Commission on Human Rights by Luis Kutner in behalf of Madame Ruth Tshombe, acting for her husband Moise Tshombe, former prime minister of the Congo. Copies of the petition were served on all U.N. missions and Washington embassies and legations. It was directed to Algeria as the principal respondent where Tshombe was detained after being air-kidnapped and ordered for extradition to the Congo where he had been "tried" *in absentia,* found guilty of treason, and sentenced to death. In the same petition for World Habeas Corpus, Spain, which had granted him political asylum, and the United Kingdom, from whose charter-licensed airplane he had been kidnapped, were asked to intervene in Tshombe's behalf.

It is clearly within the competence of the General Assembly to make recommendations concerning violations of human rights, among which detention of persons without trial is recognized as one of the most important. The more effective achievement of World Habeas Corpus by the general acceptance of legal obligations as provided in the Covenant of Civil and Political Rights and of a world court with jurisdiction to issue a writ of habeas corpus (see draft proposal, Kutner, *Habeas Corpus*, p. 266) is undoubtedly desirable, but must be considered a long-range problem. It requires as prerequisites relaxation of international tensions, a world atmosphere of peace and mutual confidence among states, a considerable convergence of cultural and legal concepts throughout the world, the establishment of conditions of stability and civil order in most countries, and experience in the application of the principle nationally, regionally, and by ad hoc recommendations of the United Nations. Until much progress is made in establishing these conditions, pressures by states with a culture, ideology, and a legal system that attaches high priority to civil liberties to induce other states to accept this priority are more likely to induce resistance and conflict and the charge of encroachment on domestic jurisdiction than to forward the cause of human rights.

If we are to have a world of peacefully coexisting states, "safe," as President Kennedy said, "for diversity," sovereign states must feel free to develop their systems of values and law without external coercion but with opportunity to communicate, discuss, and understand the values of civil liberties.

With such understanding, it is to be hoped that, as world conditions improve, states will, one after another, come to appreciate the wisdom of assuring the rule of law internally as well as in international relations, and will accept the jurisdiction of a world tribunal to examine claims of unlawful detention when local remedies prove unavailing, as they have often done in controversies concerning the "denial of justice" to nations of foreign states in their territory.

We may hope that in time all states will ratify the Covenant of Civil and Political Rights approved by the General Assembly and will go further in accepting adequate international procedures for implementation, especially a tribunal, of World Habeas Corpus.

Habeas Corpus–Its Past, Present, and Possible Worldwide Future

By Leonard V. B. Sutton*

The writ of habeas corpus as used today in the United States is a civil remedy commanding that a person restrained be brought before a civil court for a determination of the legality of his detention. Historically, however, under the English common law system, upon which the American system is based, there were a number of different types of writs serving this purpose, each commanding that a person restrained be brought before a court or public official for a specified purpose. For example, the ancient writ of *habeas corpus ad deliberandum et recipiendum,* which ordered that a prisoner be removed to a different jurisdiction in which an alleged offense had been committed, is perhaps similar to the present procedures of extradition in use in the various American states. The ancient writ of *habeas corpus ad prosequendum* was used for the same purpose. The old writs of *habeas corpus ad faciendum et recipiendum* and *habeas corpus cum causa* commanded that a prisoner be removed from an inferi-

* Chairman, U.S. Foreign Claims Settlement Commission; member of the Committee for World Habeas Corpus; former member of the Colorado Bar; justice of the Colorado Supreme Court; chief justice of the Colorado Supreme Court in 1960 and 1966. Justice Sutton is a widely known lecturer and author on judicial administration, political affairs, and international relations.

or court to a superior court. Other early day writs were *habeas corpus ad satisfaciendum,* which was used in order to remove a prisoner from an inferior court to a superior court in order to execute on a judgment gained in the inferior court, and the writ of *habeas corpus ad testificandum,* which commanded that a witness in custody appear in court for the purpose of giving testimony or compelled a bankrupt to appear for examination in a bankruptcy proceeding.[1] The writ of *habeas corpus ad subjiciendum,* the source of our present procedures, commanded a prisoner to be brought before a public official for the purpose of determining the legality of his detention.[2]

The principle of habeas corpus, though often thought of as of Anglo-Saxon origin, can be traced in other legal systems as well, having arisen independently to meet a widespread human need for justice and freedom. An example of this was the process of "manifestation" which in Spanish law paralleled the early writs of English habeas corpus.[3] The former, though, was much more effective at the time and was considered unequaled as an instance of judicial firmness and integrity.[4] Still earlier, the Roman edicts of *Quen liberum hominem dolo malo retines, exhibeas* and *De libero homine exhibendo,* the latter of which can be traced into the civil law of more recent times, were striking parallels to early writs of Anglo-Saxon habeas corpus. These Roman edicts commanded that freemen who were restrained unjustly were to be brought in public before a praetor who would determine whether they should be liberated.[5] As a prerequisite for the edicts to operate, however, it had to be clearly shown that the prisoner was a freeman, since his status was not open to question in the proceeding. Nor could a creditor demand production of his debtor by the edicts.[6]

The first evidence of the use of the principle of habeas corpus in England appeared during the reign of Henry II (1154–1189) in the form of writ called *De odio et atia,* which was used to liberate persons unjustly imprisoned. Other writs securing personal property and liberty, for example, the writs of *De homine replegiande, De manucaptione capienda,* and of Mainprise[7] appeared at about the same time. These gradually merged into what were to become the various writs of habeas corpus.[8] The first royal recognition of the right embodied in the principle of habeas corpus was the signing of the Magna Charta, 15 June 1215.[9] The development of the law in this field, however, from that time until the time of Henry VI (1422–1461) remains somewhat obscure.

In any event, during the reign of Henry VI a remedy known as *Corpus cum causa* made frequent appearances. This writ was closer than De odio et atia, in form and effect, to the later writ of habeas corpus and was used primarily for release from unjust private detention. Apparently it was not until the reign of Henry VII (1485–1509) that the remedy was used against the crown.[10] By the time of the reign of Charles I (1625–1649), the process had become an admitted constitutional remedy and was referred to as a writ of habeas corpus although not yet having been broken down into the numerous forms discussed previously.[11] This line of development, though, led to the passage of the English Habeas Corpus Act on 26 May 1679.[12]

Prior to the passage of the Habeas Corpus Act in England, the power to issue the writs had been exercised by the Courts of Chancery, King's Bench, Exchequer, and Common Pleas. The right, once firmly established in English law, was, however, greatly abused, and the act when finally passed was aimed not at securing this right to the people but at eliminating the flagrant abuses of the right by government and crown lawyers.[13] The act itself, 31 Car. II, passed the House of Commons as early as 1640 but did not get approval from the House of Lords until 1679, and then only by dubious means. It is reported that one assenting member apparently managed to be counted more than once with the final vote of the 107 member house being 57 in favor of passage and 55 against.[14]

The act of 1679 authorized all four of the above mentioned courts to grant the writ of habeas corpus upon proper application, and also authorized its granting by the Lord Chancellor, the Lord Keeper, any of His Majesty's justices of any of the four benches, and the barons of the Exchequer of the degree of the coif. The jurisdiction granted was only on imprisonment for criminal or supposed criminal matters. The act was later implemented by the Statute of 56 Geo. III in 1816, which gave similar jurisdiction in other than criminal matters and also extended authority to any baron of the Exchequer and any judge of the bench of either England or Ireland.[15] It was further supplemented by the Statute of 25 Vic. 20 in 1862. The latter act prohibited any writ from issuing out of England into a colony or dominion which itself had a lawful court with the authority to grant the writ and insure its execution.[16]

The first recorded application for the writ of habeas corpus in the North American Colonies was in 1689 in Massachusetts. Though the application was refused, there was no indication that the request was considered unusual at the time. In 1692 the Assembly of Massachusetts passed an act specifically conferring upon the courts the power to grant the writ, but the enactment was disallowed by Lord Bellamont in 1695.[17] South Carolina, in 1692, also passed an act specifically putting the Statute of 31 Car. II in force.[18] In most other colonies, though no specific action was taken, the people apparently assumed that the right to habeas corpus extended to them as there were instances of application for it in a number of them.[19] The denial, on application to the British Parliment, of the authority to issue writs of habeas corpus in the Province of Quebec in 1774, however, became an additional ground for complaint at the first Continental Congress in that year, as the other colonies felt that the right, although severely abused at the time, would be flatly denied them as well.[20]

Though no provision for the right to habeas corpus was made in the American Articles of Confederation, the United States Constitution, when adopted in 1787, specifically included the right. The reference in the U.S. Constitution merely preserves the right and makes no jurisdictional grants.[21] Actual implementation of the writ came in the federal Judiciary Act of 24 September 1789, section 14 of which granted jurisdiction to issue the writ to the Federal Supreme Court, the Federal Circuit Courts, and the Federal District Courts.[22] All of the states have also made some provision for the right to habeas corpus, some by constitutional provision and others simply by statutory enactments. Thus, though originally this was essentially a common law writ, it has become entirely either constitutional or statutory in the United States of America.[23]

SUBSEQUENT DEVELOPMENT OF THE WRIT IN THE UNITED STATES OF AMERICA

The right to a writ of habeas corpus has not remained intact throughout the history of the United States. The federal Constitution provides that the privilege may not be suspended "... unless when, in cases of rebellion or invasion, the public safety may require it."[24] On 27 April 1861 President Lincoln authorized

General Scott by letter to suspend the writ should it become necessary for the public safety during the Civil War.[25] At that time there was no express authority placing the suspension of the writ among the powers of the president. In 1863, however, such a statute was passed.

The United States Supreme Court in 1866, during the time in which the writ was suspended, did issue a writ of habeas corpus in *Ex parte Milligan*[26] stating that:

> The suspension of the privilege of the writ of habeas corpus does not suspend the writ itself. The writ issues as a matter of course; and on the return made to it, the court decides whether the party applying is denied the right of proceeding any further with it.[27]

The court then went on to say that the suspension of the privilege of the writ ceases when the rebellion or other public emergency ceases, and the prisoner may be released, if in fact his claim has merit, when the suspension terminates.[28]

The writ of habeas corpus today is used in both federal and state courts in the United States for numerous purposes both civil and criminal. All uses involve a determination of the legality of a detention of one sort or another. These uses include, among others:

1. Discharge of a person charged with an act which is not a crime.[29]
2. Discharge of a person charged under a statute which is unconstitutional.[30]
3. Discharge of a person charged under an unconstitutional ordinance.[31]
4. Testing the legality of a detention on warrant before an indictment has been obtained.[32]
5. Release from arrest in violation of the right to immunity.[33]
6. Discharge of a person detained through invalid or illegal exercise of executive or administrative authority.[34]
7. Release from detention under a statute repealed prior to the alleged offense.[35]
8. Release where the court was without jurisdiction in rendering judgment or exceeded its power in passing sentence.[36]
9. Release where a delay in pronouncing sentence is sufficient to divest the court of jurisdiction.[37]

10. Where a sentence is excessive, release from that portion which is illegal.[38]
11. Release on bail by a court other than one ordering the original detention.[39]
12. Release on reduced bail where excessive bail was set.[40]
13. Attacking the legal existence of a court detaining the petitioner.[41]
14. Release from confinement in an improper or unauthorized place.[42]
15. Discharge of a person improperly in custody in lieu of another.[43]
16. Release from custody when there has been an unlawful delay in the proceedings.[44]
17. Release of a person detained under an order for the exclusion of an alien.[45]
18. Discharge of a person detained under unlawful deportation orders.[46]
19. Release of a person under civil arrest by a court with improper jurisdiction.[47]
20. Release of one detained improperly for contempt.[48]
21. Release by the asylum state of one held on interstate extradition proceedings.[49]
22. Discharge of one unlawfully detained for removal to another federal district for trial.[50]
23. Discharge of a person illegally in the custody of the military authorities as a member of the armed forces.[51]
24. Release of a person improperly under military arrest or court martial.[52]
25. Release to the military authorities of a person in custody of the civil authorities when the military authorities have sole jurisdiction.[53]
26. Release of a draftee improperly drafted or improperly classified.[54]
27. Discharge of a person committed to an institution after acquittal of criminal charges by reason of insanity, and who has subsequently regained his sanity.[55]
28. Release of a person civilly committed who has regained his sanity.[56]

29. Release from parole of a person whose freedom is significantly restrained by reason of the parole.[57]
31. Determination of controversies concerning custody of children.[59]

An even more detailed breakdown may be made today with reference to a recent rash of United States Supreme Court decisions which have involved the use of the writ of habeas corpus to attack various procedural defects in criminal trials. Among the current number of denials of fundamental fairness held assertable by means of the writ are:

1. Denial of the right to counsel at trial.[60]
2. Involuntary nature of a confession admitted as evidence.[61]
3. Evidence obtained as a result of an illegal search and seizure.[62]
4. Denial of the right to counsel at critical points in the proceedings.[63]
5. Denial of counsel during interrogation by the police.[64]
6. Pre-trial publicity prejudicial to defendant.[65]
7. Denial of the right against self incrimination.[66]
8. Denial of the right to counsel for prosecution of appeal.[67]

Both historically and currently it is apparent, as mentioned earlier, that the need for and development of the various writs of habeas corpus arose because of mankind's innate sense of justice and the need of organized governmental structures to recognize human rights, dignity, and freedom. It is really then what, in the United States, is called due process of law. This implies, of course, a public hearing or public trial with a recognized form of judgment,[68] thus securing an individual and his property from the arbitrary exercise of the powers of government, unrestrained by established principles of law, of private rights, and of distributive justice.

THE MOVEMENT TOWARD A WORLD HABEAS CORPUS

The movement toward international recognition of the remedy of habeas corpus to protect fundamental human rights has gained considerable momentum in the past few decades. It has been said that this development is based primarily upon divine law, an international theory of due process, and certain individual rights inherent in nature.[69] Whatever its origin, and admittedly it has an excellent historical pedigree, in 1928 the Permanent Court of

International Justice ruled that treaties may confer direct substantive rights upon individuals. Based upon that ruling, a number of treaties have come into effect which do just that. One example is the Hungarian Peace Treaty of 1947.[70]

Apparently the protection, on an international scale, of what today are called human rights was first provided for in article 55 of the U.N. Charter. This section pledges signatory nations to a universal respect for an observance of human rights and fundamental freedoms. Article 56, in turn, pledges members to take positive action in observance of the purposes and aims of article 55.[71] Many of these principles, however, are still in the process of being debated and implemented since there does not seem to be universal agreement by the U.N. members upon how to expedite the charter provisions as expressed in the Universal Declaration of Human Rights and Fundamental Freedoms,[72] which was proposed by the Commission of Human Rights and adopted by the General Assembly on 10 December 1948.[73]

As far as habeas corpus is concerned, article 9 of the above mentioned Universal Declaration contains a provision to the effect that "no one shall be subject to arbitrary arrest, detention or exile."[74] Neither this declaration, which does not have the effect of a treaty,[75] nor the U.N. Charter, contain any provision for implementation of the right to be free from arbitrary arrest.

The vision of an international writ of habeas corpus has only been propounded fairly recently by legal theorists. Luis Kutner, author of the concept and the well-known American leader in this field, made the following comments on the beginnings of the idea:

> The concept of an international writ of habeas corpus came into existence as a concrete proposal after the reading of *Mein Kampf* in 1931 and a view of the frightening scene of 10,000 arms raised in Roman salute to the raucous voice of a demented, self-proclaimed redeemer of the German national honor. Hitler's blueprint for arbitrary arrest, detention, and human slaughter was made available for all the world to see.[76]

The ideal, though, has caught the imagination of many persons in many lands, particularly in the United States of America, where numerous authors, lecturers, congressmen, diplomats, and legal theorists urged, during the 1950s that the right to issue writs of habeas corpus should be vested in a world court.[77] During those years a resolution was even proposed in the United States House of Representatives to the effect that the United States sponsor a treaty proposing that an international court be empowered to issue the writ of habeas corpus upon proper application even to countries detaining their own nationals. Opposition to such a stand, by the U.S. Department of State among others, was based upon the obvious loss of sovereignty by each signatory nation which would take such a step.[78]

Some other nations, however, have not been as reticent as the United States and have evidently believed the surrender of such a parcel of sovereign power to be worthwhile in the rapidly changing world of today. For example, the European Convention for the Protection of Human Rights and Fundamental Freedoms, which became effective in September 1953, provided for regional implementation of a remedy for arbitrary detention.[79] Then, too, the European Court of Human Rights came into being in 1959 as a result of the European Convention, and in 1960 that court began handling cases of a nature that would be treated by international courts of habeas corpus as proposed by Mr. Kutner.[80] The possible creation of the latter type of a court has now become the subject of considerable worldwide discussion. Its advent is believed by many authorities to be the proper beginning of a solution as to how the basic human rights of mankind to individual freedom can best be recognized and protected. For that reason the general concept and operation of such a court system will next be discussed in some detail.

Kutner's concept is for the creation by treaty-statute of regional international courts of habeas corpus. The regional courts would be created in definitive geographical regions each comprised of a number of signatory nations. Each regional court would be staffed by regional world attorneys general appointed to resist applications as well as by *amici curiae*, regionally appointed, to aid in the prosecution of petitions.[81] The court itself would consist of not less than two jurists from each signatory country, each serving a region which does not include his own country. Each region would select its own chief justice from among the member jurists.[82] The court itself would operate on general principles of fundamental fairness, and on natural law rather than legal principles drawn from any one or more member nations.[83] Apparently inherent in the legal concepts to be employed, however, would be those discussed earlier herein relating to due process of law and the right of an individual to be free from arbitrary governmental arrest and restraint.

There are many practical difficulties in trying to establish such a new judicial system in this era of great social, economic, and political upheaval. First among these is the need to change on a worldwide basis the generally accepted and long-standing concept in international law that only states can and should bring actions in international tribunals. If World Habeas Corpus is to succeed it is obvious that the detained or incarcerated individual, or someone on his behalf, must be permitted to file and prosecute that petition. As previously noted, a good start in altering thinking along the necessary lines has been made by the creation of the European Court of Human Rights. Assuming that a successful effort can be made on that point and that at least some regional blocs of states will be willing to adopt a Kutner-type treaty-statute, other obstacles also loom nevertheless on the horizon. For example, before the United States would adhere to such a court (through a proposal by the president concurred in by the Senate as for any other treaty) something probably would have to be done about the Connally Amendment to the 1946 United States Declaration of Adherence to the Jurisdiction of the International Court of Justice.[84] This is so because undoubtedly such a restriction would again be proposed for the adherence to any new court as well. But even if that obstacle did not materialize, or were defeated, there next appears to be a reluctance on the part of some nations, including the United States, to agree, on a theoretical basis, to any loss of individual sovereignty, which is, to some extent, implicit in adhering to an international judicial body. This is so even though article 95 of the U.N. Charter permits the establishment of regional international courts. An even more serious stumbling block, however, assuming that national prejudices against the creation of such courts can in time be overcome or solved, in that there does not appear to be at this time any way to enforce the mandates of such courts.[85] It has been suggested that sanctions are unnecessary. Proponents of this belief cite as examples the general success of the few international tribunals that have heretofore functioned as well as of international arbitral boards. Also, the European Common Market operations are referred to for the proposition that signatory nations will respect and adhere to the judgments of an international judicial body.[86] This position, while it may be overly optimistic, may be somewhat supported by the fact that there are very few recorded instances of disobedience to the judgments of the present International Court of Justice.[87]

History teaches us that the progress of the human race has always been one of struggle to achieve a better way of life, a more perfect justice, and a more peaceful existence. The writ of habeas corpus has been one of the most potent weapons yet devised in man's attempt to follow paths to these fundamental and rightful goals. Mankind will somehow, some way, and hopefully very soon, use this ancient, revered, and versatile remedy to serve his need for human freedom on an international basis. Surely, regional international courts of world habeas corpus are within reach, and once created and obeyed, will permit those who in good faith adhere to the precepts of the U.N. Charter to see to it that at least in their countries there is protection against arbitrary arrest and unlawful detention. Hopefully then, this safeguard can gradually but surely be extended to all men everywhere.

Notes

1. 39 C.J.S., *Habeas Corpus* § 1, note 2.
2. Scott & Roe, *The Law of Habeas Corpus*, 8 (1923).
3. For an excellent article on the history of Habeas Corpus in the Spanish concept and its modified current use in Puerto Rico, see: Amadeo, *El Habeas Corpus En Puerto Rico*, 17(1) Revista Juridica 1 (1947).
4. II Hurd, *A Treatise on the Right of Personal Liberty and on the Writ of Habeas Corpus*, 131 (1876).
5. Ibid.
6. Church, *A Treatise on the Writ of Habeas Corpus*, 3 (1893).
7. 39 C.J.S., *Habeas Corpus* § 1.
8. Church, *A Treatise*, p. 4.
9. Ferris, *The Law of Extraordinary Legal Remedies*, 22 (1926).
10. Hurd, *A Treatise*, p. 130.
11. Church, *A Treatise*, p. 4.
12. Hurd, *A Treatise*, p. 132.   13. Ibid.
14. Church, *A Treatise*, p. 22.
15. Hurd, *A Treatise*, p. 133.   16. Ibid., p. 133, note 1.
17. Church, *A Treatise*, p. 35
18. Ibid., p. 37.   19. Ibid., p. 38.
20. Ibid., p. 39.   21. Ibid., p. 40.
22. Hurd, *A Treatise*, p. 134.
23. 39 C.J.S., *Habeas Corpus* § 3.
24. Constitution of the United States of America, art. I, § 9(2).
25. Kutner, *World Habeas Corpus for International Man: A Credo for International Due Process of Law*, 36 U. Det. L. J. 235, 253 (1959).

26. 71 U.S. (4 Wall.) 2 (1866).

27. Ibid., pp. 130, 131.

28. Kutner & Carl, *An International Writ of Habeas Corpus: Protection of Personal Liberty in a World of Diverse Systems of Public Order*, 22 U. Pitt. L. Rev. 469, 507, note 251 (1961).

29. *Hill v. Sanford*, 131 F.2d 417 (5th Cir. 1942).

30. *Ex parte Novotny*, 88 F.2d 72 (7th Cir. 1937).

31. *Ex parte Martinez*, 56 Cal. App.2d 473, 132 P.2d 901 (1942).

32. *Kurnava v. United States*, 222 F. Supp. 822 (W.D. Mo. 1963).

33. *United States v. Baird*, 85 Fed. 63 (D.S.N.J. 1897).

34. *Sigurdson v. Del Guercio*, 154 F. Supp. 220 (S.D. Cal. 1957).

35. *Ex parte De La Pena*, 157 Tex. Cr. 560, 251 S.W.2d 890 (1952); *Ex parte Moore*, 44 Wyo. 92, 8 P.2d 818 (1932).

36. *Johnson v. Zerbst*, 304 U.S. 458, 58 S. Ct. 1019, 82 L. Ed. 1461 (1937); *Wilson v. Bell*, 137 F.2d 716 (6th Cir. 1943); *Graham v. Squier*, 132 F.2d 681 (9th Cir. 1942).

37. *Mintie v. Biddle*, 15 F.2d 931 (8th Cir. 1926).

38. *McKinney v. Finletter*, 205 F.2d 761 (10th Cir. 1953); *Wilson v. Bell*, supra note 36.

39. *Petition of Johnson*, 72 S. Ct. 1028, 96 L. Ed. 1377 (1952).

40. *United States ex rel Rubinstein v. Mulcahy*, 155 F.2d 1002 (2nd Cir. 1946).

41. *Ex parte Pitts*, 35 Fla. 149, 17 So. 76 (1895).

42. *Simon v. Maryland*, 227 F. Supp. 588 (D.C. Md. 1964); *Barrett v. People*, 136 Colo. 144, 315 P.2d 192 (1957).

43. *Foster v. Perry*, 71 Fla. 155, 70 So. 1007 (1916).

44. *State v. Maldonado*, 92 Ariz. 70, 373 P.2d 583 (1963).

45. *Brownell v. We Shung*, 77 S. Ct. 252, 352 U.S. 180, 1 L. Ed.2d 225 (1956); *Ex parte Fong Yim*, 134 Fed. 938 (S.D.N.Y. 1905); *Ex parte Lee Bock Fook*, 40 F. Supp. 937 (S.D. Calif. 1941).

46. *Harisiades v. Shaughnessy*, 72 S. Ct. 512, 342 U.S. 580, 96 L. Ed. 586 (1952); *United States ex rel Martinez-Agnosto v. Mason*, 344 F. 2d 673 (2nd Cir. 1965); *Sigurdson v. Del Guercio*, supra note 34.

47. *Johnson v. Lindsey*, 89 Fla. 143, 103 So. 419 (1925).

48. *John Breuner Co. v. Bryant*, 36 Cal.2d 877, 229 P.2d 356 (1951); *Lawley v. State*, 117 Tex. Cr. 14, 36 S.W.2d 1035 (1931).

49. *In re Gibson*, 147 F. Supp. 591 (D.D.C. 1957); *Davis v. O'Connell*, 185 F.2d 513 (5th Cir. 1951); *Application of Oppenheimer*, 95 Ariz. 292, 389 P.2d 696 (1964); *Krutka v. Bryer*, 150 Colo. 293, 372 P.2d 83 (1962). It should be noted, however, that in state extradition proceedings the asylum state, in the absence of a public policy to the contrary, should not inquire into the truth of the charges contained in the warrant from the demanding state. The only inquiry is whether a felony has been charged and whether the extradition papers are in proper order. The defenses to the crime itself must be asserted when the prisoner is returned for trial to the demanding state. See *Capra v. Miller*, _____ Colo. _____, 422 P.2d 636 (1967) and *Fox v. People*, Colo. _____, 420 P.2d 412 (1966).

50. *Henry v. Henkel*, 35 S. Ct. 54, 235 U.S. 219, 59 L.Ed. 203 (1914).

51. *Levin v. Gillespie*, 121 F. Supp. 239 (N.D. Cal. 1954); *Farley v. Ratliff*, 267 Fed. 682 (4th Cir. 1920).

52. *United States ex rel Singleton v. Kinsella*, 80 S. Ct. 297, 361 U.S. 234, 4 L. Ed.2d 268 (1960); *Wales v. Whitney*, 114 U.S. 564, 5 S. Ct. 1050, 29 L. Ed. 277 (1885); *DeCoster v. Madigan*, 223 F.2d 906 (7th Cir. 1965); *McKinney v. Finletter*, supra note 38.

53. *Ex parte King*, 246 Fed. 868 (D.C. Ky. 1917).

54. *Witmer* v. *United States*, 75 S. Ct. 392, 348 U.S. 375, 99 L. Ed. 428 (1955); *Bowles* v. *United States*, 63 S. Ct. 912, 319 U.S. 33, 87 L. Ed. 1194 (1943).
55. *Richey* v. *Baur*, 298 S.W.2d 445 (Mo. 1957).
56. *Ex parte R. R.*, 140 N.J. Eq. 371, 54 A.2d 814 (1947); *Ex parte Cloutman*, 47 Cal. App.2d 77, 117 P.2d 378 (1941).
57. *Jones* v. *Cunningham*, 83 S. Ct. 373, 371 U.S.' 236, 9 L. Ed.2d 285 (1963).
58. *Hill* v. *Hilbert*, 92 Okla. Cr. 169, 222 P.2d 166 (1950); *State* v. *Hutchinson*, 246 Ala. 48, 18 So.2d 723 (1944).
59. *Pugh* v. *Pugh*, 133 W. Va. 501, 56 S.E.2d 901 (1949); *Ex rel Pruyne* v. *Walts*, 122 N.Y. 238, 25 N.E. 266 (1890).
60. *Gideon* v. *Wainwright*, 372 U.S. 335, 83 S. Ct. 792, 9 L. Ed.2d 799, 93 A.L.R. 2d 733 (1963).
61. *Jackson* v. *Denno*, 378 U.S. 368, 84 S. Ct. 1774, 12 L. Ed.2d 908, 1 A.L.R.3d 1205 (1964); *Fay* v. *Noia*, 372 U.S. 391, 83 S. Ct. 822, 9 L. Ed.2d 837 (1963).
62. *Mapp.* v. *Ohio*, 367 U.S. 643, 81 S. Ct. 1684, 6 L. Ed.2d 1081, 84 A.L.R.2d 933 (1961).
63. *White* v. *Maryland*, 373 U.S. 59, 83 S. Ct. 1050, 10 L. Ed.2d 193 (1965); *Hamilton* v. *Alabama*, 368 U.S. 52, 82 S. Ct. 157, 7 L. Ed. 2d 114 (1961).
64. *Miranda* v. *Arizona*, 384 U.S. 436, 86 S. Ct. 1602, 16 L. Ed.2d 694 (1966); *Escobedo* v. *Illinois*, 378 U.S. 478, 84 S. Ct. 1758, 12 L. Ed.2d 977 (1964).
65. *Sheppard* v. *Maxwell*, 384 U.S. 333, 86 S. Ct. 1507, 16 L. Ed.2d 600 (1966); *Rideau* v. *Louisiana*, 373 U.S. 723, 83 S. Ct. 1417, 10 L. Ed.2d 663 (1963).
66. *Malloy* v. *Hogan*, 378 U.S. 1, 84 S. Ct. 1489, 12 L. Ed.2d 653 (1964).
67. *Douglas* v. *California*, 372 U.S. 353, 83 S. Ct. 814, 9 L. Ed.2d 811 (1963).
68. In this connection see *La Plata River and Cherry Creek Ditch Co.* v. *Hinderlider*, 93 Colo. 128, 25 P.2d 187 (1933).
69. Kutner, *World Habeas Corpus*, p. 242.
70. Kutner & Carl, *An International Writ*, p. 536.
71. Kutner, *World Habeas Corpus: A Legal Absolute for Survival*, 39 U. Det. L. J. 279, 282 (1962).
72. E. g., see Report of the American Bar Association's "Standing Committee on Peace and Law Through United Nations" of May 1967 and its comments and recommendations on four of the proposed conventions already submitted to the United States Senate (Genocide, Supplementary Slavery, Abolition of Forced Labor, and Political Rights of Women); and see its comments on other conventions not yet submitted to the Senate for its advice and consent. As far as is known no convention has yet been proposed by an official United Nations Commission on a worldwide habeas corpus system.
73. Kutner, *A Proposal for a United Nations Writ of Habeas Corpus and an International Court of Human Rights*, 28 Tul. L. Rev. 417, 420 (1954).
74. Kutner, *A Legal Absolute*, p. 295.
75. Kutner, *A Proposal for a U.N. Writ*, p. 420.
76. Kutner, *A Legal Absolute*, p. 288.
77. Ibid.   78. Ibid., p. 289.
79. Kutner, *A Proposal for a U.N. Writ*, p. 421; Kutner & Carl, *An International Writ*, p. 538.
80. Kutner, *A Legal Absolute*, p. 306.
81. Ibid., p. 319.   82. Ibid., p. 322.
83. Kutner, *W.H.C. for International Man*, p. 243.
84. Kutner, *A Legal Absolute*, p. 290. It should be noted in this connection that the Connally Amendment consists of only the eight italicized words which appear at the end of the following quotation, from the United States' Declaration of Acceptance of the Jurisdiction of the World Court, viz.: "This declaration shall not apply to . . . (b) Disputes with regard to matters which

are essentially within the domestic jurisdiction of the United States of America *as determined by the United States of America."* The net effect of this amendment is not only to give the United States what amounts to a veto over which cases it will permit to come before that court but also, under the doctrine of reciprocity, a state sued by the United States has the same right of determination. If it is assumed that any regional world court joined by the United States would have a similar restriction placed on the declaration of adherence, or, that article 92 of the U.N. Charter is revised so that an appeal would be possible from a regional court to the International Court of Justice, then the original "veto" power could still be exercised.

85. Ibid., p. 292.   86. Ibid., p. 292, 295.   87. Ibid., p. 325.

World Habeas Corpus, World Law, and Sovereignty

By Andrew Lee*

From the dawn of civilization to the present time, states have risen and fallen, always through struggle and war. Twice in the last half century we have been involved in struggles of the fiercest character. Yet side by side with this, there has always existed a desire that things should be otherwise; there have always been statesmen exalting peace. All over the world today men hunger for peace. How are they to find it? It is certain that the search will be difficult; it is by no means certain that it will be successful. Yes it is safe to say that the need to examine the problem has never been greater than it is today, at a time when the agencies of destruction have grown so portentously and when the consequences of war on the grand scale might be little less than mutual annihilation. In so examining it, we can measure more accurately the possibilities by looking at the record. We can avoid previous errors, if we review the story. We can gain a new sense of proportion as to what is involved. Looking at the matter historically, the earliest recipe prescribed to deal with it is the fortification

* Dr. Andrew Lee is dean of the Department of Law, Soochow University, Taipei, Taiwan; chairman, World Conference of Lawyers of the Committee for the Republic of China.

and extension of international law. As a matter of fact, though many people do not realize it, there has been a substantial growth of international law in the last hundred years, particularly in the last fifty years. There are widely accepted principles of international intercourse, and there is a vast body of treaties which are in essence legal documents governing the relations of the signatories to one another. Some of these treaties are truly international agreements, such as, for example, the Charter of the United Nations or the protocol creating the International Court of Justice. Some are more restricted in their scope, but all of them are drafted in legal terms and all of them are subject to legal interpretation. It is foolish to say that international law is a mere figment of the imagination. It is equally foolish to say that its rules are constantly broken. As a matter of fact, within a wide area they are observed with as much regularity as the rules of municipal law; and when they are broken, the attempt is usually made to justify the breach on some legal ground.

But at the same time, it is true that experience does not suggest that the growth of legal principles has brought about a peaceful world or prevented the outbreak of conflicts of large dimensions. Clearly the development of international law has not been adequate to restrain the forces of violence. There are reasons why this is so. One of the reasons lies in the limited scope of the rules of law accepted by the international community. These rules are nothing like, or as extensive as, the rules that govern the relations of individuals in a civil society. The great nations of the world, even the nations of the West, have shown a very limited disposition to submit their disputes to an international tribunal.

There is nothing strange about this. In international adjudication, there are lacking some of the assurances that exist in the case of adjudication before national tribunals. In the latter case, it is possible to define the principle governing a given situation, if not perfectly at least with a good deal more precision than in an international controversy. It is possible to have the case considered by regularly established tribunals, construing statutes, and constitutions, and organized in a judicial *hierarchy*. In general, both parties to the dispute will acquiesce in the ultimate decision and will, within limits, have the machinery to enforce it. None of these factors exists in the same sense in the field of international law, There is an international court of justice, but no hierarchy of courts. The International Court of Justice has no power to enforce its decisions.

But the difficulty lies deeper still. It lies in the fact that states have never admitted, and do not now admit, that their activities and relations with other states are inevitably controlled by legal principles. The notion of submission to law runs counter to the notion that each state is sovereign.

Let us look at one argument that is universal: the argument that the acceptance of world court jurisdiction of World Habeas Corpus may involve *loss of sovereignty*. The fact is that every country is jealous of its sovereignty. This is certainly one of the roadblocks to world peace. It is the notion that any national sovereign is not within the law but is the ultimate source of law. If this idea were true, it would follow that there could not be any kind of international law or order binding on any national ruler. *But this belief is certainly not true!* The assertion that submission of international disputes to a World Court of World Habeas Corpus is a sacrifice of sovereignty is an outright misuse of the term sovereignty. It is a rhetorical cliché with proved demagogic appeal. But it will not stand up on analysis. Here is the reason: International disputes involve usually rights of two sovereign countries, say Country A and Country B. Country A has sovereignty within its own jurisdiction and over rights within that jurisdiction. But Country A does not have sovereignty over Country B's rights, and B's rights are involved in the dispute just as much as A's.

Suppose that China has a treaty under which Chinese citizens are granted certain privileges within the United States. Suppose a dispute arises in which China alleges that these privileges were denied in a particular case. If China submits this question to the International Court of Justice, has it forfeited its sovereignty? What sovereignty did China have to make the United States take an action it did not want to take within its own borders?

What really happens when a country accepts international adjudication is not that it diminishes its sovereignty but that it uses its sovereignty to obtain something of value. In the loose use of the term one could just as well say that a nation loses some of its sovereignty every time it makes a treaty. It would be nearer the truth to say that the country uses its sovereignty by putting it to work to obtain values that can be secured in no other way. If a country has only one major product, such as sugar, and would like to have automobiles and refrigerators, it will probably make an international trade agreement. In so doing it will give up its sovereign right to bar the entrance of those automobiles and refrigerators into its territory. In return it will gain the privilege of sending its sugar into the territory of another country—which until then had the sovereign right to turn the sugar back from its borders. It never occurs to anyone to characterize all this as a "sacrifice of sovereignty."

Similarly, if nations use their sovereignty to create an efficient dispute-settling mechanism, they will have used their power to gain something of value—something indeed that is of much greater value than commercial goods. If nations accepted settlement of disputes under law, the world would gain a substantial advance toward peace.

It is certainly the intention of the countries at the time of forming the United Nations and enlarging the membership of the International Court of Justice to take a step forward toward settlement of international disputes by peaceful legal means as the normal and regular method. Now, our main concern is, while of course doing everything possible to alleviate them, to keep them from breaking into international violence and war. We are concerned with the question not whether the parties are willing to submit these disputes today to judicial settlement but whether the questions themselves are of a quality that is inherently suitable to adjudication. In other words, it is important for the direction of our future efforts to know whether the problem is "Can't" or "Won't." If it is "Can't," our efforts to build peace through law could better be directed elsewhere. If it is "Won't," our efforts should be redoubled until "Won't" becomes "Will."

It is true that the task of building law structure of peace is one of great difficulty. But, difficult or not, we have no choice. We have had occasion in the past to learn the lesson that tasks that for years seemed impossible of realization have eventually yielded to hard work and patience.

There is a rabbit story which aptly sums up this theme of doing the apparently impossible. The old man was telling the little boy about the time a rabbit climbed a tree. The little boy objected, "But, father, you know rabbits cannot climb trees." "Yeah, I know that," said the old man, "but a fox was right behind the rabbit, and the rabbit was just obliged to climb that tree."

Jean Jacques Rousseau, the great French philosopher, once said, "The best way to teach your child not to lean out of the window is to let him fall out. Unfortunately, the defect of this system is that he may not survive to profit by his experience." The world has been learning about international relations for centuries by a process of periodically falling out of the window. Injuries have been severe but never quite fatal. But one more fall may be our last. We must profit by our experience, for we may not be given another chance.

Like the rabbit, so we too, in the presence of appalling danger, may do the apparently impossible and build the law structure of peace which many believe is now the last, best hope of the world.

History has taught us, moreover, that new concepts of law sometimes evolve out of seemingly hopeless situations. So the only responsible answer that free men can give to this challenge is that the struggle for world law must go on with increased intensity.

We want peace with justice. We want a world that doesn't live under the fear of the bomb, a world that acknowledges the rule of law, a world in which no nation can play bully and no nation need live in fear.

World Peace Through Law and World Habeas Corpus are not slogans of visionaries and idealists; it is the cherished objective of the realist. It is the program of all those interested in a life free of fear, in a life dedicated to the development of the individual rather than his destruction, in a life dedicated to securing the advantages of economic progress rather than the poverty of economic waste

We must, therefore, show the peoples of the world, by every means of precept, education, and example, that just as in our municipal societies, so in world societies, it will, in the end, be possible for the people of the world to sleep peacefully in their beds, in the knowledge that the law, impartially and authoritatively, protects them. This may not happen in our own time. It may not be achieved in the time of our children. But we can all of us help to advance toward it, so that perhaps in the time of our children's children the ideal will be realized.

World Habeas Corpus: The Ecuador View

By GUSTAVO SALGADO*

WHEN WE LOOK at the world scene, it is indeed discouraging to find out that, in spite of so many international organizations and public treaties, and above all the Declaration of the Fundamental Rights, intended directly or indirectly for the protection of human rights, many states and their authorities, in the name of a sovereign and unrestricted power, persecute, arrest, try, torture, condemn, and kill or imprison citizens and commit other offenses against their persons and property. The international organizations and the public treaties seem to be powerless or insufficient to take an effective and prompt action to stop the unceasing succession of arrests, trials, tortures, executions, confiscations, most of them arbitrary and illegal. Commissions composed of impartial and unbiased men are appointed to study the events on the spot, to submit a comprehensive report, and to suggest the measures to be taken. But very often they are not admitted by the governments involved and cannot perform their duties. The cases are so recent, not to be forgotten, and we cannot but mention some of them: Hungary, Tibet, Soviet Russia, East Germany, Cuba, Red China, et al.

* Professor, international law, Central University, Quito, Ecuador. Author of "Jurisprudence of the Ecuadorean Foreign Ministry," "The Case Nestor Borja, an Essay on International Law," and "Wills and Donations." Former legal adviser to the Ministry of Public Works, legal adviser to the Superintendency of Banks, assistant general attorney of the Republic.

Remedies provided by the domestic legislation of a state to prevent or correct offenses of authorities against life, freedom, and property seem to be poor and ineffective. And these remedies do not work at all if the dictator of a country or the political party in power becomes at the same time the legislative, the executive, and the judicial branch of the government, and he dictates his own laws, applies them in his own way, and interprets them as he likes. The Cuban case speaks for itself and needs no additional comment.

On the other side, the international public opinion, the press, law-abiding citizens, legal and judicial circles, and all sensible men cannot remain silent and helpless before so many offenses committed in the name of a state by their authorities and, chiefly, before the most frequent of them, the loss of personal liberty by means of arbitrary detention or arrest. Some remedy must be devised of such effectiveness and coerciveness that the authorities of any state will not fail to comply with it. There is no need to say that such remedy is habeas corpus, or as it is named in the domestic legislation of the different countries, no matter if its scope is broader or narrower than the habeas corpus writ as it was transplanted from England to their colonies and possessions, first, and then to the laws in force of several Latin-American republics and other countries of the world. A short examination of the situation, operation, and prospects of habeas corpus remedy in the republic of Ecuador is opportune here.

THE HABEAS CORPUS REMEDY IN ECUADOR

This remedy was first established by the National Assembly of 1928–1929, which enacted a new fundamental law (or Political Constitution)[1] for this country after some years of *de facto* government. But the application of this remedy depended on the enactment of a special law that was promulgated some years later, in 1933.[2] The political events of 1935 and subsequent years put an end to the fundamental law of 1928–1929 and with it the habeas corpus remedy. Ecuadorean administrations of the years 1935–1945 reenacted the Political Constitution of 1906, which did not provide for habeas corpus. After a succession of unstable or de facto governments, a National Assembly was convoked in August 1944 with the main task of enacting a modern constitution or fundamental law. This law, promulgated in April 1945, provided for habeas corpus and entrusted the mayors of cities and chairmen of municipal councils with the application of the remedy and the trial of prisoners who alleged that they were illegally arrested.[3] Again this constitution was repealed by the political events of March 1946 and Ecuadorean citizens were convoked immediately to elect deputies for a new national assembly which would discuss and promulgate a new fundamental law, because the Constitution of 1945 was described by the president of the republic as too much restrictive of his powers.

The National Assembly met on the 10 of August 1946 and, after the approval of its procedure, began the discussion of a draft constitution prepared by a special commission appointed by the president of the republic. The assembly enacted the new constitution on the 31 of December 1946, and this fundamental law is still in force notwithstanding several political events that imperiled its existence. The Constitution of 1946 again provided for habeas corpus remedy and again entrusted mayors of cities and chairmen of municipal councils with the upkeep and application of the remedy;[4] and, to this effect, the same assembly amended the law for local governments, concerning the powers of mayors and chairmen of municipal councils, and adjusted it to the new political constitution.[5]

I thought it opportune to sum up the historical evolution of habeas corpus remedy in Ecuador in order to show that this institution is comparatively of recent date in our country and is not yet firmly entrenched in the conscience of Ecuadorean citizens. Besides, it is necessary to emphasize that the enactment of habeas corpus remedy is not the result of any political struggle to attain it, so that it may be described as a popular conquest. It is rather a political "grant" effected by progressive lawmakers anxious of putting our country on the same footing as the most advanced countries as far as social and political guarantees are concerned.

The application of habeas corpus by mayors and chairmen of municipal councils has never been so easy and smooth as it seems when we read article 187, paragraph 4, of our Constitution. And this is especially the case with Quito and Guayaquil, the most important cities of this country. The mayoralties of Quito and Guayquil are always coveted by leading politicians, either because they can from these posts prepare their candidacy to the presidency of the republic (that is why they are called the "antechambers" of the presidency) or because, if they are opponents of the government, they can build an easy and strong opposition from their posts thanks to the relative independence enjoyed by municipal councils. The national government can do practically nothing against a mayor or a municipal council even when this has become a stronghold of the political opposition.

When as a result of political activity against the national government a person has been arrested—and this happens mainly in Quito and Guayaquil—he immediately takes recourse to habeas corpus and applies to the mayor of the city. The examination of a habeas corpus case by a mayor is not based upon precedents, as it may be assumed, although a municipal council always has a legal advisor or so-called procurator. The trial of a habeas corpus case depends chiefly on the political position of the mayor with respect to the president of the republic. If the mayor's attitude toward the executive is friendly or neutral, he tries the case very simply: he directs the police authority to appear before him with the prisoner and demands him to produce the arrest order properly executed. If everything is normal, he confirms the arrest order and closes the hearing. If something is illegal or irregular, he directs to release the prisoner. But as a rule he does not examine the reason for the arrest of the prisoner, with what offense he is charged, nor the proceedings, witnessess, depositions, etc.

But if, on the other hand, the mayor of Quito or Guayaquil is unfriendly to the president of the republic, he examines carefully the proceedings. If the offense with which the prisoner is charged is punishable or not, he qualifies the witnesses' depositions and tries to find errors or gaps in order to blame the police authorities and to release the prisoner.

In this way the mayor hopes to weaken the national government, to increase his popularity, and to enhance his probability of success in a next election campaign where he shall be nominated as a senator or deputy or vice president and even president.

As a consequence of this fact, it is necessary to point out that the most important cases of habeas corpus have had political implications, and the public follows them with keen interest. Cases of persons arrested in connection with ordinary offenses generally do not arouse the interest of public opinion, and many of them are ignored altogether.

THE REQUEST FOR RELEASE

Besides the habeas corpus remedy proper, our code of criminal proceedings offers another remedy to persons illegally arrested or detained. Article 418 of the Code of Criminal procedure, which provides for it, reads as follows:

Any individual who, in violation of the provisions of this Code, is arrested or imprisoned may apply for his release to the judge higher than that who has decreed the deprivation of liberty. If the complaint is filed with the supreme or the superior court the president of the court shall take cognizance of same. If the deprivation of liberty has been ordered by police chiefs, police commissioners, or local commissioners (tenientes políticos), the complaints shall be brought before the criminal judges of the corresponding district. The application shall be brought in writing. Immediately after submission of the application the competent judge shall direct the appearance of the *detenu* or prisoner and shall hear his statement which shall be recorded and the record of proceedings shall be undersigned by the judge, the recording secretary and the complainant or a witness if he does not know how to sign. On the basis of this statement the judge shall request all information necessary to complete his opinion and to secure the legality of his decision, and within forty-eight hours he shall decide what he thinks lawful. His decision shall be added to the record of proceedings mentioned in the foregoing paragraph. If the deprivation of liberty proves illegal, the judge shall direct the immediate release of the complainant, and the authorities or employes charged with the custody of the detenu or prisoner shall comply with the order necessarily. The judge who has ordered the illegal arrest or detention of an individual shall be dismissed from his duties, and to this effect the judge or court that took cognizance of the petition or complaint referred to shall give immediate notice to the authority or body empowered to decree the dismissal. The judge who misuses the power granted by this article shall be liable to the same penalty of dismissal. Those charged with the custody of the prisoner who shall not comply with the order dealt with in the fifth paragraph of this article shall also be dismissed. What is provided for in the foregoing paragraphs is understood without prejudice to the criminal responsibility for the arbitrary detention.

This remedy, request for release *(recurso de libertad)*, does not originate with the Political Constitution but with the code of Criminal Procedure. In the opinion of an Ecuadorean jurist, the request for release "constitutes the second great column for the defense of individual liberty against arbitrariness. In the category of legal remedies it is of a lower quality than habeas corpus and, as far as its scope is concerned, it is more restricted."[6]

Contrary to habeas corpus, it is only the *detenu* or the prisoner who may take recourse to the request for release and not any individual. It rests on when the detention or the imprisonment has infringed the rules of the Code of Criminal Procedure. It is easy to infer that the rules are those of article 150 of the same code, the requirements for a lawful provisory detention. But there are also other rules that may be infringed, with the result of having a person under an unlawful arrest.

It is interesting to point out that this remedy is included in the code of Criminal Procedure of 1938 and was confused with the habeas corpus writ; and when twenty years later some Ecuadorean jurists discussed the subject, the opinions were conflicting until the Legislative Commission and the National Congress established definitely the request for release as a remedy independent from habeas corpus provided for by the Political Constitution.

A writer who advocates the independence of the request for release from habeas corpus draws the following conclusions:

> Habeas corpus has its judge and the request for release has another judge. Habeas corpus is an administrative remedy of a very wide scope, while the other is a more limited remedy. We must remember that habeas corpus lies against detentions, arrests or imprisonments ordered by any competent authority. The request for release applies only to cases of detention and imprisonment—not arrests—ordered by judges of the judiciary. The first one comprises the judiciary at large and, besides, extends to other branches of government like the military jurisdiction . . . As to the authority who takes cognizance of a case of habeas corpus and misuses his powers it has practically nothing to fear. On the contrary, a judge is responsible for any misuse of his powers when he takes cognizance of a request for release. The likeness of both remedies as to the personal appearance of the detenu, the hearing of the case, the examination of the documents on the basis of which he was detained, arrested, or imprisoned, are not sufficient ground for the one to exclude the other.[7]

PROSPECTS OF HABEAS CORPUS IN ECUADOR

Our personal opinion is that both habeas corpus and request for release have not yet entrenched firmly in the conscience of our people. They are remedies, and useful ones; but people look at habeas corpus as an extraordinary remedy applied for on occasion of or as a result of political events. Those who take recourse to habeas corpus are as a rule leaders of political parties or individuals arrested in connection with a politcal event, a workers' strike or any disturbance of this kind. A habeas corpus hearing becomes very often a political forum where the mayor, the audience, and, by means of the press and radio, the people can listen to the most ardent speeches against the national government by prisoners and their lawyers. And very often also the mayor's decision is an outspoken or a tacit protest against the chief of state or his subordinates and agents. It is no exaggeration to say that the release or commitment of the prisoner is less important than the violence of the attacks and denunciations against the national government and, first of all, the president of the republic.

If it is not a political prisoner who takes recourse to habeas corpus, it is someone connected with a sensational event. For instance, after the burning of the building of the newspaper *El Comercio* in 1949, an Argentinian citizen was arrested; he then applied for habeas corpus. And some months ago the police arrested a group of young people who were practicing guerilla warfare in the vicinity of Quito, and among them a teacher or leader who proved to be an Argentinian citizen was also arrested. This one took recourse to habeas corpus, but the remedy was denied to him by the mayor of the capital because he found that the proceedings were legal and correct. This case was again sensational because many people believed that the Cuban embassy, Cuban and Communist agents, and foreign money and propaganda were involved, and public opinion awaited important international disclosures.

This is sufficient proof that habeas corpus is still regarded as an extraordinary remedy in important cases and for important people. It is not yet a popular remedy, so to say, resorted to by everybody who is illegally arrested or thinks he is illegally arrested as a result of ordinary offenses. As long as habeas corpus is a political weapon to intimidate the national government and its authorities and agents, it will not be a popular remedy. It is still an expensive remedy because political prisoners are generally well-to-do people, opponents of the government who can afford to pay high fees to the best attorneys—politically biased also—and who prepare pleadings that are tantamount to speeches delivered by the most uncompromising opponents in a parliament. Probably this kind of speeches and pleadings were heard when habeas corpus was first established under the Tudor kings, but this is a real proof that habeas corpus in Ecuador is yet at an earlier stage of development. As far as request for release *(recurso de libertad)* is concerned, although it is an older remedy than habeas corpus, it has not the salient features of the latter; and, for all practical purposes, we can maintain that it has been superseded by the habeas corpus writ.

AN INTERNATIONAL WRIT OF HABEAS CORPUS

On this background of protection of personal liberty in Ecuador, we have long been interested in the proposal of World Habeas Corpus by Luis Kutner that seeks to establish world protection of personal liberty in a world of diverse systems of public order. Kutner's proposal is designed undoubtedly to introduce a revolutionary change in the protection of personal liberty by means of an international writ of habeas corpus and the establishment of an international court of habeas corpus, and circuit courts, whose division would correspond not only to geographical propinquity but also to the main diversities in legal tradition, culture, religion, and history.

From this corner of the world where we live and observe the events, it is rather urgent to assess the opportunity and immediate necessity of the author's proposal for the protection of personal liberty. No doubt that Cuba, Tibet, Hungary, the countries behind the Iron Curtain, etc., are what we call "neuralgic points" of the world that badly need direct protection of an international nature to assist thousands and thousands of people illegally arrested or imprisoned, tried, tortured, persecuted, or killed. Mr. Kutner's proposal certainly tends to assist them. If it could be implemented on an international basis, it should be a blessing for those who live terrorized by police states.

But we want to speak for Ecuador. We even dare not speak for Latin-American countries although our legal tradition, culture, religion, and history are more or less the same. Contrary to a general opinion, most Latin-American countries do not know one another, or their knowledge is deficient and superficial. We know much more of the United States, France, Italy, Spain, than of Brazil, Paraguay, Guatemala, etc. By a natural tendency we are more interested in big and advanced countries than those which are on the same stage as we are. For this very reason we are very cautious in generalizing our observations on Mr. Kutner's proposal to other Latin-American countries.

NEED FOR A CHANGE IN CONCEPTION

From the point of view of the doctrine of international law, we think that the author's proposal requires a radical change of a conception that has been rooted a long time among jurists, statesmen, and students of international law, namely that international law is concerned with states, independent and semi-independent, colonies, ethnic groups, national minorities, and so on, but not with the individual as such. So far the individual has been the concern of other branches of law, but international law has considered the individual when he represents a member of the community of nations.

It is true in the last decades a certain change in conception is taking place of which the best fruits are the Universal Declaration of the Human Rights and the U.N. Treaty on Genocide. It is also true that the number of international treaties and conventions dealing with economic, social, and labor matters are increasing every day, to the extent that we can say that inter-American relations especially are more and more centering around economic, social, and labor matters. But we are not far from a stage of international law on which the individual, that is his rights, are preserved and guaranteed by both international and municipal law.

The precondition for the materialization of Luis Kutner's proposal is an advanced degree of evolution of international law where the states or the community of nations have created an appropriate machinery for the preservation of personal liberty and the application of coercive measures against those states, or their authorities, which impair personal liberty. As a matter of fact, no state has reached that high stage; but gradually we are approaching it, if not all states some of them at least.

SOVEREIGNTY AND NONINTERVENTION OR INTERDEPENDENCE

This theoretical consideration has a practical and very important consequence. If the states have not reached the stage described above, they are not prepared either to accept the interference of an international organization in what they call their internal affairs. Countries with a long democratic tradition would of course gladly sacrifice a part of their sovereignty for the sake of a high standard of international justice and a full preservation of personal liberty.

But newly independent states in Africa and Asia are very proud and jealous of their national independence, so we think they should be convinced to accept an interference such as the proposed international court of habeas corpus implies. Needless to say that totalitarian states like those behind the Iron Curtain might resist this kind of international court of habeas corpus and the international writ of habeas corpus, not exactly because they are jealous of their national sovereignty but because they are afraid of disclosing to an international commission their inner weaknesses and the arbitrariness on which their legal, political, and economic systems are founded.

In Latin-American countries this matter, sovereignty v. interdependence, is of a tremendous importance. Theoretically, every day our statesmen and diplomats are proclaiming that the conception of absolute sovereignty and independence is obsolete and that the time has arrived for the new conception of a fruitful interdependence of states for the progress and welfare of their peoples. Every day they are proclaiming and requesting the financial and technical assistance of industrially advanced countries to overcome the present stage of economic and social underdevelopment. And every day we are trying new forms of association and cooperation like free zones of trade, common market, and customhouse union to promote the exploitations of our resources to our benefit. Yet all these new forms of association imply the renunciation of a part of our sovereignty and independence.

On the other hand, the very existence of the inter-American system is founded on the respect and equality among states and on the principle of nonintervention in the internal affairs of the members of our regional community. This is a reality which we cannot ignore and that has been very often the source of misunderstandings and disputes in this continent.

The inter-American system carries thus two conflicting principles within itself. The American states proclaim constantly that they aim at the full exercise of representative government by means of democratic and genuine elections. A just application of this principle presupposes the possibility that the regional organization may intervene whenever a member government denies its people the right to elect their representatives in free, genuine, and secret elections; whenever a member government assumes dictatorial powers or uses terrorist and repressive methods against its own people. But as soon as the regional organization tries to take a step in this direction, the dictator, or the de facto government affected, invokes the principle of absolute sovereignty and nonintervention in what they regard as internal affairs of their exclusive jurisdiction. They flatly refuse any right to fact-finding commissions that may try to investigate a dispute or a violation of rights and reject any recommendation or suggestion aimed at the restoration of individual guarantees and rights.

Some of the state members have even threatened with the withdrawal from the inter-American system if the other American states insist in the application of friendly measures designed to restore the gradual exercise of the democratic government. We have cases so recent and blatant that we are relieved of mentioning them here. Even the action of the United Nations is also impaired by the existence of the Organization of American States, for whenever on the request of an American state the United Nations wanted to intervene directly, the O.A.S. alleged that it has exclusive jurisdiction on inter-American relations and has immediately taken cognizance of a case.

These are the main difficulties for the establishment and effective functioning of an international court of habeas corpus in this area of the world. We sincerely want to see that these difficulties are solved or eliminated in a future as near as possible.

Notes

1. Political Constitution, part II, chapter XIII, article 151:
   "The Constitution guarantees the inhabitants of Ecuador, mainly, the following rights: (8) The right to habeas corpus. Any individual who on the assumption of infringement of the foregoing provisions, believes that he is unlawfully detained, tried or imprisoned, may take recourse by himself or by anybody on his behalf to the authority appointed by stature. This authority shall direct that the detenu shall appear before him, and his decree shall be complied with by all who keep jails or arrest posts. Upon examination of the case he shall decree his immediate release, or he shall cause the legal rights to be restored, or he shall commit the detenu to the competent judge. He shall try the case summarily, correcting any mistake by himself or referring it to the competent official for correction.
2. Public Law for Habeas Corpus, 1933, given by the Congress of the Republic of Ecuador.
3. Political Constitution (April 1945), article 141: (5) . . . The state guarantees: The right to habeas corpus. . . .
4. Political Constitution, 1946, chapter II, On ordinary individual guarantees,

article 187: The state guarantees the inhabitants of Ecuador: (4) The right to habeas corpus. . . .

5. Amendment to the public law on local governments, November 27, 1948, article 35.

6. Public Law for Habeas Corpus, 1933.

7. Ibid.

The Legal Ultimate for The Unity of Mankind*

By Luis Kutner**

World Habeas Corpus . . . the difference between civilization and tyranny.

Sir Winston Churchill†

We in this country, in this generation are—by destiny rather than choice—the watchmen on the walls of world freedom.

John F. Kennedy††

It is Fitting that, in this 750th anniversary year of the Magna Charta, the cardinal principles of justice, based on impartial judicial administration, should now be on the threshold of internationalization. Long prior to 1215, and with sickening repetition subsequent thereto, justice was delayed and denied. Indi-

* Presented at the Inter-American Bar Association and American Bar Association Conference, San Juan, Puerto Rico, May 20-28, 1965.
** Member, Illinois Bar; president, Commission for International Due Process of Law; author of World Habeas Corpus, Due Process of Economy, Due Process of Outer Space Law, Habeas Proprietatem, and other proposals; former lecturer and associate professor of law, Yale University; lecturer University of Chicago Law School and others; former consul for Ecuador; former consul general for Guatemala.
† Meeting at Claridge's, London, 1950.
†† From President John F. Kennedy's last undelivered address, Dallas, Texas, November 22, 1963.

vidual grievances have been lost in the quicksand of sovereign indifference. The concept that the individual is no longer an object of international law, but the subject thereof, has yet to be concretely implemented before an authoritative and competent international tribunal.

Within a short time, there will be published a world law code sponsored by the World Peace Through Law Center. Publication will coincide with the Washington World Conference. The code will contain the text of all treaties of general application, the expansions of the flesh of the U.N. Charter, and probably the treaties which have been ratified by at least twenty-five nations. The vanguard of legal thinking will structuralize the lengthening shadow of legal concepts concerned with the collective responsibility of guaranteeing and preserving the integrity and dignity of man. It will forecast that principles are giving way to enforceable laws.

WORLD PUBLIC ORDER

It should be a matter of great pride for the lawyers of the world concerned with international law that they are exercising virile leadership in overcoming diplomatic reluctance and ambiguity. The delicate veil of international affairs is being pierced in the progress towards a world realistically engaged in waging the peace, where human beings may grow to their full stature without hurtful interference by their native state or international aggressor. International, hemispheric and regional bar associations are mutually concerned with the exercise of judicial power in the enforcement of law in the world community. The limited activity of the International Court of Justice, notwithstanding its availability for the juridical settlement of controversies arising between sovereign states, is giving way to the idea that the settlement of international disputes must build a library of precedent law.

The annihilation of approximately one hundred million human beings since 1917, and the nationalization and expropriation of foreign investments by emerging new nations, beg the question as to need for international judicial machinery to provide available remedies against personal detention and seizure of property without due process of law.

International organizations, international arbitral machinery, and the international character of the International Court of Justice and the European Court of Human Rights offer the world states the grand opportunity of freeing themselves from national embarrassment in resisting the impleméntation of legal remedies for wrongs committed against person and property. International due process of law, bottomed on competent judicial machinery, can ultimately command respect and confidence among diverse and competitve political and legal systems.

World public order requires accessible world legal machinery. Jurisdictional acceptance must precede the knowledge of how to correct and prevent wrongs. Offenses against international law must be codified by ratified treaties so that aroused national feelings can be overcome or minimized in the event that a nation or its leaders are summoned before an impartial international tribunal. In due course, the conscience and intelligence of mankind will attain the stature of accepting international jurisdiction as a matter of course. By this method nations can reach the dignity of being recognized as civilized. Groundless fears of those who are still laboring under the delusion of invasions of sovereignty will be abdicated in favor of affirmative, simple, and fair legal procedures furnished by international statute-treaties.

A LEGAL BEACHHEAD

The concept of World Habeas Corpus was first proposed in 1931. The catalyst was Hitler's *Mein Kampf* and the exposure of the author to the oral and written sppeches of Joseph Goebbels, Hermann Goering, Ernest Roehm, and Adolph Hitler. The author was frustrated in attempting to sound the alarm to the Nazi blueprint for human decimation and in attempting to create a rule of law, a personal legal beachhead for mankind. The inevitability of the rising tidal wave of national socialism was clear to few men in its expiation of German guilt in World War I, repudiation of the Treaty of Versailles, and determination to create a bloodbath in order to cleanse the guilt.[1] The monstrosity of the Nazi mentality was not comprehended. The Jews were to be removed from Germany. *Mein Kampf* spelled out the blueprint for all the world to see. Arbitrary detention and murder was to be the order of the day. The love of law was to be flouted. But the conscience of the world remained sound asleep.

At the International Bar Association Conference in Mexico City, during the summer of 1964, the author presented an exhaustive paper on World Habeas Corpus and International Extradition.[2]

The consensus of the Mexico conference was, as the author urged, that there should be broader remedies for the protection of individual human rights than those which the extradition process affords. The following resolution was passed:

> This first Plenary Session of the Tenth Biennial Conference of the International Bar Association recommends to the Council of the IBA that they should request all the Association's affiliated bodies to proceed with studies of the laws of extradition and habeas corpus (and similar procedures in relation thereto), in their own countries with a view to formulating proposals which in particular may effect improvements in:
>
> (a) Making available recourse to judicial controls where executive use is made of immigration and deportation powers in cases where the appropriate procedure would be the extradition process.
>
> (b) The possibility of making available as an ultimate remedy in appropriate cases to a person unjustly affected by the extradition process, access to some extra national tribunal; bearing in mind that this session considers that habeas corpus and similar procedures in relation to extradition are merely a facet of the wider and universal problem of the effective protection of human rights.

A REALISTIC CONCEPT

The concept of World Habeas Corpus is based on the premise that man is the subject and ultimate beneficiary of domestic and international law, and should have the liberty, integrity, and freedom of his person guarded and guaranteed by regional accessible international courts created by the constitutionally ratified world treaty-statute without impairment of the sovereignty of each signatory state. There is little need for argument to establish the fact that there has been a systematic and deliberate denial of human rights which has a direct relationship to the preservation of world peace. Peace and security cannot be assured in a world where people who are denied their individual rights are pressed to measures of violence against their oppressors.[3]

In sponsoring the concept of World Habeas Corpus, Dean Roscoe Pound stated that "all states need not be merged in a great world state, in which their personality is lost, in order that their conduct may be inquired into and ordered by authority of a world legal order."[4] In support of the same concept, Honorable William J. Brennan, Jr., has stated:

The all-important—indeed the most important—end of a world rule of law, the securing of individual liberty, can be obtained without the creation of a world state.

All that seems necessary is that the United Nations signatories ordain by a simple treaty statute a structure and scheme for securing international due process of the nature of national due process familiar to every American: a prompt and speedy trial; legal assistance, including assistance for the indigent; prohibition of any kind of undue coercion or influence; freedom to conduct one's defense; the right to a public trial and written proceedings; the presumption of innocence and the burden upon the State to prove guilt beyond a reasonable doubt; security against cruel and unusual punishments. These standards of due process, and thus of effective justice, only words now in the Universal Declaration of Human Rights, have their counterparts in our own U.S. Constitution. The vital difference, however, is that our nation has vitalized them for our people through a national forum and a national procedure for their enforcement. . . .

Why should we not internationalize the writ of habeas corpus along these lines to enforce the guarantees of the Universal Declaration of Human Rights? The research . . . has demonstrated that it can be done. Professor Kutner has performed an invaluable service for the world in blueprinting a plan for world habeas corpus including a judicial structure and a procedure. He proposes doing this within the present United Nations structure through a treaty-statute. It is a concrete program whereby the now only morally binding Universal Declaration of Human Rights would be made, by the voluntary consent of the nations of the world, a legally binding commitment enforcible in an international court of habeas corpus which would function through appropriately accessible regional courts. Regional world attorneys general would either prosecute or resist application for the writ. Of perhaps equal or greater importance, in the reflection of what happens in our States under the regime of Federal habeas corpus, the sovereign nations would commit themselves to enforce the guarantees of the Declaration in their own tribunals, authorizing review of their decisions by the international court of habeas corpus. Thus individuals would have relief in the international tribunal only upon a proper showing either that relief was wrongly denied under available remedies in the courts of the member state, or that that state provided no such remedies.[5]

THE MEXICO CONFERENCE

It was the consensus at the Mexico Conference of the International Bar Association that individual security, vis-à-vis national security, is meaningless except in terms of international security. To carry the syllogism further, the securing of human liberty becomes a problem international in scope. Safe-guarding individuals, whether they are citizens or aliens, against arbitrary actions of a host state has been subject to repeated frustration. One need not belabor the more than 40,000,000 human beings extinguished by the Soviets since 1917, the 26,000,000 by the Red Chinese, the 6,000,000 Jews and 2,000,000 Catholics by the Nazis, and the millions of others unrecorded by various unilateral tyrannies, to emphasize the urgency of international implementation of human rights which heretofore has been looked upon as a matter essentially within the jurisdiction of the sovereign state. Uncontrolled naked force is out of place in an era which seeks to create protective cloaks of international charters and agreements, or in a world which gives more than lip service to the concept of respect for human dignity. Past efforts of various conventions to protect human rights have proven abortive because of the multiple and competing systems of public order which prevail. The Communist order in eastern Europe and Asia and in the Caribbean must be considered in addition to the basic legal systems of the National Chinese, Hindu, Japanic, Germanic, Slavic, Mohammedan, Romanesque, and Anglican nations.[6] The contemporary world, ever growing with continued explorations of outer space, angrily suggests that any hesitancy in creating a world rule of law is fraught with the peril of human extinction. Military and economic coercion has become unrealistic and intolerant. The global community must not delay in the subjugation of coercion to authoritative and sanctionable human rights.

The time scale of humanity, catapulting 340,000 years of man's development and 50,000 years of man's recorded history, surviving and absorbing extinguished ancient civilizations, evolving 2,000 years of Christianity and more than 5,000 years of Judaism, has achieved the intensity of the moment of decision. Iron Curtains cannot check the invasion of ideas of liberty. As Thomas Paine wrote,

> An army of principles will penetrate where an army of soldiers cannot. It will succeed where diplomatic management would fail; neither the Rhine, the Channel, nor the ocean can avert its progress; it will march on the horizon of the world, and it will conquer.[7]

THE ROOTS ARE DEEP

World Habeas Corpus is a tangible recognition of the need to codify the principle that man is born with certain inalienable rights. The roots are deep. The parliament of man is obligated to the great events leading up to the decalogue of Moses, the Talmudic recordings, the events leading up to the Magna Charta, the rational propaganda of Jean Jacques Rousseau, John Locke, Jacques Maritain, Thomas Jefferson, Benjamin Franklin, Samuel Adams, the English Bill of Rights, the first Habeas Corpus Act of 1679, the Bills of Rights in the colonial American state constitutions, the French Declaration of Rights of Man and Citizens (1789), the first ten amendments to the Constitution of the United States (the so-called Bill of Rights, 1791), the Declaration of Independence, the Atlantic Charter, the conferences at Moscow, Cairo, Teheran, and Dunbarton Oaks, the drafting conferences of the U.N. Charter at San Francisco (April-June 1945), the Universal Declaration of Human Rights, the Genocide Convention, the European Convention for the Protection of Human Rights and Fundamental Freedoms (28 November 1950), the European Court of Human Rights, the European Commission of Human Rights, and the United Nations Philippine meeting on Human Rights, (17-28 February 1958), to name but a few.

The concept that individuals should have an equal capacity to act on the international level with that of international organizations is today *a fait accompli*. Sovereignty arguments are overcome in the thousands of mixed arbitral tribunal decisions, International Court of Justice judgments and orders, in the organizational capacity to sue and be sued, to make contracts, to hold property, and in organizational liability to or immunity from judicial process.[8]

THE UNIVERSAL POSTAL UNION

One of the great international organizations of all time is the Universal Postal Union.

H. G. Wells once said, [it] "is surely something that should be made part of the compulsory education of every statesman and publicist." When it was established in the 1870s, there was little experience to serve as a guide. Free from the influence of political considerations—largely because of its subject matter—and unbound by previous models, the organization sought matter-of-factly to create an appropriate pattern of operation.[9]

It has been said that the history of international postal service is the real story of civilization—of discovery, exploration, and conquest, of international trade and of settlement in new lands. Since the dawn of civilization, communication in one form or another is known to have existed. From the relays of horsemen used by King Darius of Persia in 500 B.C. to those used by the pony express in 1859, postal service has been a vital cog in the machinery of civilization.[10] The international union and uniformity of rates between countries reached its grand congress at the Paris Conference in May 1863, where an international agreement was set out along the lines of the Austro Postal Union in 1842. Toward the end of 1868, the Universal Postal Union, composed of the entire civilized world, commenced to be structuralized. A General Postal Union was finally concluded at that time between the European Middle East countries and the United States. The Universal Postal Congress, administered by an executive council, consultative committees, and an international bureau, and working in harmony with the United Nations and other international organizations,[11] has been more than effective in emphasizing the fact that the international organization for standardization has become the ultimate in blending national autonomy with aspects of supranationality. The question of the surrender of sovereignty is not raised, and any dispute is submitted to the International Bureau for final arbitration.

The reasons underlying the peaceful existence of the Universal Postal Union imply greater reasons for human dignity and liberty via World Habeas Corpus. It is not an exaggeration to say that this organization has become the indispensable element in the business, social, and political life of contemporary civilization. Its international mechanisms have stimulated many innovations of international relations, and it has become a durable supranational governmental institution, rendering obsolete the arguments against surrendering sovereignty.[12]

THE EVOLUTION OF THE LAW

The law, as an ancient and venerable institution, has now evolved to the concrete stage at which human beings can have adequate and genuine representation in the international community. The reasons are no longer obscure, nor are they tenuous, even in this day of precarious world relationships and competing political systems. Civilizations can endure only if they produce the institutions of justice and rules of law in creating binding and responsible international capacities. The common ground on which all civilizations meet is that they are composed of human beings. International personalities may be in flux, but the "subjects of international law are—like the subjects of national law—individual human beings."[13]

The experience of states in protecting individuals against arbitrary deprivation of liberty has been exhaustively presented in previous writings of the author.[14] Article 9 of the Universal Declaration of Human Rights reads, *inter alia,* "No one shall be subject to arbitrary arrest, detention or exile."[15] The legal tradition of procedural remedies similar to habeas corpus forms part of the law in less than one-third of the signatory members of the United Nations.[16] The actual efficacy of the principles of World Habeas Corpus is in the process of building citational precedent in the recently emerged states admitted to the United Nations.[17]

The code of criminal procedure of the U.S.S.R. contains several provisions with respect to the integrity of the person. Optimism is increasing that the promise may be fulfilled in fact (art. 6, art. 138, art. 158). A most illuminating note is found in the Soviet Penal Code, article 115:

> The illegal arrest of any person, or illegally compelling a person to appear before judicial or investigatory authorities [is punished with] deprivation of liberty for a term not exceeding one year. Compelling a person under interrogation to give evidence by use of illegal methods on the part of the person conducting the interrogation; holding a person in custody, as a preventive measure, for personal reasons or from motives of self-interest [is punished with] deprivation of liberty for a term not exceeding five years.[18]

In Tokyo, Japan, in 1960, the Seminar on the Role of Substantive Criminal Law in the Protection of Human Rights and the Purposes and Legitimate Limits of Penal Sanctions was organized by the United Nations in cooperation with the government of Japan.[19] The consensus of the seminar was that remedies should be available to individuals whose human rights had been infringed upon, and that substantive criminal law could insure the protection of human rights as set forth in the Charter of the United Nations, in the Universal Declaration of Human Rights, and in national constitutions. The seminar, together with the Seminar on the Protection of Human Rights under Criminal Law and

Procedure in Santiago, Chile, in 1958, spelled out the collective responsibility of all nations for establishing a competent legal implementation of the rights which protect the individual from wrongful accusation and illegal or arbitrary arrest and detention.

WORLD PEACE THROUGH LAW

The Athens World Conference on World Peace Through the Rule of Law[20] demonstrated beyond a peradventure of doubt that lawyers the world over could play the dominant role in substituting the rule of law for the rule of force in international relations. The agreements reached and the program adopted emphasized that law must replace force and that the world must find concrete means to obtain this objective. The program adopted strengthens optimism that international legal institutions, through the expansion of international law, can maintain the peace.

The plenary and working sessions amply buttressed the multifaceted approach of world peace through law, with topics ranging from *Pacem in Terris* to increasing the use and usefulness of the International Court of Justice, the creation and jurisdiction of stabilized courts, law rules to encourage international investment, law to facilitate economical areas of trade, incresing the scope and effectiveness of arbitration and consultation, and other means of resolving any disputes, developing law rules and legal institutions for disarmament programs, creating law for outer space and space communications, the United Nations and political regional organizations as the source of law rules and legal institutions, international cooperation and legal education and research, encouraging international unification of private law, organizing lawyers internationally for effective cooperative action, stating the general principles of international law, and structuralizing a world legal order based on law and laws in relation to world law. The Athens World Conference is a fulfilment of the prophecy of Roscoe Pound that "we cannot expect the development of human nature to stop where we now find it."[21]

It becomes almost trite to assert that law is the only discipline that can and actually does dominate all other disciplines in dealing with man, property, or nations. Today there are afoot the manifest forces making for universality in law. As Roscoe Pound suggested:

Shall we say that today there is quest of a universal regime of justice? May we conceive of law as transcending and putting limits to organized force? Does our quest of a universal justice involve a quest of universal law? Is a law of the world possible?

Since the Hebrew prophets men have dreamed of a general and perpetual peace. In the modern world this has taken the form of a planned legal order; a world wide regime of adjusting relations and ordering conduct under the control of some agency of organized society. But force is wasteful, and there are ethical and economic objections to even an ideal universal regime of force. All experience shows that the regime of forcible maintenance of peace and order is likely to get out of hand and work mischief. But we are thinking of an ideal regime for an actual world and must take for granted something from which the ideal regime may derive efficacy for its purpose.

Must the effectuating agency of necessity take the form of a politically organized society? This is generally assumed. Since the sixteenth century there has been a rooted belief that organized force of a politically organized society was a necessary prerequisite of a regime of justice. Hence plans for a universal regime of justice have taken the form of plans for a world wide political organization—a universal super-state.

Plans for universal peace since the "grand design" of King Henry IV of France in 1603 have been many. They have been religious or political or consensual.

In the nineteenth century these were succeeded by a system of particular arbitrations and later by general plans of arbitration of particular disputes. These presupposed a doubtfully existent international law, or where there were special treaties for arbitration, often formulated certain rules for the case in hand. In the present century we have seen what may be called embryo super-states projected, partly political and partly judicial.

Behind these plans toward a universal peace we may see two conflicting ideas: the Germanic cult of the local, self-governing community—what Beseler called Kleinstaatismus, or, as I translate it "Mainstreetism"—and what came to be the Roman belief in a universal empire.

Have we not since the seventeenth century, which was obsessed by the Roman autocratic universal state, expected a universal political organization to bring about a universal justice according to law, whereas perhaps the law must come before the regime of adjudication, not so much however, in the form of rules as in the form of universally recognized principles.

. . . What seems most significant is the general giving up of the extreme localism of the Anglo-American lawyer of the last century. There was and there long had been a cult of the local law. Every one seemed to hold as a matter of course that the law of the time and place had a sufficient basis in the local political sovereignty and was to be thought of in terms of that sovereignty. Its basis in an independent political sovereignty justified it and all its details.[22]

In a recent article Henry Luce quoted Lord Hailsham's expectations for the future: "I see a world where freedom under law is the rule and not the exception for mankind. In that world the sums now spent on arms are devoted to education and research, to the elimination of disease, to the rescue of deserts from the sand ... and to the enjoyment of the good things of life by the suffering millions of mankind."[23]

Philip C. Jessup admirably referred to Baron von Asbeck's vision of the purpose of the study of international law: " 'To explore how the present law has come to be what it is, how it is involved in a process of reform and extension and intensification, in order that we may be able to assist in the building, stone upon stone, in storm and rain, of a transnational legal order for states and peoples and men.' "[24]

Justice Jessup continued: "It is indeed true that 'no one is asking for a complete rejection of what we know as international law. No one is asking that the books be burned and that we start afresh in rejection of the lessons history has given as to the rules which minimize friction.' In his distinguished contribution to the series of lectures in honor of Dag Hammarskjöld, Secretary General U Thant made a plea for a world 'made safe for diversity,' and the same plea was echoed by the President of the United States in his State of the Union message. In a world so oriented, none need despair that there will be general international realization of the common interest or that the timeless tide will flow toward uniformity in the law of nations."[25]

AMPARO

Another procedural remedy designed to secure personal liberty is *amparo*, which first attained its juridical maturity in Mexico.[26] Amparo (deriving from the Spanish word *amparar* which means to aid or help) is a summary legal procedure used not only to prevent a violation of personal liberty but also to prevent any infringement of individual constitutional rights by any law or authority whatever. For example, it is the proper recourse against slavery, arbitrary detention, or any restrictions upon freedom of thought, speech, press, assembly, education, or choice of occupation.[27] The function of amparo is to restore the injured party to the full enjoyment of his liberties "by means of reconstituting the situation to its former state if the act complained of were a positive one, or if the act were negative, by obligating the authority to respect the guarantee and to comply with that which such guarantee demands.[28] Amparo is of a much broader nature than the writ of habeas corpus and combines many features of such Anglo-Saxon writs as habeas corpus, mandamus, and certiorari.[29]

Mexico and Chile have not adopted the institution of habeas corpus but use amparo to secure individual personal liberty. Although Costa Rica, Guatemala, and Panama provide for the writ of habeas corpus, they also have amparo to cover those cases where habeas corpus does not lie.

A. *Who may file an application for amparo?* These states give the right to petition for amparo to everyone;[30] such petition may also be filed by any person acting on behalf of another.[31]

B. *With respect to whom may the writ be brought?* Chile offers relief through amparo only to those who have been illegally arrested, indicted, or imprisoned.[32] In Costa Rica,[33] Guatemala,[34] Panama,[35] and Mexico,[36] amparo is available whenever anyone's constitutional rights are threatened by an official act.

C. *For what type of acts in violation of what standards?* Under Mexican law amparo may be granted in civil and labor cases as well as in criminal matters if any basic constitutional guarantee has been violated.[37] It is proper recourse against any application of the penalties prohibited by article 22 of the Mexican Constitution (prohibitions against cruel and unusual punishment, excessive bail, etc.). It also lies on behalf of anyone who is threatened with deportation, exile, or loss of life or personal freedom by an official act other than a judicial proceeding.[38] Amparo can be used only against official acts or laws; it does not lie for actions of private individuals.[38] It is, however, the correct remedy against administrative decisions that cause damage that cannot be repaired by means of an appeal or a legal defense.[40]

The scope of protection afforded by amparo is essentially the same in Costa Rica, Guatemala, and Panama as it is in Mexico.[41] In Chile, however, the writ of amparo is primarily directed toward

securing certain specified rights to detained persons;[42] thus
Chilean amparo seems to resemble habeas corpus more closely than
does Mexico's.

D. *By what procedures?* Amparo may be sought in Mexico only
when no other judicial recourse is available and when the petitioner is threatened with an irreparable injury.[43] The laws regarding
the use of amparo in penal matters are rather similar to the rules
concerning criminal appeals under U.S. law.[44] To prevent the
possibility that a person may simply be detained in prison without
ever being given the chance to present his case to a judge, the
Mexican Constitution requires that upon the expiration of a maximum of ninety-nine hours after the initial arrest, every detained
person must be released unless the jailer has received a formal
judicial order for commitment of the prisoner. Any official who
fails to comply with this provision is subject to penal sanctions.[45]

An amparo proceeding is initiated in Guatemala by filing a
petition for such relief;[46] where desirable, the judge may hold the
hearing in the place of detention.[47] In Chile, an application for
amparo must be given priority over all other cases and the court
must decide the matter within twenty-four hours.[48] In addition,
the Chilean Code of Criminal Procedure requires that five days
after the initial arrest, a detained person must either be released or
formally charged with an offense.[49]

E. *Orders the court may make.* Mexican law obligates the court in
an amparo case to make such orders as are necessary to restore the
petitioner to the full enjoyment of his individual constitutional
rights. However, the court may declare a law unconstitutional
only insofar as its application to the particular case is concerned;
such a decision cannot affect the general constitutionality of the
statute.[50]

A decision to grant amparo in Guatemala has the effect of
immediately suspending the illegal order or official act and discon-
tinuing the effect of such measure,[51] but such decision is not *res
judicata.*[52] Chilean judges in amparo cases have several alternatives.
They may correct any legal defects themselves or may report such
defects to the authority who should correct them. In addition, the
judge may either order the *detenu* immediately released or place
him at the disposal of the proper court.[53]

F. *Enforcement of amparo decisions.* Aside from the general provisions enabling courts to enforce any of their orders, the constitution of Guatemala specifically provides that any act which impedes, restricts or in any way obstructs the exercise of the right of amparo is punishable.[54] Legal responsibility is imposed upon any court that fails to entertain a petition for amparo.[55] The laws of the Federal District of Mexico expressly forbid the police to arrest anyone who has been released under amparo.[56]

This analysis shows that personal liberty may be protected by amparo as adequately as by habeas corpus. At least on the level of formal authority, the above survey indicates that habeas corpus or its functional equivalent is presently operative in thirty-eight countries. The mere fact that these remedies are working more or less effectively in numerous states of such diverse traditions and backgrounds casts doubt upon Mr. Delignieres' contention that habeas corpus is meaningless outside a system of common law.

Structure of the Proposed International Court of Habeas Corpus

In order to root such international protection in the diverse patterns of law, the world should be divided into nine circuits (or arenas). Aside from the practical consideration of geographical proximity, the delineation of these circuits ought to correspond approximately to the main diversities in legal traditions, culture, religion, and history.[57] A circuit court of habeas corpus would be located in each one of these regions and hear cases arising within its own arena. The following circuits would be established:[58]

1. The Communist-Orient Circuit—Communist China, North Viet-Nam, Outer Mongolia, and North Korea;

2. The U.S.S.R.-Eastern Europe Circuit—the Soviet Union and the Communist states of eastern Europe, including Yugoslavia;

3. The Western Europe Circuit—the non-Communist states of western Europe, Great Britain, Greenland, Iceland, Ireland, Cyprus, Crete, and Israel;

4. The Islamic Circuit—the Arabic states of the Middle East, Pakistan, the predominantly Moslem states of North Africa, and Algeria;

5. The Southern Africa Circuit—the African states outside the Islamic circuit;

6. The Non-Communist Orient Circuit—India, Japan, Burma,

Ceylon, Nationalist China, South Korea, Thailand, Nepal, Non-Communist Viet-Nam, excluding Indonesia and the Philippines;

7. The Austral-Oceanic Circuit—Australia, the Philippines, New Zealand, the South Sea Islands, Indonesia, etc.;

8. The Latin American Circuit—all Latin states within the Western Hemisphere, including Cuba, Haiti, the Dominican Republic, etc.; and

9. The Anglo-American Circuit—Canada, the United States, Puerto Rico, and British and North American possessions in the West Indies.[59]

This proposed division sacrifices the unity of the British Commonwealth legal system for the sake of regional contiguity; still, it may be noted that the Commonwealth members have been placed in circuits in which the other states have been considerably influenced by Anglo-American jurisprudence, as in the case of Australia and the Philippines or India and Japan. In case of a dispute regarding the arena to which a nation should belong, the state involved should have the right to make the final decision. As power alignments in the world community change, a state should likewise be free to shift to the circuit of its choice.

Presiding over the entire world would be a supreme international court of habeas corpus to hear appeals from the circuit courts.

COMPOSITION OF THE TRIBUNALS

A. *The Circuit Courts.* Each circuit court should be composed of seven judges, of whom at least four must be nationals of a state located within the arena over which the particular circuit court has jurisdiction. Of course, it may be objected that this proposal already "packs the court" in favor of the decisions of the national governments within any one arena, but such a compromise seems essential if there is to be a possibility of states agreeing to participate in this type of international tribunal. In addition, this scheme will insure that the decisions of the courts develop in accord with the realities of the conditions existing within the individual arenas.

To reflect accurately the relative basis of power (people, resources, and territory) within the arena, at least one national from each of the world's predominant states should sit as a judge in the circuit court having jurisdiction over that state. Thus, on the U.S.S.-R.-Eastern Europe Circuit Court, one judge must be a citizen of the Soviet Union; in the Communist-Orient Circuit, one judge would be from mainland China; in the Western Europe Circuit, one judge should be French and one judge British; in the Anglo-American Circuit, one judge from the United States; in the Non-Communist Orient Circuit, one judge must be Indian and one judge Japanese; and on the Austral-Oceania Circuit Court, one judge from the Philippines and one from Australia.

The remaining judges on each circuit court must be chosen from states outside the territory of the arena in question. To avoid undesirable duplication in philosophies, the other three judges on the U.S.S.R.-Eastern Europe Circuit would have to be nationals of states outside both that circuit and outside the Communist-Orient Circuit. The additional three judges on the Communist-Orient Circuit should be likewise from nations outside both this circuit and the U.S.S.R.-Eastern Europe Circuit. In exchange for this concession, it should be agreed that at least one judge on the Anglo-American Circuit Court will be a citizen of 'a Communist state.

To obtain a list of candidates for these judicial positions, each nation which is a member of the court system should submit three names of outstanding jurists of their country. From these lists, the member nations within an individual circuit-arena should select four judges who are nationals of states within the arena (local judges) and three from outside the arena (nonlocal judges) to constitute the circuit court for their region. If the states within a particular circuit cannot reach an agreement as to who the judges shall be, then they should be chosen by lot from the respective lists of "local" nominees and "nonlocal" nominees.

From the remaining candidates not appointed to any of the circuit courts, the judges of each circuit court shall select seven nominees from outside their arena (nonlocal judges) to sit within that circuit as screening judges, i.e., to determine whether a petition discloses a *prima facie* case.

B. *The Supreme Court.* The supreme court should be composed of nine justices—one justice for each circuit-arena. The justice must be a national of a state within the circuit he represents, and he should be chosen by a simple majority vote of the judges composing the circuit tribunal for that region.

PROCEDURE OF THE TRIBUNALS

A. *Invoking the Authority of the Circuit Court.* Any detained person anywhere or any other person on his behalf may invoke the jurisdiction of the circuit court, as soon as one has been established for the region where he is confined. It would not be necessary that the state detaining him be a member of the international court of habeas corpus nor that the state involved even agree to submit to the jurisdiction of the court. It would be irrelevant whether the detaining government is considered a "state" under the technical rules of international law. However, the authorities of the detaining government would have, of course, the right to intervene before the tribunal to defend their action in detaining the petitioner, even though that nation is not a member of the court. In order for any state to interpose a defense, it must bring the detenu before the court. The refusal of a state to intervene or to permit the detenu to appear before the court in person will not prevent the tribunal from proceeding with the case and deciding on the basis of the available evidence. If the court decides the petitioner should be released, it may depend upon its own prestige and other enforcement measures to pressure the detaining authorities into compliance with its order.

B. *Exhaustion of Local Remedies.* In accord with traditional international prescription, the petitioner would have to show that he had previously exhausted all local remedies, except where such action would be obviously futile.[60] The application of this rule is necessary to bring the work of these tribunals within manageable proportions and to show some respect for state sovereignty by allowing each nation the first opportunity to provide relief. Naturally, this requirement should not be applied if the municipal laws of the state permit the prisoner to be detained without any right whatever to have his case reviewed by an impartial decision maker.

C. *Orders the Tribunal May Take.* The circuit courts should have the power to make one of three alternative decisions: (1) to continue the detention; (2) to order the petitioner released at once; or (3) if the detention is illegal due to a procedural defect, the court may, in its discretion, order the case remanded to the national courts for correction or retrial. Moreover, the circuit courts would have the power to determine only the legality of the detention of the individual petitioner; their decisions would not affect the constitutionality or validity of any municipal or state law, except insofar as the individual petitioner may be concerned. This regulation would eliminate the heart of the objection that such international courts could drastically modify the effect of domestic legislation.

D. *Voting Requirements for a Decision.* On the circuit court level, a simple majority would be sufficient to render a decision. In practice this would mean, for example, that the four "local judges" on the Communist-Orient Circuit Court would be sufficient to order a detention continued. On the other hand, the three "nonlocal" judges would have to swing only one of the "local judges" to their side in order to obtain the controlling vote.

E. *Appeals to the Supreme International Court of Habeas Corpus.* A decision by a circuit court to release the petitioner should be final and not subject to appeal. But a holding that the detention is legal and may be continued should be appealable by right to the supreme international court of habeas corpus, if three of the circuit court judges dissented from the decision of the lower court. Under this system, the three "nonlocal" judges could use their combined power against any bloc voting of the "local judges" by making such blanket decisions automatically open to review by the upper court. Where only two of the circuit court judges have dissented, the supreme court should have the power to review the case at its discretion in a manner comparable to certiorari in the United States. The upper court should also have the option to review determinations by the circuit court to remand the case to the state courts for correction.

For the supreme international court of habeas corpus to overturn the decision of the lower courts, at least six of the justices would have to vote for reversal. There should also be a presumption in favor of the reasonableness and validity of the circuit court's decision. This requirement of six votes to reverse the circuit court's judgment would again weigh the decision-making process in favor of the particular system of public order under which the petitioner is detained. Russia, for example, could have her internal decisions upheld by merely securing the vote of the justices from the U.S.S.R.-Eastern Europe Circuit, the Communist-Orient Circuit, and two other justices, e.g., from the Islamic Circuit, the Latin American Circuit or the Non-Communist Orient Circuit. On the other hand, if six or seven justices from the other circuit regions all vote to release the petitioner, it should constitute rather clear proof as to how world public opinion stands on the case. In spite of the obvious defects in this distribution of voting power, it seems the only realistic method of devising an acceptable plan for such an international tribunal.

STANDARDS AGAINST WHICH THE VALIDITY OF THE DETENTION SHOULD BE TESTED

A. *On the Circuit Court Level.* In view of the profound diversities existing among the major systems of public order, it would be futile to seek an absolute and all-inclusive definition of "arbitrary" or "illegal" detention. Instead, the circuit courts of habeas corpus should determine if, under all the factual conditions and circumstances existing within the particular arena, the continued detention of the petitioner is reasonable. What is "reasonable" will naturally vary from one arena or region to another. Implicit in this basic test of reasonableness is a balancing process which would weigh the relative importance of the values sought to be protected against the risks involved. The attention of the decision makers must be focused on all the relevant factors in context which should rationally affect the decision. As McDougal and Feliciano stated:

> The realistic function of . . . rules, considered as a whole, is, accordingly, not mechanically to dictate specific decision but to guide the attention of decision-makers to significant variable factors in typical recurring contexts of decision, to serve as summary indices to relevant crystallized community expectations and, hence, to permit creative and adaptive, instead of arbitrary and irrational, decisions.[61]

Under the category of values for which protection is claimed, the following questions should be considered:

1. What is the nature of the substantive rights for which the petitioner is asking protection (right to counsel, right to a fair trial, right to free speech, etc.) ?

2. What is the relative importance of the claimed right to individual human dignity (e.g., the right to a fair trial seems more basic to humanity than freedom of assembly) ?

3. What values are the detaining government claiming to safe-guard (public order, internal security, etc.) ?

4. How essential is the detention of this petitioner to secure the value demanded by the government in question (perspectives, identifications, and expectations of the peoples living within that arena) ?

5. Is the purpose of the conflicting claims to expand and obtain new values or to conserve and protect existing ones?

6. Do the claimants seek to expand, preserve, or narrow the substantive rights or values already guaranteed by formal authori-ty? At this point the courts should examine (a) the existing international prescription and standards, such as "denials of jus-tice," "general principles of law recognized by civilized nations," etc.,[62] as well as (b) the municipal laws of the detaining state and the relevant norms of other nations within the same system of public order.

Under the category of risks involved, the decision-makers should consider: the possible threat to the security of the state; the proba-bilities of increasing the tensions of the cold war; the risk of precipitating or expanding violence; the relative willingness of the detaining government to accept intervention by the world commu-nity and to comply with its decision, etc. In addition, the judges should consider all possible alternatives, e.g., whether the detaining state might consent to releasing the petitioner on condition that he be exiled, and the possibilities that the state would be willing to free him into the custody of another state in exchange for a prisoner held by the latter state.

Essential to this balancing process is a profound understanding of the jurisprudential system under which the particular arena operates. In the U.S.S.R.-Eastern Europe arena, the decision-makers should aim toward the greater realization of human dignity within the framework of the Marxian conception of an ideal society, whereas the judges in the Arabic region should strive toward the ideal within the structure of the Islamic religious con-ceptions, and the judges in the North American arena should attempt to perfect the Anglo-American conceptions of "equality under law," democratic constitutionalism, etc. At the present time, it would be absurd for an international habeas corpus court to try to secure the right of free speech to an anti-Communist in the Soviet Union. On the other hand, since the formal authority of the U.S.S.R. already guarantees various rights of procedural due process, she may be willing to submit to some international enforcement and gradual expansion of these procedural rights. The supervisory powers of the international court could assure that the formal guarantees in Soviet law are respected in practice, e.g., insuring that the petitioner really was accorded the right to counsel upon notification "of the termination of the investigation." The tribunal could likewise be the checking force to see that the Soviet state prosecutors actually make, within the prescribed time limit, the required decision as to whether this particular prisoner ought to be further confined. In this way the possibility could be avoided that a certain prosecutor might in advance merely hand over to the police authorities a detention order signed in blank, rather than making a careful determination in each individual case. It may thus be possible to obtain within the Soviet orbit both "due process of law" and some degree of freedom to Communists who deviate only slightly from the official policy.

In contrast, a rather high level of protection should be secured in the Latin American arena, since the formal authority (constitutions) of all these states guarantees a multitude of individual rights and liberties, and the practice of most of these states is more or less in accord with such formal authority. The recent downfall of six leading dictators in Latin America, together with the vigorous agitation against the remaining despots, shows clearly that these people are politically maturing and demanding recognition of all basic human rights. Hence, the level of development in this arena is probably sufficient to permit an international court of habeas corpus to force a recalcitrant Latin American government to grant the fundamental freedoms to its subjects. In this arena the circuit court of habeas corpus should protect even such substantive rights as the freedom of expression of thought.

Where the legal suspension of certain rights is involved (as in the Preventive Detention Act or state of siege cases), the circuit courts should make the following inquiries: Was it necessary for the security of the state to supend this *particular* right in reference to this *particular* individual? What are the allowable limits of executive discretion in this matter? Have those limits been overstepped? Mr. Vallarta suggests that even during times of emergency the following guarantees should not be suspended: the right to a full defense, the injunction against imposing punishment without a trial, the prohibition against ex post facto laws and the proscriptions against cruel and unusual punishment.[63] Other basic privileges which should be added to this list are: the right to be confronted with adverse witnesses, the right to have confessions obtained by force or by inquisitional methods thrown out of court and the right to remain silent.[64] In addition, the circuit court should decide whether the emergency which gave rise to the suspension has in fact ceased to exist, so that the individual guarantees should be considered effective again.

B. *Standard on Appeal to the Supreme International Court of Habeas Corpus.* The test for the legality of the detention which the Supreme Court should apply is not what the individual justice feels is right or fair; rather, the only question on appeal should be: under all the conditions, factors, and variables existing in the arena of the individual circuit court, was the decision of the lower court so unreasonable as to require its reversal? As stated above, there should be a presumption in favor of the lower court's decision.

If the legality of the detention is determined on the basis of the variable factual contexts existing within the particular systems of public order, the application of this test would result in different standards of protection for each arena. Probably in certain circuit-arenas the scope of human rights accorded international protection would be quite minimal at first. However, as internal conditions stabilized and economic, social, and political institutions progressed within such regions, the decision makers of the individual circuit courts could foster and encourage the evolution and expansion of the range of personal freedoms to be protected within their region.

ENFORCEMENT OF THE DECISIONS OF THE INTERNATIONAL COURT OF HABEAS CORPUS

While this proposed court system will not immediately achieve any revolutionary reforms in the area of human rights, it will serve two crucial functions: (1) provide review of individual detentions by a judicial decision maker, and (2) offer a method by which the case may be brought to the attention of the world community. The enforcement of decisions would rest primarily upon the voluntary compliance of the state involved. Since a decision would be rooted in the norms of the legal system of a particular arena, the probable incidence of willing obedience by national officials should be quite high. Past experience has shown that states generally do comply with international judicial decisions, even though no specific enforcement procedures exist.[65] In addition, the courts would be the beneficiaries of the entire force of world public opinion. Both the Poznan trials[66] and the Oatis matter[67] demonstrated its powerful effect when properly mobilized against a specific injustice.

In the event a state refuses to obey the court's orders, resort should first be had to the appropriate regional organization, if one has been established in that area.[68] For instance, in the Western Hemisphere, the circuit tribunals could invoke the authority of the Organization of American States, and in Western Europe that of the European Community or NATO, so that these bodies might make recommendations regarding sanctions to be taken against the offending nation. This arrangement again places the emphasis upon the regional development of the international court of habeas corpus in accordance with the diverse patterns of law existing in the world.

If this procedure proves ineffective, recourse could then be had to the Security Council under article 34 of the U.N. Charter, which permits that organ to "investigate any dispute, or any situation which might lead to international friction or give rise to a dispute." Where necessary, the Security Council could impose either economic or military sanctions against the recalcitrant state.[69] In case the Security Council is unable to act because of the veto, the General Assembly[70] should take jurisdiction over the matter by virtue of the Uniting for Peace Resolution.[71]

On the question of what kinds of enforcement actions these respective international organizations (regional organizations, Security Council, or General Assembly) will employ, the standard should be one of "reasonableness" in the light of all the circumstances. Under the category of risks to be considered would be the expectations of expanding violence, the degree of force necessary to accomplish the ends or goals sought, and the probable success of the action. If the decision makers determine that armed force may be met with extreme violence, then probably only the ideological, diplomatic, and economic instruments of strategy should be used.[72] Examples of diplomatic sanctions would be expulsion of the offending nation from the United Nations,[73] severing of diplomatic relations by other member states, withdrawal of privileges other states had previously granted on the basis of reciprocity to the violator-state, etc. Among the ideological measures which could be directed against a state which refused to comply with the tribunal's decision would be formal censure by international organizations, hostile propaganda against the target state, and severing of telegraphic and telephonic communications with that state. A wide variety of economic strategies might be used, including embargoes, breaking off of all trade relations with the guilty state, revocation of tariff concessions, freezing of assets located outside the territory of that state, etc.

If international organizations fail to act in a particular case, then the decision as to the application of sanctions reverts to the officials within the individual nation-states. In such event, the power elites of each state should be guided by the same standards established above for directing the decision of the world community. Secretary of State Dean Rusk said:

> It is fashionable, when discussing international adjudication, to stress its deficiencies—the lack of sanctions, the so-called primitive state of international law, and the lack of willingness to entrust political disputes to judicial settlement, to name but a few. But these alleged deficiencies have not hindered the development of international adjudication as much as is often assumed. International courts and arbitral tribunals have managed to resolve a number of contentious disputes between nations.
>
> These disputes have not resolved the great struggles of our day. However, these struggles are probably not well suited for the processes of judicial settlement in any event. Those who seek a world in which all disputes between nations are entrusted to courts for settlement seek more than we can reasonably hope to attain in today's world. There are disputes, however—important, thorny, incapable of settlement by the states concerned—which the International Court of Justice has resolved. In earlier times these disputes might not have been resolved peacefully. The lack of sanctions has not prevented compliance with the Court's rulings. The border dispute between Honduras and Nicaragua is one example. More recently, the Court disposed of a long-festering dispute between Cambodia and Thailand.
>
> But nevertheless, it is widely agreed, and rightly so, that the number of legal disputes submitted to international adjudication is too small. There are no doubt many reasons for this. The United States would like to see more nations submit to the compulsory jurisdiction of the Court. In this connection, I should add that the present Administration, like its predecessors, would like also to see the Connally Amendment repealed. Finally, we regret the reluctance of U.N. Members to

accord the International Court of Justice compulsory jurisdiction to settle disputes arising from treaties concluded under the auspices of the United Nations.

There is one area in which international adjudication has proved especially valuable and effective. I refer to the role of the International Court of Justice in rendering advisory opinions. There has developed, though not fully enough, a tradition of referring constitutional issues arising under the charters of international organizations to the Court for adjudication. More important, there has arisen also a tradition of accepting the Court's opinions as law and acting upon them.

The Court has rendered 12 advisory opinions—ten requested by the General Assembly, one by the UNESCO Executive Board, and one by the Assembly of IMCO. These opinions have been accepted by the organs which sought them and they have been given effect. They have had a marked impact on the constitutional development of international institutions, particularly on the most important institution, the United Nations.

The advisory opinion in the *Reparations* case, for example, confirmed the Organization's capacity to maintain an international claim against both Member and non-Member States for injuries suffered by its agent. The case stands for the proposition that the founding fathers conferred upon the United Nations a legal status in the world community, and this simple proposition has been important.

The Court has performed a similar service in adjusting relationships between the component parts of the Organization itself. The advisory opinion concerning the awards made by the U.N. Administrative Tribunal is a case in point. Others are the advisory opinions regarding the admission of new members.

It should not be surprising that the Court's power to issue advisory opinions has been so important—more important, perhaps, than its power to decide contentious disputes. A primary fact of post-war international life has been the growth and development of international machinery and institutions for coping with the issues of the day. When it renders advisory opinions, the Court is functioning as an integral part of this machinery. Particularly when its advisory opinions concern the United Nations—the Organization's relation to the world community and its Members, and the allocation of power between its component parts—is the Court participating in the on-going institutional processes which characterize international life today. In this role, the Court has a clearly defined job and is uniquely suited to perform it. The issues tend to be framed more cogently, and the standards for solving them developed more fully, than when the issues are settled without benefit of the Court's participation.

I would hope that the effectiveness of the Court would encourage increasing resort to its procedures and that in this manner the role of law in international life would be enhanced. . . .[74]

Conditions for the Establishment of the
International Court of Habeas Corpus

The United Nations should exercise vigorous leadership to persuade member nations to accept a treaty establishing an international court of habeas corpus. Once a sufficient number of states have adopted the treaty so as to institute the circuit courts in three arenas, the international court of habeas corpus system should become effective, and the established circuit courts may begin to function.

A circuit court should come into existence when the treaty has been signed by at least four nations within a circuit-arena, including the state or states which are entitled by right to have one of their nationals seated as a judge on the local circuit court (e.g., the Soviet Union in the U.S.S.R.-Eastern Europe Circuit, India and Japan in the Non-Communist Orient Circuit, etc.). However, in the Anglo-American Circuit, the circuit court would be created upon the signature of only two nations, Canada and the United States. Moreover, the requirement that a judge from a Communist state be seated on the Anglo-American Circuit Court will not take effect until a circuit tribunal is established in either the Communist-Orient arena or in the U.S.S.R.-Eastern Europe arena.

Upon the establishment of the circuit courts in a minimum of seven arenas or regions, these lower tribunals shall select the justices for the supreme international court of habeas corpus, which shall start operating at once.

This plan would set the court system in motion almost immediately. Ratification of the treaty by merely ten or twelve states (e.g., the United States and Canada, four Latin American countries, England, France, and two other western European nations) would be sufficient for three circuit courts to "open for business." The increased respect accruing to those states which will have already submitted to this international justice should be a considerable inducement to the remaining nations to join the court with all due speed.[75]

This proposal for an international court of habeas corpus does not purport to offer ideal protection of human rights immediately. But since the entire proposal is predicated upon the cultural and political myths prevailing within each diverse system of public order, its structure would permit the different peoples of the world, each in its own fashion, to work toward the maximization of values and ultimate goals of all humanity.

PACEM IN TERRIS

In February 1965 world leaders gathered to examine the requirements for peace in the context of the encyclical of Pope John XXIII, *Pacem in Terris*. Almost without exception, all of the participants,[76] including those who had prepared special papers, were in agreement with the premise of Pope John XXIII that there was "the need to safeguard and ennoble human destiny." While the business of peace had become the most important business in the world, the strongest ties still concerned man with the integrity of human destiny. This outstretched hand of the Christian spirit manifested supreme confidence in the power of man to eliminate the combustibles of world conflict and to develop comprehensive rules of conduct which could be of immediate value in safeguarding individual liberty. It was agreed that, if individual liberties were protected from danger, then the sanctity of conscience, the right to dissent, would create a political climate which would guarantee religious liberty. Trespasses against the person had to be met with immediate remedies. The worldwide spread of tolerance, together with modern techniques of instant communication and interchange of knowledge, could potentially make the world a unitary community.

Since the spirit of science is the spirit of progress, since it seeks no static Utopia, it opens a clear path toward new horizons and higher peaks for man to climb in living peacefully with his fellow man. That "we are our brother's keeper" can achieve full meaning, in that the hate and beast in man may be negated by the sublime realization that man is the "cosmic individual" and, as such, is to be afforded absolute sovereignty of his person. Anything less is a corruption of justice and a repudiation of the natural law of God, the supreme force and strength in the universe. Kotaro Tanaka, retired chief justice of the Supreme Court of Japan and now sitting on the International Court of Justice stated:

> Since World Habeas Corpus is the guide for the light of world intelligence, I believe the rule of law (World Habeas Corpus) should cover all the world and, in particular, there must be no vacuum in the pro-

tection of fundamental human rights. I think it is the primary requirement in the national and international societies and, from the
viewpoint of such belief, I quite agree with the International Court
of World Habeas Corpus.[77]

The international courts of habeas corpus, the procedural structure for the concept of World Habeas Corpus, offers a vehicle for
dialogue between a citizen or alien and the state wherein he
resides. *Pacem in Terris* recognized that Catholics themselves were
to a great extent out of contact with the rest of the world, enclosed
in their own spiritual and religious ghetto. One of the chief contributions of Pope John's brief pontificate is that he opened the
ghetto and told Catholics to get out and talk to other people, to
Protestants, Jews, to Hindus, and even to Communists. He realized
that without this climate of openness, the communication essential
to prepare for a climate of mutual trust was out of the question. As
Thomas Merton convincingly stated:

> [W]here there is a deep simple all embracing love of man, of the
> created world, of living and inanimate things, then there will be re-
> spect for life, for freedom, for truth, for justice. There will be humble
> love of good. But where there is no love of man, no love of life, then
> make all the laws you want, all the edicts and treaties, issue all the
> anathemas, set up all the safeguards and inspections, fill the air with
> spying satellites and hang cameras on the moon. As long as you see
> your fellow man essentially to be feared, mistrusted, hated and de-
> stroyed, there cannot be peace on earth. And who knows if fear alone
> will suffice to prevent a war of total destruction? Pope John was not
> among those who believed that fear is enough.[78]

The conference on *Pacem in Terris* manifested monumental
support for articles 55 and 56 of the U.N. Charter. Article 55
provides "the United Nations shall promote: ... (c) universal
respect for, and observance of, human rights and fundamental
freedoms for all without distinction as to race, sex, language, or
religion." Pursuant to article 56, "all members pledge themselves to
take joint and separate action in cooperation with the Organization for the achievement of the purposes set forth in Article 55."

The eloquent statement of Vice President Hubert H. Humphrey
demonstrated statesmanship and leadership:

> The Pope did not write a Utopian blueprint for world peace presup-
> posing a sudden change in the nature of man. Rather, it represents a

call to action to leaders of nations presupposing a gradual change for human institutions . . . to build a world community.[79]

Grenville Clark, who co-authored with Louis Sohn *World Peace through World Law*, suggested that "nations must grant powers to a separate international body sufficient, to curb the destructive impulse of any one nation, and such powers can only be honestly described as those of government, i.e., world government."[80] Herman Kahn, the Rand Corporation's nuclear strategist, felt that "a rather bad world government might be better than no world government."[81] Luis Quintinilla of Mexico gave great weight to the need for emphasis on the rule of law. Israel's Abba Eban urged mankind to rise above national boundaries. Russia's Yevdni Jekov, leading Soviet historian, and other members of the Soviet orbit of influence thought war could no longer settle idealogical conflict between great nations. Senator Fulbright's forthright summation pierced the ambiguity of some arguments by proposing a plan for mutual tolerance and urging "the cultivation of a spirit in which nations are more interested in solving problems than in proving theories."[82] The consensus of the participants was that the "human nation" of the world was in need of workable ground rules and not diplomatic vaccums.

PACTA SUNT SERVANDA

In due course, the Connally reservation will give way to the fact that durable international rules of law can arise only from the explicit consent of states. Since every treaty is a limitation of, but not an impairment of, sovereignty, this is a standardized rule of international law that must exist in a working international community. A world convention to adopt the world treaty-statute of the World Habeas Corpus is of immediate necessity. It can demonstrate that the sanctity of the contractual nature of the treaty-statute will be respected. There is ample precedent that other international tribunals are successful without an extrinsic system of enforcement.

International arbitral boards and special international guards have proven successful without formal enforcement procedure. Hans Morgenthau has found that in the thousands of such decisions rendered in the last century and a half, voluntary execution was refused by the losing party in no fewer than ten cases.[83]

"Seldom has a State refused to execute the decision of a court which it has recognized in a treaty. The idea of law, in spite of everything, still seems stronger than the ideology of power."[84]

World Habeas Corpus provides the concrete structure and procedural process suggested by Dag Hammarskjöld in his dedication to the principle that a sovereign state must regard and protect the fundamental rights of individuals. In urging the cooperation of the International Law Association with the United Nations, Mr. Hammarskjöld declared:

> To turn aside from the United Nations now because it cannot be transformed into a world authority enforcing the law upon the nations would be to erase all the steady, though slow and painful, advances that have been made and to close the door to hopes for the future of world society, toward which present efforts and experiences should be at least a modest stepping stone.[85]

A great parallel for World Habeas Corpus as a step towards a world parliament was suggested by Winston Churchill in addressing the Strasbourg meeting with respect to a council of Europe:

> I have always thought that the process of building up a European parliament must be gradual and that it should roll forward on a tide of facts, events and impulses, rather than by elaborate constitution making. Either we shall prove our worth, weight and value to Europe, or we shall fail. We are not making a machine, we are growing a living plant.[86]

World Habeas Corpus is conscious of the salient premise that mankind is the sum of human beings and is always moving forward from within. The unification of mankind under a rule of law is the inexorable goal of inevitable change. Progress toward cloaking mankind with a rule of law against arbitrary detention may be checked but never ultimately denied. As a conscious part of the human race, man must conclude that he is not born individually, he is born of society, lives and grows in society. Man is obliged to society and causes society to evolve. Man's progress is not circumscribed by race, language, creed, or country. Mankind embraces all of man from the first to the last man on earth.

CONCLUSION

World Habeas Corpus does not pretend to be the panacea for all the ills of mankind. It is merely a remedy to correct and prevent arbitrary or wrongful detentions of human beings. Based upon a treaty-statute, duly ratified, it will have an extraterritorial basis, and will develop regional human communities into legal communities. As such, each of these will be able to coordinate other legal communities having common elements, growing into the larger and superior legal community. This will ultimately achieve the status of a competent legal community *when* it becomes self-governing and is the highest legal power in relation to its individual members recognized by its collective signatory members. Sovereignty will be retained and not be impaired even though, under the rule of law, a signatory member becomes a limited subordinate community. The duty and obligations created by this superior legal order are imposed on a subordinate community merely as a collective unit being responsible for the correction of arbitrary detention of an individual.

World Habeas Corpus can become a new definition of the term international due process of law. There is sufficient legal tradition and precedent to demonstrate that the world has a collective obligation as a self-governing community to maintain the integrity and dignity of citizens in its subordinate communities. The world has long sought a solution to the most vexatious of all problems, namely, the wanton destruction, annihilation, and imprisonment of human beings. High sounding principles and lamentations have failed to concretize a legal structure. It is this that World Habeas Corpus attempts to do in a very practical and concrete way.

The time for acceptance of World Habeas Corpus has now arrived. It cannot be delayed. It can carry mankind further toward unity than any material and technical contributions or financial assistance. It is a force of conscious progress stimulating mankind to individual freedom. World Habeas Corpus responds to the present age that is ever wakening, ever transforming. The lowest individual in the world is entitled to liberty, equality, and fraternity as guaranteed to him by the very nature of his being, a human being.

Senator Everett McKinley Dirksen has said, "There is nothing as strong as an idea whose time has come." It can become the canopy for the enlarged, compassionate "great society" envisioned by President Lyndon Baines Johnson.

Notes

1. The United States Senate refused to ratify the Treaty on 19 March 1919 and in March 1920 displayed remarkable international naiveté. The peace was political and prophetically cast a shadow over the figure of the League of Nations. It dramatized the human tragedy of Woodrow Wilson whose enthusiastic optimism for world control of war was dissented to by the United States. The Peace Conference at Versailles was a gathering very ill-adapted to do more than carry out the vengeance and bitterness of the war to their logical conclusions. The Germans, Austrians, Turks, and Bulgarians were permitted no share in its deliberations; they were only allowed to accept the decisions it dictated to them. It was a conference of conquerors. From the point of view of human welfare, the place of meeting was particularly unfortunate. It was at Versailles in 1871 that, with every circumstance of triumphant vulgarity, the new German Empire had been proclaimed. The suggestion of the melodramatic reversal of that scene in the same Hall of Mirrors was overpowering.

2. Mr. Kutner's paper represented the American Bar Association.

3. Cong. Rec. A6774 (daily ed. 13 Sept. 1962) (remarks of Senator Estes Kefauver); Address by Mrs. Lord, Commission of Human Rights, 12 May 1953 in U.N. Doc. No. F/CN/4/690 (1953); Kutner, *World Habeas Corpus for International Man: A Credo for International Due Process of Law,* 36 U. Det. L.J. (1959).

4. As quoted in address by Hon. Justice William J. Brennan, Jr., *International Due Process and the Law,* Law and Layman Conference, American Bar Association, 7 Aug. 1962 in 108 Cong. Rec. A6774 (daily ed. 13 Sept. 1962).

5. Address by Hon. William J. Brennan, Jr., *International Due Procéss and the Law,* Law and Layman Conference, American Bar Association, 7 Aug. 1962 in 108 Cong. Rec. A6774-75 (daily ed. 13 Sept. 1962).

6. McDougal & Feliciano, *International Coercion and World Public Order: The General Principles of the Law of War,* 67 Yale L.J. 771 (1958) ; McDougal & Feliciano, *A Map of the World's Law,* 1929 Geographical Rev. 114.

7. As quoted in Kutner, *World Habeas Corpus* 133 (1963). and Kutner, supra note 3, at 243.

8. Many other self-executing provisions are demonstrated in the international personalities of Euratom, the European Coal and Steel Community, the International Geophysical Year, the International Committee on Space Research, the International Refugee Organization, the International Labor Organization, the International Monetary Fund, the World Bank, the International Financial Corporation, the International Chamber of Commerce, the International Industrial Development Conference for Asia, the International Law Conference sponsored by the American Society of International Law (February 1956), the International Bar Association Conference, and the Conference for Protection of Investments Abroad in Time of Peace (Cologne, 1958). *Yearbook, International Organizations* (1964 ed.).

9. Winslow, *The Universal Postal Union,* Int'l Cong. 1 (No. 552, March 1965) (editor's introduction).

10. See generally Menon, *Cursus Publicus,* Int'l Cong. 3 (No. 552, March 1965).

11. The other organizations include the World Health Organization, the International Atomic Agency, the International Labor Organization, the International Civil Aviation Organization, and the International Air Transport Association. These do not include more than one hundred governmental organizations other than the United Nations family or the nearly one thousand

nongovernmental organizations. Fewer than two hundred of the latter account for some 700,000,000 persons. Ibid., pp. 49-59.

12. Ibid., pp. 60-64.

13. St. Korowicz, *The Problem of the International Personality of Individuals,* 50 Am. J. Int'l L. 533, 561 (1956). See generally Clark & Sohn, *World Peace Through World Law* 524 (1958); Goodrich & Hambro, *Charter of the United Nations* 322-24 (1949); Heilborn, *Das System des Volherrachts* 84 (1896); Lauterpacht, *International Law and Human Rights* 27 (1950); Wright, *Introduction to World Habeas Corpus* (1958). This principle has been and is accepted by many scholars, including Grotius, Pufendorf, Fiore, Bluntschlei, Heilborn, de Martin, Wilhelm Kaufman, John Westlake, Hefier De Lapredelle, Renard, Alfred Verdoss, W. Ivor Jenning, DeLouter, Simon Rundstein, Reeves, Bourquin, Jean Spirapoulos, James Leslie Brierley, Jacques Dumas, Aachely, Roscoe Pound, Quincy Wright, Philip Jessup, Charles S. Rhyne, Kotara Tanaka, Caroline K. Simon, Myres S. McDougal, Herbert W. Briggs, Charles Fenwick, Charles Cheney Hyde, Paul Guggenheim, Allan Stevenson, William J. Brennan, Jr., Oppenheim, Hersch Lauterpacht, Ballador Pallrei, Marcel Siebert, Harold D. Lasswell, Hans Kelsen, Walter F. George, Estes Kefauver, and many, many others.

14. Kutner, op. cit. supra note 7; Kutner, *World Habeas Corpus and International Extradition,* 41 U. Det. L.J. 525 (1964); Kutner, *World Habeas Corpus: A Legal Absolute for Survival,* 39 U. Det. L.J. 279 (1962); Kutner & Carl, *An International Writ of Habeas Corpus: Protection of Personal Liberty in a World of Diverse Systems of Public Order,* 22 U. Pitt. L. Rev. 469 (1961); Kutner, supra note 3.

15. U.N. EcoSoc Council Off. Reg. 20th Sess., Supp. No. 6, at 28 (E/2731 & Corr.) (1955).

16. Including Argentine Rep. Const. art. 29; Bolivian St. Const. art. 8; Brazil Const. art. 141 §§ 22, 23; Burma Const. art. 25(2); Chile Const. art. 16; Rep. China Const. art. 8; Costa Rica Const. art. 48; Cuba Const. art. 29 (now suspended); Dominican Rep. Const. art. 6 § 12; Ecuador Const. art. 164; Basic Laws Fed. Rep. Germany art. 19(4); Political Stat. Guat. art. 16; Honduras Const. art. 32; India Const. art. 32(2); Ireland Const. art. 40 (4) (2); Japan Const. art. 34; Nicaragua Const. art. 41; Paraguay Const. art. 24; Philippines Const. art. III § 1(14); Habeas Corpus Act, 1679, 31 Car. 2, c. 2 (Australia, New Zealand, Pakistan, United Kingdom); British North America Act, 1952 (Canada). Texts of the above cited and others can be found in 1 Peaslee, Constitutions of Nations (2d ed. 1956) .

17. These nations include Cameroun, Central African Republic, Chad, Congo (Brazzaville), Congo (Leopoldville), Cyprus, Dahomey, Gabon, Ivory Coast, Malagasy Republic, Mali, Niger, Nigeria Senegal, Somalia, Togo, Upper Volta, Mauretania and Tanzia.

18. *U.N. Yearbook on Human Rights* 229 (Supp. 1959) .

19. 1960 Seminar, Tokyo, Japan, 10-24 May 1960. The participants at the seminar were Australia Cambodia, Ceylon, China, Federation of Malaya, Hong Kong, India, Indonesia, Iran, Japan, Nepal, New Zealand, Pakistan, Philippines, Republic of Korea, Republic of Viet Nam, Sarawak, Singapore, Thailand and Afghanistan. Of the nongovernmental organizations in consultative status with the Economic and Social Council, the World Federations of United Nations Associations were alslo represented, as were the International Bar Association, International Criminal Police Organizations, International Federation of Women Lawyers, International Law Association, the Pan Pacific and Southeast Asia Women's Association, International Society of Criminology, Inter-

national Commission of Jurists, International League for the Rights of Man, International Association of Legal Scientists, World Federation for Mental Health, and a representative of the Secretary General of the United Nations.

20. Mr. Charles S. Rhyne was chairman of the conference.
21. Address by Dean Roscoe Pound, *A World Legal Order*, Fletcher School of Law and Diplomacy, 27 Oct. 1959.
22. Ibid.
23. Luce, *The Way of the Law: The Road to the Mountains of Vision*, 45 A.B.A.J. 482 (1959) (quoting Lord Hailsham).
24. Jessup, *Diversity and Uniformity in the Law of Nations*, 58 Am. J. Int'l L. 341, 342 (1964).
25. Ibid., p. 358. (Footnotes omitted.)
26. There is some debate as to the origin of this institution. Some authorities have claimed it is an outgrowth of the old Spanish system of *fueros* (rights). Vallarta, *El Juicio de Amparo* 3 (1881). Another writer contended that it is a Mexican adaptation and modification of the United States writ of habeas corpus. Aguilar Arriaga, *El Amparo de Mexico y sus Antecedentes Nacionales y Extranjeros*, 52 Mexican Thesis 1 (1942).
27. Vallarta, op. cit. supra note 26, at 39.
28. Ibid., p. 82.
29. Tucker, *The Mexican Government of Today* 118 (1957).
30. Chile Const. art. 16; Costa Rica Const. art. 48; Political Stat. Guat. art. 80; Pan. Const. art. 51; The Protection of Rights Act, art. 17, Mex. Memo.
31. In Mexico, if the injured party is unable to submit the application, any other person, "including even a minor or a married woman," may do so in his behalf. In that case, the court must take all measures necessary to bring the person before the court and request him to endorse the application for the remedy. If the party concerned endorses the application, the court must proceed with the matter; but if the party does not endorse the application, the petition is considered void. The Protection of Rights Act, art. 17, Mex. Memo.
32. Chile Const. art. 16.
33. Costa Rica Const. art. 48.
34. Political Stat. Guat. art. 80.
35. Pan. Const. art. 51.
36. Protection of Rights Act, art. 17, Mex. Memo.
37. Mex. Const. art. 107 § III(a).
38. Protection of Rights Act, art. 17, Mex. Memo. Amparo is also the procedural device used in Mexico whenever a local or state authority has invaded the sphere of federal jurisdiction. Vallarta, op. cit. supra note 26, at 19-21.
39. Vallarta, op. cit. supra note 26, at 49.
40. Mex. Const. art. 107, § IV.
41. Costa Rica Const. art. 48. In Panama, amparo may be granted on behalf of any person "against whom a mandatory or restraining order, violating the rights and guarantees held sacred by this Constitution is issued." Pan. Const. art. 51. The Guatemalan Constitution makes this remedy available to maintain or restore the constitutional rights of an individual; to obtain a ruling in a specific case that an order or act of any authority is not binding on the petitioner because it contravenes or restricts any of his constitutional rights; or to seek a ruling in a specific case that an order or resolution which is not a legislative act (e.g., an administrative ruling) does not apply to the petitioner because it would violate a constitutional right. Political Stat. Guat. art. 80.
42. For example, § 306 of the Chilean Code of Criminal Procedure provides that amparo will be granted in any of the following cases: where a warrant of arrest or order of imprisonment is issued by an authority not empowered to

make an arrest; where such warrant is issued in cases other than those provided by law, or if the formalities prescribed by law have not been complied with in issuing the warrant; where the warrant has been issued without good cause, or where all the requisite legal conditions have been fulfilled but it is not established by the proceedings that it is necessary to detain the person concerned; or where the person detained in custody has not been interrogated within the statutory period of twenty-four hours. Chile Memo.

43. The Mexican Constitution states that amparo may be granted in judicial matters, whether civil, penal or labor, only in the following cases. Mex. Const. art. 107 § III(a). This remedy lies against final judgments or awards if no other ordinary recourse is available by which these judgments may be modified or amended, provided that the violation of the law resulted in judgment or award. If the violation occurs during the course of the trial, it must have affected the defense of the petitioner to the extent of affecting the verdict, and the objection must have been duly noted and protest entered against the denial or reparation. In addition, if the error is committed in the first instance, it must have been invoked in the second instance as a violation of the law. The remedy also lies "against acts committed during the suit whose execution is impossible of reparation, acts exercised outside the suit or after the termination thereof when all recourse has been exhausted." Mex. Const. art. 107 § III(b). Amparo is also available against acts which affect persons who were not parties to the suit.

44. If amparo is sought because of a violation of the guarantees of article 16 of the Constitution (i.e., the right of a criminal defendant to be brought before a magistrate without delay, etc.), the petitioner must seek recourse through the appellate court of the court which committed the error or through the respective district courts. The attorney general is a party to all amparo suits unless he decides to abstain from the case on the ground that it lacks public interest. Mex. Const. art. 107 §§ XII, XV. Judgments of amparo are reviewed by the Supreme Court either when the constitutionality of a law is challenged (i.e., in case of controversies arising out of laws or acts of the federal authorities which limit or encroach on the sovereignty of the states, and all controversies arising out of the laws or acts of the state authorities which invade the sphere of the federal authorities) or when, in criminal cases, the only claim is a violation of article 22 of the Constitution (prohibiting cruel or unusual punishment, excessive fines, and capital punishment except for certain specified grave offenses). Mex. Const. art. 107 § VIII. In all other cases, there is no right to appeal the decision of a circuit court in an amparo matter. Final sentences in penal suits must be stayed as soon as the judge is notified that an application for amparo has been filed. Mex. Const. art. 107 § X.

45. Article 107, § XVIII, of the Mexican Constitution provides that all detained persons must be brought before a magistrate within twenty-four hours for a preliminary examination. If the jailer does not thereafter receive an order of committal from the judge within seventy-two hours after placing the prisoner at the court's disposal, this fact must immediately be brought to the attention of the court. If within the next three hours the jailer does not receive a committal warrant, he must release the detenu.

46. Political Stat. Guat. art. 80 § C.

47. Political Stat. Guat. art. 81.

48. An extension of six days is allowed if it is necessary to conduct an investigation in a place other than that where the court is sitting. An amparo decision may be appealed to the appropriate court of appeal and from that court directly to the Chilean Supreme Court. Chile Const. art. 16; Code Crim. Proc. § 306, Chile Memo.

49. This time limit is extended to ten days in case of arson. Code Crim. Proc. §
    251, Chile Memo.
50. Vallarta, op. cit. supra note 26, at 49.
51. Political Stat. Guat. art. 80 § C. The Constitution demands that the judical
    interpretation be liberal in amparo cases and the judges in these proceedings
    may dispense with evidence they deem unnecessary. Political Stat. Guat. art.
    84.
52. Political Stat. Guat. art. 85.
53. Chile Const. art. 16.
54. Political Stat. Guat. art. 83.
55. Political Stat. Guat. art. 85.
56. Reglamento de la Policia Preventiva, Federal District, art. 70, Mex. Memo.
57. In prior articles the author suggested that there be seven circuit courts. The
    increase to nine circuits is to accommodate all the rapidly emerging new and
    distinct patterns of law in the world community.
58. Since the completion of this article, more than thirty new nations have
    emerged and have been admitted to the United Nations. The bulk of these
    nations would probably be included within the jurisdiction of the South
    Africa Circuit (i.e., Mali Federation, Upper Volta, Ivory Coast, Togo, Da-
    homey, Cameroon, the Central African Republic, Gabon, Congo Republic,
    Niger, Chad, Republic of the Congo, and Malagasy Republic). Malaya would
    most likely choose to join the Non-Communist Orient Circuit, while as indi-
    cated above, Cyprus would probably become part of the Western Europe
    Circuit. As pointed out, in case of disagreement, any of these states would be
    free to make the final decision themselves.
59. See F.S.C. Northrup's conclusion that there are seven major cultural-legal
    units in the contemporary world: (1) the Asian solidarity of India, Ceylon,
    Burma, Thailand, Indo-China, South Korea, and Japan, rooted in the basic
    philosophical and cultural similarity of non-Aryan Hinduism, Buddhism,
    Taoism, and Confucianism; (2) the Islamic world, rooted in the religious and
    philosophical faith and reconstruction of a resurgent Islam; (3) the non-
    Islamic, non-European African world, rooted in its lesser known culture; (4)
    the continental European Union, grounded in a predominantly Roman Cath-
    olic culture with a secular leadership that has passed through the liberalizing
    influence of modern philosophical thought; (5) the British Commonwealth,
    with its predominantly Protestant British empirical philosophical traditions
    combined with the bond of unity derived through clasical education, English
    law, the Church of England, and its royal family; (6) Pan America, rooted in
    the liberal constitutionalism of the common law of the United States on the
    one hand, and the modern equivalent of Cicero's liberal Stoic Roman legal
    universalism on the other hand, as expressed in governments and even edu-
    cation, under secular leadership; and (7) the Soviet Communist world, com-
    prising the U.S.S.R., her eastern European Satellites, mainland China and
    North Korea. Northrup, *The Taming of Nations* 286-87 (1954).
60. In order to contend successfully that international proceedings are inappro-
    priate, the defendant state must prove the existence, in its system of internal
    law, of remedies which have not been used. The views expressed by writers
    and in judicial precedents coincide in that the existence of remedies which
    are obviously ineffective is not held to be sufficient to justify the application
    of the rule. "Remedies which could not rectify the situation cannot be relied
    upon by the defendant State as precluding an international action. . . . [I]t
    is hardly possible to limit the scope of the rule of prior exhaustion of local
    remedies to recourse to local courts." Ambatielos (Greece v. United Kingdom),
    in 50 Am. J. Int'l L. 674 (1956) .

61. McDougal & Feliciano, supra note 6, at 815.
62. Guides for measuring the obligations of states may be found in precedents of mixed arbitral boards, international custom and transnational tribunals, as well as in the principles to which states have given at least lip service in international declarations. As Hans Kelsen has pointed out, "the present day international law [developed] out of customs and agreements, and in this legal system custom was for the most part formed by the practice of the courts themselves." Kelsen, *Compulsory Adjudication of International Disputes*, 37 Am. J. Int'l L. 392, 400 (1944). Another recognition of such traditional sources of international law is article 38 of the Statute of the International Court of Justice authorizing the court to apply "international conventions," "international custom," "the general principles of law recognized by civilized nations," "judicial decisions and teachings of the most highly qualified publicists of the various nations," and principles of equity.
63. Vallarta, op. cit. supra note 26.
64. See Rogge, *Why Men Confess* 28 (1959).
65. See § XVIII and note 83 infra.
66. The whole episode of the Poznan trials and the surge of feeling inside and outside Poland to which they gave rise show what may be done by the force of public opinion directed to a clear issue of justice, provided that there is a favorable climate of opinion and freedom from the kind of outside interference the tragic consequences of which we have seen in Hungary. More particularly, the Poznan trials are interesting and important as illustrating the appeal which a threatened violation of fundamental principles of fair trial may make to the legal profession throughout the world. *Poznan Trials, Hungary, Middle East and Vienna Conference*, International Commission of Jurists, Bull. No. 6, Dec. 1956, p. 1 (editorial).
67. Many persons believe that the continual pressure of public attention attracted by the petition for United Nations' Habeas Corpus was an important factor in obtaining Oatis' release. Representative John V. Beamer stated, "I believe that the Kutner petition was greatly instrumental in assisting me in speeding Oatis' release." 104 Cong. Rec. 7131 (1958). See 104 Cong. Rec. 1236 (1958) (remarks of Rep. Beamer).
68. Article 52, paragraph 1, of the U.N. Charter authorizes such regional arrangements or agencies to deal with matters "relating to the maintenance of international peace and security as are appropriate for regional action." Paragraph 2 requires that members entering into such arrangements "shall make every effort to achieve pacific settlement of local disputes through such regional arrangements or by such regional agencies before referring them to the Security Council."
69. Article 41 authorizes the Security Council to call upon the members of the United Nations to apply such measures as are necessary to give effect to its decisions. These may include complete or partial interruption of economic relations and of rail, sea, air, postal, telegraph, radio, and other means of communications, and the severance of diplomatic relations. Where these kinds of measures are inadequate, article 42 of the United Nations Charter permits the Security Council to take such action "by air, sea or land forces as may be necessary to maintain or restore international peace and security. Such action may include demonstrations, blockade, and other operations by air, sea or land forces of Members of the United Nations."
70. Articles 10 and 13 of the United Nations Charter give the General Assembly the right to make recommendations for the purpose of "assisting in the realization of human rights and fundamental freedom for all. . . ."
71. Article 1 provides: If the Security Council, because of lack of unanimity of

the permanent Members, fails to exercise its primary responsibility for the maintenance of international peace and security in any case where there appears to be a threat to peace, breach of the peace or act of aggression, the General Assembly shall consider the matter immediately with a view to making appropriate recommendations to Members for collective measures, including in the case of a breach of the peace or act of aggression, the use of armed force, when necessary to maintain or restore international peace and security. . . . U.N. Gen. Ass. Off. Rec. 5th Sess., Supp. No. 20, at 10 (A/1775) (1950).

72. For example, the General Assembly Resolution of 18 May 1951 recommended that every state apply an embargo on shipments to areas under the control of Chinese Communists and North Korean authorities, of "arms, ammunition and implements of war, atomic energy materials, petroleum, transportation materials of strategic value, and items useful in the production of arms, ammunition and implements of war." U.N. Gen. Ass. Off. Rec. 5th Sess., No. 20A, at 1 (A/1775/Add. 1) (1950).

73. Article 6 of the Charter allows expulsion of a member "which has persistently violated the Principles contained in the present Charter."

74. Remarks of Secretary of State Dean Rusk, Presentation of the Manley O. Hudson Medal of the American Society of International Law to Judge Philip C. Jessup of the International Court of Justice Washington, D.C., Nov. 14, 1964, in Dep't of State Press Release No. 493, Nov. 17, 1964; 51 Dep't State Bull. 802 (1964); 59 Am. J. Int'l L. 382 (1965).

75. Other administrative details could be worked out through negotiation by the prospective members of the court system. For example, in reference to the matter of the expense of maintaining the court, the following formula might be used: One half the cost of maintaining each circuit tribunal shall be equally divided between those states which are entitled to have a national judge on the local circuit, e.g., one-fourth of the cost of the Non-Communist Orient Circuit would be borne by India and one-fourth by Japan; one-fourth of the cost of the Western Europe Circuit by Great Britain and one-fourth by France; one-fourth of the Austral-Oceania Circuit cost by the Philippines and one-fourth by Australia. The United States, the U.S.S.R. and Communist China should each pay one-half the expenses for their respective circuit courts. The remaining expenses of the individual circuit tribunals should be equally divided between all other member states within that arena. The cost of maintaining the Supreme International Court of Habeas Corpus could be shared equally by those states which have become members of the court system and are entitled by right to have a national sitting on their local circuit court.

76. Among those who participated in the three-day conference were: Vice President Hubert H. Humphrey; U Thant, United Nations Secretary General; Mohammed Zafrula Kahn, Judge of the International Court of Justice and former President of the United Nations General Assembly; Barbara Ward, economist and author; Senator J. William Fulbright; Ambassador Adlai Stevenson; Arnold Toynbee, historian; United States Supreme Court Chief Justice Earl Warren; Justice Philip Jessup of the World Court; Paul Henri Spaak, Foreign Minister of Belgium; Robert Hutchins, who acted as Chairman; Protestant theologian Paul Tillich; Japan's pacifist Kenzo Takayanagi; S. O. Adebo, Nigerian Chieftain Ambassador to the United Nations; Pietro Ninno, Vice Premier of Italy; Luis Quintanilla of Mexico; Adam Schafft of Poland; Linus Pauling, double Nobel prize winner; Semyon Tsarapkin of Russia; Soviet delegate Zhukov, Xavier Derian of France; and high government officials from the Soviet Union, Poland, Yugoslavia, Great Britain, and Japan, as well as African and Latin American nations.

77. Address by Kotaro Tanaka, Conference on *Pacem in Terris*, Feb. 1965.
78. Merton, *Challenge of Responsibility*, Saturday Rev., Feb. 13, 1955, pp. 28-30.
79. Address by Vice President Humphrey, Conference on *Pacem in Terris*, Feb., 1965.
80. Address by Grenville Clark, Conference on *Pacem in Terris*, Feb., 1965.
81. Address by Herman Kahn, Conference on *Pacem in Terris*, Feb., 1965.
82. Address by Senator Fulbright, Conference on *Pacem in Terris*, Feb., 1965.
83. Morgenthau, *Politics Among Nations* 296 (3d ed. 1963). As Briggs has pointed out, "treaties are more regularly and more honestly observed than violated and the use or threat of force ordinarily has nothing to do with it." Briggs, *The Law of Nations* 20-21 (2d ed. 1952). Mixed arbitral boards and special international courts have for centuries resolved all kinds of problems without formal enforcement machinery. Goodrich and Hambro have indicated that "in no case did the parties refuse to carry out a judgment of the Permanent Court of International Justice." Goodrich & Hambro, *Charter of the United Nations, Commentary and Document* 485 (rev. ed. 1949). Mr. S. Rosenne has written: "The general presumption that a State will observe its conventional obligations and more particularly will comply with the decision of the Court is equally valid in relation to the execution of the decisions of the Court [i.e., the International Court of Justice]." Rosenne, The International Court of Justice 84 (1957). He further claimed that although England was not successful in her efforts to secure satisfaction of the judgment against Albania in the *Corfu Channel* case, much of the difficulty was due to conflicting claims to property sought to be attached. See discussion of the *Monetary Gold* case, Rosenne, op. cit. supra at 97. See McNair, *The Law of Treaties* 351 (1st ed. 1938); see notes 66 & 67 supra and extensive citations in Kutner, *World Habeas Corpus: A Legal Absolute for Survival*, 39 U. Det. L.J. 279, 295 n.48 (1962).
84. Kelsen, supra note 62, at 400.
85. As quoted in 52 Prog. Am. Soc'y Int'l L. 39 (1958).
86. Address by Sir Winston Churchill, Strasbourg, Aug. 11, 1950.

Appendix

WORLD HABEAS CORPUS

TREATY-STATUTE OF THE INTERNATIONAL COURT OF HABEAS CORPUS*

Preamble

Whereas, The people of the world concerned with the security of the human person are deeply sensible of their duty and proceed with confidence in their declaration to coordinate, clarify and integrate all public order systems concerned with human liberty by establishing a world community and all component regions under the rule óf law, in order to guarantee human liberty, rights and fundamental freedom for all without distinction (or discrimination) as to race, sex, language, religion, or nationality; and

Whereas, The world concern for the security of the human individual is greater than principles of jurisdiction derived from territorial sovereignty, nationality, and other technical concepts; and

Whereas, It is the overriding aim to aid in the implementation of the universal order of human dignity by recognizing that the several social processes of the globe are imbedded in the larger context of singular world systems of order; and

Whereas, Adherence to human individual security refers to maximum demands for the maintenance of a public order which affords full ópportunity to preserve and increase all values by legal procedures free from acts or threats of coercion and oppression;

Resolved, That we, the people of the member nations of the International Court of Habeas Corpus, in order to more fully establish the sanctity of human liberty, provide for the security of the individual and guarantee human rights, do adopt the principle of international due process of law and definitive legal method of the International Court of Habeas Corpus with power to issue the international writ of habeas corpus, and establish this treaty-statute for the International Court of Habeas Corpus and accessible regional courts.

Article I

The International Court of Habeas Corpus is hereby established and empowered by the signatory member nations of this treaty-statute with jurisdiction to process

---

* Proposed before the American Bar Association, August 25, 1959, and amended since the emergence of twenty-nine new states.

petitions for the international writ of habeas corpus by and on behalf of individuals when their individual security is violated without due process of law as defined herein.

Chapter I. *Organization of the Court*
Article II

The Court shall be composed of a body of distinguished jurists of international stature and high moral character, who possess the qualifications required in their respective countries for appointment to the highest judicial offices, or are jurisconsults of recognized competence in international law.

Article III

1. The Court shall consist of two distinguished jurists from each of the signatory member countries to this treaty-statute.

2. There shall be nine permanent justices on each of the nine international tribunals of equal competence and jurisdiction, with their boundaries and jurisdiction in the following nine international circuits:

   (1) The Communist-Orient Circuit—Communist China, North Viet Nam, Outer Mongolia and North Korea;

   (2) The U.S.S.R.-Eastern Europe Circuit—the Soviet Union and the Communist states of eastern Europe, including Yugoslavia;

   (3) The Western Europe Circuit—the non-Communist states of western Europe, Great Britain, Greenland, Iceland, Ireland, Cyprus, Crete and Israel;

   (4) The Islamic Circuit—the Arabic states of the Middle East, Pakistan, the predominantly Moslem states of North Africa and Algeria;

   (5) The Southern Africa Circuit—the African states outside the Islamic circuit;

   (6) The Non-Communist Orient Circuit—India, Japan, Burma, Ceylon, Nationalist China, South Korea, Thailand, Nepal, Non-Communist Viet Nam, excluding Indonesia and the Philippines;

   (7) The Austral-Oceania Circuit—consisting of Australia, the Philippines, New Zealand, the South Sea Islands, Indonesia, etc.;

   (8) The Latin American Circuit—all Latin states within the Western hemisphere, including Cuba, Haiti, the Dominican Republic, etc.; and

   (9) The Anglo-American Circuit—Canada, the United States, Puerto Rico, and British and North American possessions in the West Indies.

3. The signatory member nations shall define the boundaries of each of the international circuits.

4. In addition to the nine circuit courts there shall be nine chief justices to sit in review, one from each circuit.

5. The remaining jurists shall be distributed to each of the circuit courts for functions of or acting as associate justices for the purpose of examining each petition for the international writ of habeas corpus for its legal sufficiency.

6. A person who for purposes of membership in the Court could be regarded as a national of more than one state shall be deemed to be a national of the one in which he ordinarily exercises civil and political rights.

Article IV

1. Each signatory member nation to this treaty-statute shall designate two nationals of its own state to become upon such designation members of the International Court of Habeas Corpus.

2. Within two months after the twenty-eighth nation of the world accepts this treaty-statute there shall be a convention of the designated members of the International Court of Habeas Corpus.

3. The convention shall select or designate from its membership seven justices for each of the regional courts and in addition thereto it shall select or designate nine chief justices who shall sit in review.

4. The remaining members shall be distributed by the permanent membership of the Court to each of the tribunals for functions of or acting as associate justices.

Article V

Before making these designations to the International Court of Habeas Corpus, each nation is recommended to consult its highest court of justice, its legal faculties and schools of law, and its national academies and sections of international academies devoted to the study of law.

Article VI

1. The members of the Court who are designated by the convention to be permanent members of the circuit tribunals and the designated chief justices shall hold office for nine years, provided, however, that of the judges designated at the first convention, the terms of two of the justices on each of the regional tribunals shall expire at the end of three years, and the terms of three justices shall expire at the end of six years; and provided, further, however, that of the chief justices designated by the convention the terms of three justices shall expire at the end of three years and the terms of three more justices shall expire at the end of six years.

2. The justices whose terms are to expire at the end of the above-mentioned periods of three years and six years shall be chosen by lot to be drawn by the convention immediately after the first designations have been completed.

3. The members of the Court shall continue to discharge their duties until their places have been filled. Though replaced, they shall finish any cases which they may have begun.

4. In the case of resignation of a member of the Court, the resignation shall be addressed to the President Chief Justice. This notification makes the place vacant.

Article VII

Vacancies shall be filled by the associate justices, according to the rules established by the Court.

Article VIII

A member of the Court designated to replace a member whose term of office has not expired shall hold office for the remainder of his predecessor's term.

Article IX

1. No member of the Court may exercise any political or administrative function, or engage in any other occupation of a professional nature.

2. Any doubt on this point shall be settled by the decision of the court.

Article X

1. No member of the Court may act as agent counsel or advocate in any case.

2. No member may participate in the decision of any case in which he has previously taken part as agent, counsel, or advocate for one of the parties, or as a member of a national or international court, or in any other capacity.

3. Any doubt on this point shall be settled by the decision of the Court.

Article XI

1. No member of the Court can be dismissed unless, in the unanimous opinion of the other members, he has ceased to fulfill the required conditions.

2. Formal notification thereof shall be made to the President Chief Justice.
3. This notification makes the place vacant.

Article XII

The members of the Court, when engaged in the business of the Court, shall enjoy diplomatic privileges and immunities throughout the world.

Article XIII

Every member of the Court shall, before taking up his duties, make a solemn declaration in open court that he will exercise his powers impartially and conscientiously.

Article XIV

1. The chief justices shall elect from among themselves the President Chief Justice, and each circuit tribunal shall elect a presiding justice from among its permanent justices, to hold office for three years; they may be re-elected.
2. The court shall appoint its registrar and may provide for the appointment of such other officers as may be necessary.
3. Each circuit tribunal shall appoint any amicus curiae, and there shall be an amicus curiae general to assist the chief justices.

Article XV

The President Chief Justice and the presiding justices shall be the presiding officers of their tribunals.

Article XVI

1. The seat of the Court of Review shall be established by the convention. This, however, shall not prevent the Court from sitting and exercising its functions elsewhere whenever the Court considers it desirable.
2. The seat of each of the circuit tribunals shall be established by the convention. This, however, shall not prevent the circuit tribunal from sitting and exercising its function elsewhere whenever the Court considers it desirable.

Article XVII

1. The Court shall remain permanently in session except during the judicial vacations, the dates and duration of which shall be fixed by the convention; provided, however, that the vacations of the circuit tribunals shall not be concurrent, and that a petitioner may petition for the international writ of habeas corpus to one of the other judicial circuit tribunals if he is prevented from so doing before the circuit tribunal having permanent jurisdiction over the disposition of the petition because that circuit is exercising its judicial vacation.
2. Members of the Court are entitled to periodic leave, the dates and duration of which shall be fixed at each court, having in mind the distance between the seat of the Court and the home of each justice.
3. Members of the Court shall be bound, unless they are on leave or prevented from attending by illness or other serious reasons duly explained to the presiding officer, to hold themselves permanently at the disposal of the court.

Article XVIII

1. If, for some special reason a member of the court considers that he should not take part in the decision of a particular case, he shall so inform the presiding officer.
2. If the presiding officer considers that for some special reason one of the

members of the Court should not sit in a particular case, he shall give him notice accordingly.

3. If in any such case the member of the Court and the presiding officer disagree, the matter shall be settled by the decision of the Court.

Article XIX

The full Court shall sit except when it is expressly provided otherwise by the rules of the Court.

Article XX

A judgment given by any of the circuit tribunals shall be considered as rendered by the Court, and shall be subject to review only by the chief justices.

Article XXI

The Court shall frame rules for carrying out its functions. In particular, it shall lay down all rules of procedure.

Article XXII

1. Each member of the court shall receive an annual salary.

2. The President Chief Justice shall receive a special annual allowance.

3. The presiding justices shall receive a special allowance, but in no event shall it exceed the amount allowed to the President Chief Justice.

4. The registrar and all other aides of the Court shall receive annual salary.

5. These salaries, allowances, and compensations shall be determined by the signatory member nations to this treaty-statutory member nations to this treaty-statute sitting in executive session. They may not be decreased during the term of office.

6. Regulations made by the conventions shall fit the conditions under which retirement pensions may be given to members of the Court and to the registrar, and the conditions under which members of the Court and the registrar shall have traveling expenses refunded.

7. The above salaries, allowances, and compensations shall be free of all taxation.

Article XXIII

The expenses of the Court shall be borne by the signatory members to this treaty-statute as herein set forth, half of the total expenses shall be borne by the Big Five Powers of France, Great Britain, India, Union of Soviet Socialist Republics, and the United States; half of the total expenses shall be borne equally by the remainder of the signatory members.

Chapter II. Competence of the Court

Article XXIV

1. Only individuals or groups of individuals may be parties in cases before the Court.

2. The United Nations shall be ipso facto an ad hoc committee to fact find; and upon the recommendation of the Court, or the United Nations, the Department of State of any member nation shall be enlisted to make investigations to aid the Court in its investigations, subject to and in conformity with the rules of the Court.

Article XXV

1. Any person who is detained or restrained without due process of law within the boundaries of one of the member nations to this treaty-statute shall find

original jurisdiction in the judicial circuit tribunal having jurisdiction over the place whereat he is restrained.

2. The Court shall be open to individuals detained or restrained within the boundaries of a non-member nation when such nation agrees to submit the cause to the Court for disposition.

3. When a non-member nation submits the cause to the Court for disposition, it shall irrevocably bind itself to abide by the proceedings and decision of the court.

4. When a non-member nation to this treaty-statute is a party to a case, the Court shall fix the amount which that party is to contribute toward the expenses of the Court.

Article XXVI

1. The jurisdiction of the Court comprises all cases where an individual (or group of individuals) is imprisoned, detained, or otherwise restrained for his (or their) liberty without due process of law.

2. International due process of law shall guarantee:
   a) public trial of any person accused of a violation of law;
   b) the right of any person accused to be informed in advance of trial of the specific charge made against him;
   c) the right to be confronted with the witness against him;
   d) the right of compulory process to obtain witnesses in his favor;
   e) the right to counsel of his own choice;
   f) the right not to be compelled to give testimony against himself;
   g) the right to have an interpreter;
   h) the right to communicate with his own government and to have a representative of that government present at his trial;
   i) the right not to be held twice in jeopardy for the same offense;
   j) the right to be free from prosecution by virtue of any ex post facto law;
   k) the right to be free from excessive bail;
   l) the right to be free from any cruel or unusual punishment;
   m) the right to be free from any unreasonable searches and seizures;
   n) the right to freedom of conscience and religion; freedom of thought, speech, press and expression in any other form; freedom of association and assembly; and freedom of petition.

Article XXVII

The types of confinement for which the writ shall apply will include:
   a) any violation of the standards particularized in the Universal Declaration of Human Rights;
   b) military and political crimes;
   c) charges of treason;
   d) acts charged as hostile to the respondent state by an alien visitor or resident;
   e) any crime punishable by death; or
   f) any crime established by international extradition treaty.

Article XXVIII

The orders of the International Court of Habeas Corpus shall be made effective by the sanctions and deprivations exacted in the Charter of the United Nations.

Chapter III.   Special Competence of the Chief Justices

Article XXIX

The Chief Justices of the International Court of Habeas Corpus shall permit appeals from decisions of the circuit tribunals when it appears to at least one-third of the judges of this appeal court:

a) that a decision of a circuit tribunal may be inconsistent with a prior decision of the same issue of law by the Court of Review of the International Court of Habeas Corpus or by one of the circuit tribunals;

b) that a circuit tribunal may have wrongfully decided a question of law;

c) that a regional court may have exceeded its jurisdiction;

d) that a circuit tribunal may have deprived a person of a right or privilege guaranteed by International Due Process of Law;

e) that a regional court may have made a fundamental error resulting in a denial of justice.

Chapter IV.   Procedure and Disposition of Petition

Article XXX

Each petition for the international writ of habeas corpus shall be made to the circuit tribunal of the International Court of Habeas Corpus having jurisdiction over the place where the person unlawfully detained is located.

Article XXXI

The petition shall be signed by the person for whose relief it is intended, or by some person in his behalf, and verified by affidavit.

Article XXXII

The petition shall state in substance:

1. That the person in whose behalf the writ is applied for is imprisoned, detained or restrained of his liberty, and the place where, naming all the parties if they are known, or describing them if they are not known.

2. The cause or pretense of the restraint, according to the best knowledge and belief of the petitioner.

3. That there had been an exhaustion of all available sovereign remedies, or that there are no available remedies, or that the case is an extraordinary one which empowers the Court to take original jurisdiction.

Article XXXIII

Unless it appears from the petition itself, or from the documents thereto annexed, that the party can neither be discharged, admitted to bail nor otherwise relieved, at least a majority of three associate justices may find that a petition is legally sufficient, and upon so finding, they shall be empowered to issue a show cause order upon the respondent nation, ordering it to file its motion as to why the international writ of habeas corpus should not issue.

Article XXXIV

The show cause order shall be issued under the seal of the Court and shall require the respondent to answer within ten days; provided, however, that the Court may extend the period, if, in the opinion of the Court, more time is required by the respondent nation.

Article XXXV

The respondent nation upon whom such order is served shall state in its return plainly and unequivocally:

1. Whether the subject party is at the time of issue of the order, or was, and at what time prior or subsequent to the date of the order, under the control, restraint, or in custody of the respondent.

2. The cause of such imprisonment or restraint.

3. By virtue of what authority the subject party is held, and if by some written warrant or writ of any kind, the original shall be produced and exhibited upon the return of the order.

4. If the person upon whom the order is served has had the party in his custody or control or under his restraint, at any time prior or subsequent to the date of the order, but has transferred such custody or restraint to another, the return shall state particularly to whom, at what time, for what cause and by virtue of what authority such transfer took place.

Article XXXVI

If the respondent nation moves to dismiss the petition for insufficiency, the petitioner shall be allowed to file an answer.

Article XXXVII

If the respondent nation fails to show cause within the time so ordered, or if the Court finds that the cause shown is not a legally sufficient one, the Court shall be empowered to issue the international writ of habeas corpus.

Article XXXVIII

1. The Court shall also issue a subpoena to summon witnesses to appear before the Court at the time and place where such habeas corpus is returnable, unless the Court shall deem it unnecessary, and it shall be the duty of the officer to whom the subpoena is issued, to serve the same, if it be possible, in time to enable such witnesses to attend.

2. The writ may be served by any person appointed for that purpose by the Court by whom it is allowed.

Article XXXIX

Service shall be made by leaving a copy of the original writ with the chief executive officer of the respondent nation, or with any of his under officers who have authority to act directly on his behalf, or who are directly answerable to the chief executive in the normal course of their official duties.

Article XL

The respondent nation shall, at the time of making the return, bring the body of the party, if in his custody or power or under his restraint, according to the command of the writ, unless prevented by the sickness or infirmity of the party.

Article XLI

When, from the sickness or infirmity of the party, he cannot, without danger, be brought to the place appointed for the return of the writ, that fact shall be stated in the return, and if it be proved to the satisfaction of the Court, the Court may so proceed or make such other order in the case as law and justice require.

Article XLII

Whenever it shall appear by the petition that anyone is illegally held in custody and restraint, and that there is good reason to believe that such person will be taken out of the jurisdiction of the circuit court to which petition was made, or will suffer some irreparable inury before compliance with the writ can be enforced, the Court may cause the executive officer of the respondent nation to take the party into his direct supervisory custody.

Article XLIII

Upon the return of the international writ of habeas corpus, the Court shall, without delay, proceed to examine the cause of the imprisonment or restraint, but the examination may be adjourned from time to time as circumstances require.

Article XLIV

The party imprisoned or restrained may deny any of the material facts set forth in the return and may allege any other facts that may be material in the case, which denial or allegation shall be on oath; and the Court shall proceed to its established rules of procedure.

Article XLV

The hearing shall be under the control of the presiding officer or, if he is unable to preside, of the senior judge present.

Article XLVI

The hearing in Court shall be public.

Article XLVII

1. Minutes shall be made at each hearing and signed by the registrar or by one of his assistants appointed for the circuit tribunals. They shall be kept on record.
2. These minutes shall be authentic.

Article XLVIII

The Court shall make orders for the conduct of the case, shall decide the form and time in which each party must conclude its arguments and make all arrangements connected with the taking of evidence.

DATE DUE

DEC 8 71			

DEMCO 38-297